34 95

D062125b

34 95

Along Route 66

Along Route 66

Quinta Scott

University of Oklahoma Press : Norman

Also by Quinta Scott
(with Howard S. Miller) *The Eads Bridge,* rev. ed. (St. Louis, 1999)
(with Elaine Viets) *St. Louis: Home on the River* (Memphis, 1995)
(with Elaine Viets) *Images of St. Louis* (Columbia, 1989)
(with Susan Croce Kelly) *Route 66: The Highway and Its People* (Norman, 1988)
(with M. M. Constantin) *Sidestreets, St. Louis* (St. Louis, 1981)

The publishers have generously given permission to use extended quotations from *The Grapes of Wrath* by John Steinbeck, ©1939, renewed 1967 by John Steinbeck. Used by permission of Viking Penguin, a division of Penguin Books USA Inc.

Library of Congress Cataloging-in-Publication Data

Scott, Quinta, 1941–
    Along Route 66 / Quinta Scott.
       p. cm.
    Includes bibliographical references and index.
    ISBN 0–8061–3250–7 (alk. paper)
    1. Roadside architecture—West (U.S.) 2. Architecture, Modern—20th century—West (U.S.)
3. United States Highway 66. 4. Roadside architecture—West (U.S.)—Pictorial works. 5.
Architecture, Modern—20th century—West (U.S.)—Pictorial works. 6. United States Highway
66—Pictorial works. I. Title: Along Route Sixty-six. II. Title.

NA725 .S39 2000
720'.978'0904—dc21
                                                                                    99–054653
                                                                                         CIP

The paper in this book meets the guidelines for permanence and durability of the Committee on Production Guidelines for Book Longevity of the Council on Library Resources, Inc. ⊚

Text design by John Coghlan

1 2 3 4 5 6 7 8 9 10

In memory of my parents,
Tirzah Perfect Dunn
Frederick Wallace Dunn

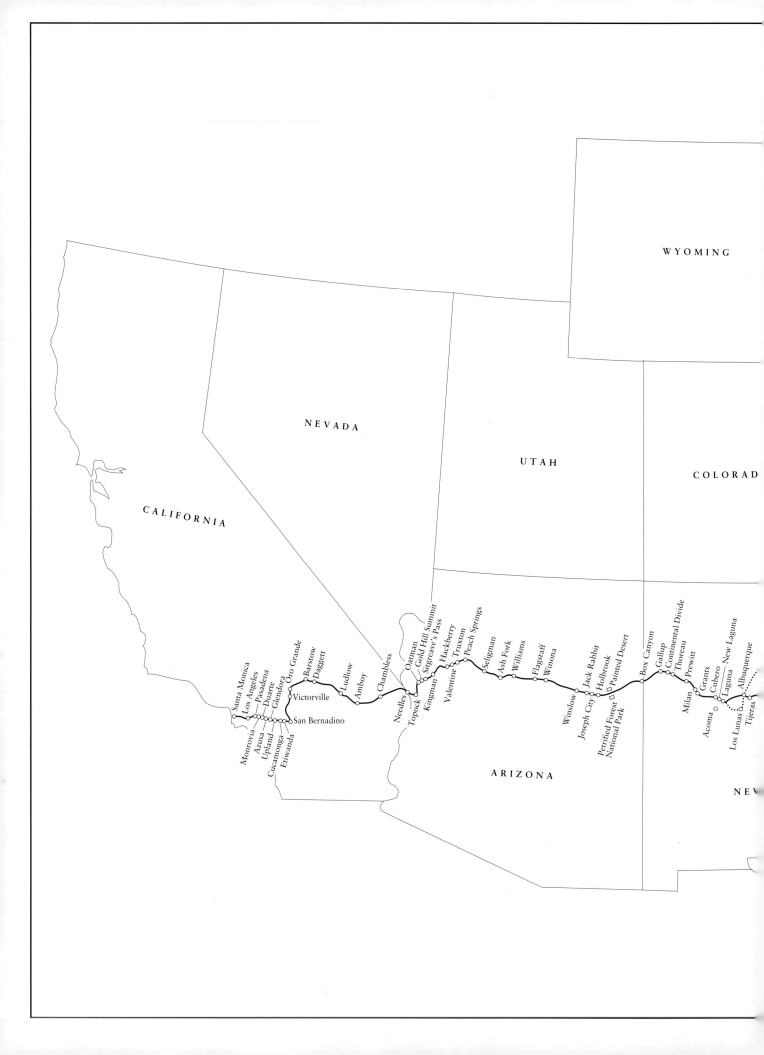

SOUTH DAKOTA

MINNESOTA

WISCONSIN

IOWA

NEBRASKA

MISSOURI

Chicago
Cicero
Joliet
Braidwood
Odell Gardner
Pontiac
McLean Bloomington
Broadwell Lincoln
Springfield Elkhart
Farmersville
Litchfield
Benld Mt. Olive
Staunton
Worden
Hamel
Edwardsville Mitchell
Pond St. Louis
Gray Summit
St. Clair Villa Ridge
Sullivan Stanton
Fort Leonard Wood Rolla Cuba
Gascozark Doolittle
Lebanon Clementine
Conway Devils Elbow
Carthage Hazelgreen
Springfield Marshfield
Galena Halltown
Baxter Springs Phelps
Commerce Joplin Avila
Vinita Miami
Afton
Claremore
Tulsa Catoosa
Stroud
Davenport
Chandler
Arcadia
Luther
Wellston
Oklahoma City

KANSAS

ILLINOIS

Clines Corners
Santa Rosa
Cuervo Newkirk
Tucumcari
Glenrio
Adrian
Vega
Wildorado
Amarillo
Conway
Groom
Alanreed
McLean
Shamrock
Texola
Sayre
Elk City
Canute
Clinton
Weatherford
Hydro Bridgeport
Hinton Junction Geary
El Reno

OKLAHOMA

TEXAS

MEXICO

U.S. Highway 66
.... 1926
———— 1939

Contents

Acknowledgments

Many, many people helped move this project along. Dozens of folks patiently told me their stories and their histories along Route 66. When Susan Croce Kelly and I did the oral research for *Route 66: The Highway and Its People*, we literally knocked on the doors of old gas stations, motels, and cafés and asked, "Who built this building?" When we located that person, we tape-recorded our interview. Then we played the old college game: Who do you know? One by one, our informants passed us down the road, and we learned how they invented American auto tourism. When I wrote the first draft of this book, I drew much of my information, particularly architectural information, from these tapes.

On the final draft, I developed a new strategy for locating informants: Yahoo!'s People Search. If I had a name, I learned I could log onto the Internet, call up Yahoo!, type in a name and a town, and get a phone number. Seventy-five percent of the time the person I needed to talk to answered the phone. Occasionally I needed the help of local reference librarians who were always willing to comb city directories for a name or, failing that, to give me the name and number of the local historian, who was invariably willing to help. Kate Anthony of the Amarillo Public Library, John Vittal at the Albuquerque Public Library, and many anonymous librarians in towns along the road were always ready to help. City planners and engineers in the building departments of Upland, Glendora, Duarte, and Barstow, California, helped me flush out owners and construction dates of buildings in their towns.

Details, details, details. Numerous patient friends along the road filled in details. Terry Sykes in the interlibrary loan department of the St. Louis Public Library was tireless in tracking down material for me. Maggie McShan, who researches history for the love of it for the Needles (California) Historical Society, provided names and information on businesses in Needles and the Mojave Desert. John R. Hill, director of the Oklahoma Route 66 Museum in Clinton, always gave encouragement and direction. Once again, Ruth Sigler Avery filled in with information about her father-in-law, Cyrus Stevens Avery. Marian Clark, who wrote the wonderful *Route 66 Cookbook,* helped me date the demise of the Old English Inn in Tulsa. Joe Winkler, who presides over the Map Room at the St. Louis Public Library, and Ann Little, who came to Bridgeport, Oklahoma, as a bride, helped me nail down exactly where Bridgeport used to be. Joe Smith, who grew up in Santa Rosa, New Mexico, accepted my phone calls whenever I had a question about his part of the world, as did Glenn Johnson in Kingman, Arizona, and Pauline Bauer in Albuquerque. Paul Milan in Grants, New Mexico, told me the story of his family's motel and then helped me find other business owners in Grants. Bud Gunderson confirmed that the little gas station in Thoreau had belonged to his father in Grants. Bill Tomlinson of the Mojave River Museum in Barstow, California, dug out the information on the Ludlow Mercantile and then passed me along to Beryl Bell at the Daggett (California) Historical Society.

Esley Hamilton, the preservation historian with St. Louis County, read the very first chapter, supplied information on the Coral Court in St. Louis, and pointed me in the direction of the research that has been done on Missouri Ozark sandstone construction. He then researched the title history of the Park Plaza Courts in St. Louis and came up with the name of the original owners. This enabled me to track down Mickey Stroud in Waco, Texas, who told me the history of the Park Plaza Courts chain. Keith A. Sculle, Illinois Historical Preservation Agency, and Heath Henry, Tulsa County (Oklahoma) Historical Society, also helped with the work on the Park Plaza Courts. Finally, the Texas Collection, Baylor University, supplied me with a reproduction of the postcard of the Alamo Plaza in Waco, Texas, thus enabling me to complete the visual links between the Alamo Plaza facade and its numerous imitators along 66, including the Park Plaza Courts.

Charles Lee Cook, manager of the Shady Rest Motel in Tulsa, measured one of his cabins for me to see if it conformed to the plans and specifications of a cabin published in *Popular Mechanics* in July 1935. Close enough.

Robert Rubright read the first draft of the first chapter and encouraged me to go on. Jeffery Smith read both the first and the final drafts, made many good suggestions, and wrote letters of support. Marti Lattimore and Jim Hamilton took the first draft along on their honeymoon and brought back a report on the condition of the buildings illustrated. Then they wrote a letter of support. John A. Jakle and Alan Gowans read the first draft and encouraged me to complete the work.

John N. Drayton, director and editor-in-chief of the University of Oklahoma Press, read the first chapter and encouraged me to finish. He then ushered me through the review process, at one point asking me to defend the project, a process that was most helpful. Randy Lewis, Jean Hurtado, Ursula Daly, and Jo Ann Reece of the Press patiently answered my questions as I completed the manuscript. Finally, Ursula Smith showed me the value of a good manuscript editor as she shepherded me through the editing process with great good humor and many pats on the back.

The Design Arts Program of the National Endowment for the Arts awarded me a fellowship in 1981 that funded the photography for the first book—*Route 66: The Highway and Its People*—and this book. The Josephine Perfect and Charles Ulrick Bay Foundation matched the fellowship. I would like to thank Robert Ashton, director of the foundation, and Frederick Bay and Synova Bay Hayes, board members, for their continuing support.

Bess and Al Long provided me with my Oklahoma home in Geary and, like the loving friends they are, indulged me in onion-fried burgers in El Reno.

Finally, my husband, Barrie H. Scott, an architect, took a week off and went over the manuscript with me line by line, correcting the architectural details, helping me understand the lingo and how a building goes together, and then helped me put it all in plain English. He gave me love and support and his father's 1941 *Architectural Graphic Standards,* where I learned about adobe and other building materials of the period.

QUINTA SCOTT

St. Louis

Along Route 66

The Architecture of America's Highway

It was the way out. Invented on the cusp of the depression, Route 66 was the road out of the mines, off the farm, away from troubled Main Street. It was the road to opportunity. And, after Americans had overcome the depression and won the war and good times boomed, Route 66 was the ultimate road trip. None of the great continental highways established in 1926—U.S. 20, U.S. 30, U.S. 40, U.S. 50, or U.S. 60—ever captured our collective imagination the way this highway did. U.S. 66 and the Lincoln Highway, U.S. 30, are the only national highways that have attracted historical associations dedicated to documenting their routes and erecting signs that mark them. U.S. Highway 66 started in Chicago and went south through the Illinois prairie; it turned west at St. Louis and went through the ancient Ozark hills into the Great Plains; it continued through some of the most romantic parts of the Southwest into California's Mojave Desert; it ended in Los Angeles at the edge of the Pacific Ocean.

U.S. Highway 66 died with the passage of the Federal Aid Highway Act in 1956, which established and funded the interstate highway system. It had been created in 1926 by a joint board of the American Association of State Highway Officials, which designated and numbered the roads that would be included in the federal highway system. In those thirty years, 1926 to 1956, legendary events along the highway turned U.S. Highway 66 into Route 66. It began with the Bunion Derby in 1928, a cross-country footrace that started in Los Angeles, headed east along U.S. 66 to Chicago, and ended in New York. The footrace was promoted by C. C. Pyle and the U.S. Highway 66 Association and was followed daily in newspapers across the country. It fixed Route 66 in the national consciousness. The race was won by Andy Payne, a Cherokee from Will Rogers's hometown, Claremore, a stop on U.S. 66 in Oklahoma.

In 1934 and continuing through 1935 and 1936, when the great winds blew away the topsoil from the drought-stricken plains of Nebraska, Kansas, Oklahoma, and Texas, migrants poured down 66 in their cars and trucks, looking for a better life in California. Dorothea Lange photographed them, Woody Guthrie wrote songs about them, John Steinbeck wrote a novel about them, and John Ford followed with the movie.[1] In 1946, ex-marine Bobby Troup packed up his wife, Cynthia, left the family music business in Harrisburg, Pennsylvania, and traveled down U.S. 66 to Los Angeles to try his hand at song writing. On the way he lifted the names of towns from his road map and strung them together into one of the most enduring songs of the postwar period.[2] In the early 1960s, as the dual-lane, interstate highways replaced the twisting, narrow ribbon of concrete that was U S. 66, Sterling Silliphant sealed the myth of Route 66 in our imaginations with his weekly television series about two guys traveling from adventure to adventure in a red Corvette.[3]

It is too easy to say that the heyday of the old road was a simpler, better time and that that is why we are so intrigued by Route 66. There was nothing simple about living through the depression and the dust bowl, or World War II, or the threat of nuclear annihilation that was the cold war. While the myth of Route 66 may be the story of the Bunion Derby, *The Grapes of Wrath*, and "Get Your Kicks," the reality of Route 66 was about making a living, about using architecture—buildings and signs—to make people "Stop: Fill it up, have a bite, stay the night."

In 1972 architect Robert Venturi alerted architects and historians to the character of American roadside buildings and their signs in *Learning from Las Vegas*, his study of the architecture of Las Vegas, Nevada. Venturi described what he saw as "the rule of Route 66"—the enormous neon sign beckoning the traveler off the road to a modest motel, gas station, or café.[4] In the last three decades, the many authors who have published books on the architecture of the American roadside have concentrated on bizarre examples: tamale stands in the shape of a tamale or chili parlors in the shape of a chili bowl, what Venturi called the "Duck" in American roadside architecture—so named after a Long Island store in the shape of a duck—where the building is the sign.[5] Or they have looked at individual building types—gas stations, motels, diners, and drive-ins. No one has taken the length of a single highway and looked at its architecture, at how that architecture developed, and at the regional influences on it.

If they did, what they would find is that the roadside buildings are not as bizarre or exciting as the architectural histories would have you believe. The building designers along U.S. 66 and other American highways reached back to the vernacular styles of late-nineteenth-century and early-twentieth-century rural and suburban houses. The folks who built their motels and gas stations on 66 drew on what they knew: the architecture of the Ozarks built of local sandstone; the architecture of the Great Plains—the Western Bungalow that appeared in Kansas in the 1870s and was carried south to Oklahoma Territory twenty years later; and the architecture of the Southwest, variations on the Spanish Colonial styles—the Spanish Mission, the Spanish Pueblo, and the Casa—that had been the way of building in New Mexico, Arizona, and California since the eighteenth century and before.[6] Occasionally motel owners in California drew on the work of the Greene brothers, who developed the Craftsman Bungalow in Pasadena at the turn of the century, a style that spread across the country in the teens and twenties.[7]

The builders on 66 were local miners, farmers, and townspeople who flocked to the roadside during the depression when it offered opportunities that could not be found in the mines, on the farm, or in town. There was a living to be made from families like the Joads of John Steinbeck's *Grapes of Wrath* who were escaping the Great Plains in search of a better life in the West. Many of those who trekked west during the dust bowl days never made it to California but settled on the roadside and built successful businesses. However they got there, they made a good life along 66, where their architecture reflected local traditions and the difficulties of the times, where they built quickly using simple structural systems and materials available at the local supply store—wood frame, masonry, or structural clay tile before World War II, concrete block after the war. Whatever they chose, they finished their buildings in stucco or wood siding.

U.S. 66 was successful because of the efforts of one person. As a member of the Joint

Board of the American Association of State Highway Officials that laid out the United States system of highways in 1926, Cyrus Avery of Tulsa, Oklahoma, persuaded his colleagues on the board to route a road that connected Chicago to Los Angeles through his hometown. In doing so, the board ignored historical routes, most notably the Santa Fe Trail through Kansas to Santa Fe, New Mexico, and instead directed travelers across semipopulated stretches of the Missouri Ozarks and the Great Plains—Oklahoma, the Texas Panhandle, and eastern New Mexico. Once he had the road laid out, Avery called it "the Main Street of America" and established the U.S. Highway 66 Association to promote it as the best route to California.[8]

It was. While New Mexico and Arizona may have been empty in 1926, the region west of Denver in central Utah and Nevada is *still* empty. Anyone who has driven west along northern routes to California—U.S. 30, U.S. 40, or U.S. 50—understands the success of 66. Even today, I-70, the interstate highway that replaced U.S. 40 and U.S. 50, comes to a lonely halt at its intersection with I-15 in the middle of a Utah desert. In the teens and the twenties, the road west in winter had you making your way across narrow, often snow-blocked passes in the Colorado Rockies—Berthoud Pass just west of Denver or Monarch Pass in central Colorado—to get to Utah and Nevada. From there the drive to California was across sixty miles of desert and up over a mountain, and sixty miles of desert and up over a mountain. That went on for two states until the traveler reached the Sierra Nevada on the Nevada-California border. It was not and is not an easy drive.

As blistering as the summer was in California's Mojave Desert, as dense as the ice fog could be at Clines Corners, New Mexico, as fierce as the hailstorms were in the Texas Panhandle, as dangerous as the sleet could be in Oklahoma and Missouri, 66 was the best route to California. And, although snow occasionally blocked 66 at Flagstaff, Arizona, the road that began in the Windy City ended, after all, in Tinsel Town, where there were two mild seasons—day and night. No wonder 66 was a success; no wonder it provided a way out for the millions who traveled west and for the thousands who stayed and made their living off the passing millions.

Almost every building constructed on Route 66 between 1926 and 1956 lost its economic viability the day President Dwight David Eisenhower signed the 1956 highway act. The long, double ribbons of limited-access highways that replaced 66 bypassed every little town between Chicago and Los Angeles, leaving the small Mom-and-Pop businesses—the motels, the cafés, and the gas stations on old 66—without direct access to their customers. This did not happen right away; it took thirty years to complete the interstate highway system. It happened little bit by little bit. Those enterprises that would not or could not adapt to the new way of doing business demanded by the layout of the interchanges on the new highways suffered a loss of clientele within hours of the opening of the bypass around their towns.

Almost every building lost its aesthetic respectability the day President Lyndon Baines Johnson, encouraged by his wife, Lady Bird, signed the Highway Beautification Act of 1965, which outlawed billboards on the new interstates. Lady Bird was responding to the cry put forth by Peter Blake from his respected position as editor of the *Architectural Forum*, a leading professional journal of the sixties, when he attacked the aesthetics of roadside businesses, their buildings, their signs, and their billboards in his book *God's Own Junkyard*, published in 1964. Without the billboards, Mom and Pop had no way of notifying travelers on the interstate that they had a cozy cabin waiting for them in the next town. Business fell off; buildings began to deteriorate. Hence, until the late seventies, architects and architectural historians ignored or, even worse, sneered at America's roadside architecture.

By 1980, when historians began looking at roadside architecture in general and U.S. 66 in particular, the buildings along 66 were in pretty bad shape. The interstate highways were nearing completion. Only in Arizona and parts of Texas did the highway still go along Main Street. The triple punch dealt by Eisenhower's interstates, Johnson's beautification act, and Blake's diatribes led to the mansarding of the American roadside—the application of mansard roofs and other architectural decorations to highway buildings in an effort to make them visually respectable and economically viable under new conditions. Where the interstate left sections of the old highway totally abandoned, with a separation of several miles between the two, the architecture of the 1926–56 era survived without alteration. These stretches of highway became roadside "museums," housing relics from another era.

The architecture on U.S. 66 falls into eight overlapping regional sections, each with distinctive characteristics. First there was the local road between Chicago and Litchfield, Illinois; then there was the St. Louis urban region, which extended east and west of the city; then came the Ozark region between Rolla and Joplin, Missouri; the Great Plains between the Missouri-Kansas border and Albuquerque, New Mexico; Pueblo country, north and west of Albuquerque; the Main Street/railroad towns of western New Mexico and Arizona; the Mojave Desert west of Needles, California; and, finally, a second local stretch between San Bernardino and Los Angeles.

Within each region there were two strains of roadside architecture. The first was a truly vernacular architecture, drawing from indigenous houses in the region and often using materials available only in the region: the Illinois tavern in brick or clapboard, the Ozark Sandstone House, the Western Bungalow, the Spanish/Pueblo House, the Western Ranch House, the California Casa, and the California Bungalow. The second strain was a stylish architecture, drawing on the current fashion in roadside architecture: the revivals—Spanish Colonial, American Colonial, and Tudor; the Streamline Moderne and the International Style. The owners of these buildings, found most often within fifty miles of urban centers, frequently hired local architects or engineers to help with the design. Sometimes the architects drew on indigenous designs; most often they opted for fashion.

Of the revivals, only the Spanish Colonial grew out of indigenous architectures along 66 to become a national style. The eighteenth-century Spanish Mission and the California Casa with their enclosed courtyards lined with rooms provided the ideal model for the early-twentieth-century motel with a central courtyard. Generally constructed of wood frame or adobe brick or clay tile and covered in stucco to imitate adobe, the Spanish Colonial motel was cheap to build.[9] Along the urban stretch between San Bernardino and Los Angeles and in cities like Albuquerque, Oklahoma City, Tulsa, and St. Louis, variations on Spanish Colonial were the stylish architectures of choice in the 1920s and 1930s. Occasionally, New Mexicans found that Spanish Pueblo houses, characterized by round roof rafters, *vigas*, that penetrated the unfired brick walls and showed on the exterior, made good motel rooms when built in adobe and stucco. After World War II, the eighteenth-century California Casa, which provided the model for the American ranch house, also provided a model for the postwar motel clear across the country.[10]

The break from traditional folk architecture came as the depression eased into the forties and business owners, particularly café owners, turned to Streamline Moderne. Introduced to the American public by industrial designers Raymond Loewy, Walter Dorwin Teague, and others at the Chicago World's Fair in 1933–34 and at the New York World's Fair five years later, the Streamline Moderne style projected the future and better times.[11] The style was characterized by sleek, shiny surfaces and rounded corners molded in stucco or turned in glazed tile. The style was an outgrowth of the Spanish Colonial coupled to a depression-era fascination with the sleek curved lines used in the industrial design of cars and appliances and with factory-made materials such as glass block and structural tiles used in the construction of buildings.[12] What read as Spanish Colonial in the rounded corners of the false front over the Bond-Gunderson Trading Post in 1915 in Grants, New Mexico, read as Streamline Moderne in the similar, rounded false front over the Site Oil Company service station in 1940 in Edwardsville, Illinois.

Streamline Moderne was particularly popular in St. Louis, Tulsa, and Oklahoma City, where there was more money to spend on architecture than there was in rural regions. The urban influence on rural roadside buildings, particularly that of St. Louis, extended about fifty miles into the countryside. Hence the St. Louis region was anchored by two superb Streamline structures—the 66 Terminal Truck Stop in rural Staunton, Illinois, thirty-five miles northeast of St. Louis and the Diamonds Truck Stop at Villa Ridge, Missouri, thirty-five miles west of St. Louis.

With the end of World War II, as the forties eased into the fifties, American GIs returned home, packed up their families, moved to their suburban ranch houses, and took to the road on their annual paid vacations. Roadside entrepreneurs responded with new architectural forms—the ranch house motel designed to look like a little bit of home, the International Style motel office and café, and giant neon signs. The Museum of Modern Art in New York introduced the International Style to the American public in a 1931 show that included the design of a gas station. On the roadside the International Style was characterized by the "visual front"—large sheets of plate glass on the front of motel offices, often canted outward at the top to prevent glare, inviting the traveler inside.[13] Motel owners beckoned late-night travelers off the road with tall, blinking neon signs, brightly lit glass offices, and cozy ranch house rooms outlined in neon. Café and hamburger joint owners made their places sparkle with large expanses of canted glass topped by neon cornices on which they advertised their menus.

The coming of the interstates marked the end of an architecture based on the whims, the taste, and the sweat of the roadside entrepreneur. The straight, safe dual-lane highways that replaced 66 fenced off the wayside, carried speeding traffic past every little town, and allowed Mom and Pop only limited access to their customers at designated interchanges. It was impossible to build a motel or a gas station or a café on the roadside between towns. Towns like Bridgeport, Oklahoma, a mile-long stringtown of roadside businesses with no exit from the interstate, disappeared altogether. The only place the new highways offered commercial sites was at the interchange between the interstate and Main Street. At the same time, the first referral and franchise motels and fast-food stands appeared on the scene—the first Holiday Inn in 1952 and the first pair of Golden Arches in 1953—and with them came the beginnings of standardized roadside architecture. Cyrus Avery had called Route 66 the Main Street of America, but increasingly Mom and Pop, who owned gas stations, motels, and cafés on Main Street, lost business to those enterprises that were able to build near the highway interchanges and that snagged the traveling public before the tourists ever got to Main Street.

BUILDING TYPES

Gas Stations

When Americans took to the road in the first decade of the twentieth century, their new motorcars were fueled by gasoline, a waste product of the kerosene industry. At first motorists purchased their gasoline by the bucketful at the local livery, repair shop, or general store and funneled it into their gas tanks. In 1905, Sylanus F. Bowser took a water pump he had invented twenty years earlier and turned it into a gas pump by mounting it on a fifty-gallon container housed in a cabinet. He called his invention "the Filling Station." Other pumps followed, and soon curbside pumps proliferated outside local liveries and general stores. In Cubero, New Mexico, Sidney Gottlieb added gasoline to his inventory when automobiles began passing in front of his trading post on the Laguna Reservation. In Grants, New Mexico, the Bond-Gunderson Trading Post, which catered to ranchers, added gas pumps in front of its store in the teens. In St. Johns, Arizona, the Whiting brothers—Art, Ernest, Eddie, and Ralph—opened a gas station on the National Old Trails Road next to their box factory.[14]

In response to the popularity of the automobile and its voracious demand for gasoline, the oil industry developed distribution systems for its former waste product and a new building type—the gas station. By 1910 the basic architectural elements of the gas station were in place—an interior office and an exterior canopy covering the pumps. The exterior canopy was not always necessary and was dropped in some parts of the country to remove its obstructing columns from the pumping area. In small towns, where the service station owner fixed the locals' cars, an adjacent garage was imperative. Before the oil companies standardized their gas stations into recognizable company logos to promote brand loyalty, local entrepreneurs built their own. The Whiting brothers found they could make a little gas station for almost nothing using lumber from their father's mills, and they built a chain of them. By the mid-teens the oil companies took the basic elements—the office and the canopy—and began building standardized prefabricated glass and steel "crackerboxes" that were small, cheap, and easily assembled. Shell and Standard Oil of California were among the first to franchise out the manufacture of their crackerboxes to steel fabricators and to paint them with the company colors, thus turning them into company logos. Other manufacturers offered buildings for sale to independent dealers through catalogs.[15]

By the beginning of the thirties, the Pure Oil Company and the Phillips Petroleum Company were building standardized stations. In 1937 Texaco hired industrial designer Walter Dorwin Teague to design a station. He came up with the basic design for a Streamline Moderne building that could be built in any part of the country from whatever materials were available—porcelain-enameled steel, brick, concrete block, or frame and stucco—as long as the completed building had Texaco's sleek white finish and a cornice with three green

Prefabricated Gas Station, 1915
Carthage, Missouri

In 1914 Standard Oil of California introduced its prototype for a standardized, prefabricated steel-and-glass gas station. It, like this small prefabricated station in a private museum in Carthage, Missouri, was no more than an office and a canopy. The styles var-

ied. Though constructed of small metal parts, this station was designed to look like wood clapboard with a tile roof.[16] Photograph by author, 1979.

stripes that could be extended along a streamlined canopy. The building in its many variations was instantly recognizable as a Texaco station, even without a sign.[17]

Because the oil companies turned their stations into company logos so early and changed their logos so often, few early gas stations remain in urban areas, though a few of the home-made variety survive in rural areas and small towns. While the standardized company logos did proliferate on 66, stations built by local entrepreneurs tell us more about the regions we are passing through. While gas stations might tell us something about local folk architec-

Texaco Gas Station, ca. 1940
Glenrio, Texas

Walter Dorwin Teague designed a gas station for Texaco that could be built in any part of the country from whatever materials were available—porcelain-enameled steel, concrete block, or clay tile and stucco—as long as the completed building had a sleek white finish and a cornice with three bands of green that could be extended along the streamlined canopy. The building, even without a sign, was instantly recognizable as a Texaco station. Photograph by author, 1982.

tures, in some regions they tell us more about local materials or climate. Local gas station owners' choices of styles were regional, following, as we shall see later, the same pattern as motels. In Illinois, they built brick or wood-frame stations covered in clapboard or shingles, following local traditions where houses were brick or wood. Russell Soulsby and his father left the coal mines when they heard Illinois 16 would come through Mount Olive. By the time the road was laid out, they had set the foundation for their small clapboard Shell station. In the Missouri Ozarks folks used local sandstone. Billy Aaron and his sons cut flat slabs of sandstone from the hills just west of Rolla, which they laid up as a veneer on their station and garage.

As 66 moved out of the humid Midwest to the subhumid plains and the arid desert, station owners increased the size and depth of their canopies in order to protect themselves and their customers from the sun. It was possible to measure the intensity of the desert sun by the height and depth of the canopy. Even in the 1950s, when Texaco generally eliminated canopies from its stations, the company retained them in the Southwest to provide shade in the service area.[18] On the plains of Kansas, Oklahoma, and Texas, station operators supported their heavy canopies with thick columns from which branched massive brackets, and they covered the peaked roofs in tin shaped like Spanish tiles. In some cases they used a single pier. While they designed their canopies to protect customers from the summer sun, they raised them high enough to let in tall trucks and plenty of light.

Not so in the desert where owners designed canopies low and wide, sometimes the width of the building, so it looked like someone had cut out the front of the building itself. Occasionally they added overhangs to keep out the hot evening sun. All this wraparound shade cooled the office. At Seligman, Arizona, Tom Cook and Guy Sykes added a canopy three bays wide to the front of their Seligman Garage. In 1932 when James Albert Chambless built his gas station/motel/market at Cadiz, California, in the Mojave Desert, he raised a canopy to cover the whole front of his building. Supported by telephone poles sheathed in stucco and set on stone bases, the canopy was two bays wide and four bays long.

In the early years, campground proprietors and, later, motor-court owners operated gas stations in their complexes, with the gas station and the motor court sharing the same office. In rural areas, what started as a gas station frequently grew into a motor court with a café. In 1932 when newlyweds Leon and Ann Little bought an old gas station at the end of the Swinging Bridge over the South Canadian River at Bridgeport, Oklahoma, it came with a campground. In 1934 they packed up their ten-gallon pumps and moved south with 66 to Hinton Junction, where a new bridge had just been completed over the river. There Leon built a small station but very quickly added a café and several motel rooms. The Littles lived in a small room off the kitchen of the café. In 1940 they replaced the small station with a two-story building that included living quarters for their growing family.[19]

As the interstates were completed, in-town gas stations survived better than rural ones did. People like the Littles, whose business was located near the junction of U.S. 66 and U.S. 281, lost all their business with the opening of I-40. As interchanges were completed, the large oil companies and their distributors opened gas stations on adjacent land, skimming off the travelers on their way to someplace else. In-town motel owners who had gas stations, like Pete and Jessie Hudson in Lebanon, Missouri, gave them up. In-town gas stations like Soulsby Shell in Mount Olive, Illinois, which only provided gas, lost some of their business but continued to survive on local traffic, and frequently, in the smaller towns, their buildings survived as well. The Whiting brothers, who built their chain of gas stations on cheap land on the outskirts of towns, found themselves adjacent to the interchanges. They thrived on customers who wanted to get off the highway, get serviced, and get on their way.[20]

Motels

When Americans took to the road in the second decade of the twentieth century, they abandoned hotels that were tied to railroads and towns, took the comforts of home with them—tents, bedding, cooking utensils, and food—and set off across the American landscape, camping on the roadside. The Good Roads movement followed them and laid out an informal system of highways using colored strips and symbols nailed to fence posts and telephone poles to mark routes sponsored by their promoters. Main Street merchants, eager to draw travelers back into town, sponsored local campgrounds that offered central bath-houses and cooking facilities.

When the free campgrounds began attracting undesirable as well as desirable tenants, the merchants started charging rent for their use and opened the door to the development of the commercial campground, which rented tents and provided a central bathhouse and kitchen. Quickly the developers of commercial campgrounds added small cabins with attached garages, which offered more privacy and comfort than tents and better protected the cars as well as the people from wind, rain, hail, sleet, and snow. Soon proprietors elim-inated the tents altogether. As travelers wearied of hauling the comforts of home with them, cabin owners supplied linens and central kitchens or, better yet, opened an adjacent café. As travelers demanded more privacy and luxury, proprietors upgraded the cabins to include indoor plumbing, eliminating the central bathhouse. To round out their services to the auto tourist, they added gas stations, which they combined with the office and their own living quarters.

During the depression, many who had preferred the luxury and service offered by a hotel discovered the low cost of the motor court. Cabin owners continued to add luxuries to keep this upscale trade. Finally, for the tourist who preferred the comfort of a hotel but the con-venience of a tourist camp, enterprising homeowners along the roadside converted their houses to tourist homes. They erected signs in their front yards, advertising rooms for rent with a meal. They offered comfortable, clean rooms and a friendly atmosphere very much like the modern bed-and-breakfast.[21]

Roadside architecture, particularly motor-court architecture, represents the country's last blast of vernacular folk architecture based on regional and ethnic precedents. When the campground proprietors built their first cabins, they wanted them quick and they wanted them simple. A few bought prefabricated kits manufactured by companies such as the Economy Housing Company of Onawa, Iowa, and available in lumberyards. Others used a design for a ten-by-twelve-foot cabin published in *Popular Mechanics* in 1935.[22] For the most part, though, they built their own designs, choosing a familiar architecture and a sim-ple construction method—a wood-frame cabin finished in clapboard or stucco, or a struc-tural clay tile cabin finished in stucco. Between them, the two choices accommodated almost any style—Colonial clapboard, Western Bungalow, Craftsman Bungalow, Spanish Colonial, or Spanish Pueblo.

The builders' choices were regional. Proprietors in Illinois and Missouri turned to the white clapboard cabin set around a tree-shaded courtyard. In the Ozarks west of Rolla, Missouri, and continuing to Shamrock, Texas, builders used local sandstones that reflected the color of the land—rusty yellow and orange in the Ozarks that deepened to reds and blacks in Oklahoma and faded to pinks and grays in the Panhandle. On the Great Plains west of Oklahoma City, where wood was at a premium, they turned to manufactured mate-rials. Frequently they built Prairie or Western Bungalows, much like those that were intro-duced to the Great Plains by Russian-German immigrants in Kansas in the 1870s, with pyramidal roofs that required few long pieces of wood in their construction. In New Mexico, where the adobe house of the Pueblo Indians, who lived in villages along the Rio Grande and west of Albuquerque, was the vernacular architecture, proprietors adapted the style to

Russian-German House, ca. 1880
Schoenchen, Kansas

Russian-German families from Schoenchen in Russia settled in Ellis County, Kansas, in 1876 and began building stone houses with pyramidal roofs like those they had built in Russia. Wherever Russian-Germans settled in Kansas and Nebraska, they built this house in stone, wood frame, or adobe. It evolved into the Western Bungalow, a wood-frame, four-room house with a pyramidal roof. The style spread across the Great Plains in the late nineteenth and early twentieth centuries.[23] Photograph by author, 1988.

their motels. In Albuquerque they mimicked the Palace of the Governors in Santa Fe, essentially a Pueblo structure, built using Pueblo labor and methods and Spanish forms. In Arizona, they turned the nineteenth-century ranch house with its series of little rooms under a broad veranda into the local motel. Along the urban strip between San Bernardino and Los Angeles, proprietors found that the local Spanish mission complex provided a model for their motels.

In the early years of motel building, proprietors experimented with the plan of the motor court. They developed two models: an open plan, with cabins along a curved drive—based on the bungalow courts that had proliferated in the Los Angeles suburbs in the teens and the twenties—and a closed plan, with attached rooms lining a central court—based on the plans of Spanish missions in California and Texas.[24] Those who, like Emis and Lois Spears

Acoma Pueblo, ca. 1500
Acoma, New Mexico

Acoma Pueblo, the oldest continuously occupied village in the United States, rests on the Enchanted Mesa thirteen miles south of U.S. 66. The Acoma built parallel rows of stone and adobe—unfired clay brick—houses. The blocks were a thousand feet long and up to three stories tall. They were covered with a five-layer roof of brush and small stones supported by vigas—round poles that protruded through the walls.[25] Photograph by author, 1985.

in Lebanon, Missouri, used the bungalow plan, built their cabins along a curved drive with the bathhouse and kitchen in the center. Once they eliminated the central kitchen and bath and installed indoor plumbing in their cabins, they turned the central section into a courtyard and provided seating where, in the years before air conditioning and television, travelers gathered on summer evenings. As business improved and the site filled up, motel owners often used the green space for a pool or additional rooms. Across the front of the property, many proprietors built a café designed to appeal to guests, locals, and passersby, and a two-story building that housed the gas station, the office, and their own living quarters.[26]

With the elimination of central baths and kitchens, some motor-court builders found the Spanish Mission plan ideally suited to their needs. The closed plan with rooms lining an

Palace of the Governors, 1609
Santa Fe, New Mexico

The Spanish constructed the palace in 1609 as part of a fortress, using Pueblo Indian labor and blending Spanish architectural forms with the limitations of adobe. It was a Pueblo building using adobe walls and vigas to support the flat roof to which the Spanish added doors and windows—Pueblo Indians entered their dwellings through traps in the roof. The Spanish may also have added a colonnade that ran the length of the building, or perhaps restorers, using a theoretical recreation of the 1609 palace, added the colonnade in 1914. Motel builders in New Mexico used the palace and the pueblos from which it was adapted as models for their buildings.[27] Photograph by Fedor Ferez, ca. 1940, neg. #100767. Used by permission of the Museum of New Mexico.

interior courtyard permitted many units on a small lot. Whether it was constructed in wood frame and stucco, adobe and stucco, or structural tile and stucco, the Spanish Colonial motor court was cheap to build.[28] When William Clay Pierce of the Pierce-Pennant Oil Company built the Big Chief Hotel in Pond, Missouri, in 1928, one of a chain of motor courts between Springfield, Illinois, and Tulsa, Oklahoma, he used the Spanish Mission plan and lined a rectangular interior courtyard with attached rooms. He broke the facade into separate structures: One housed the office, another the café, and a third the gas station. Each was a variation on a Spanish Colonial house, albeit adapted to a motor court.

Builders like Pierce with the ambition to build chains used the Spanish Colonial style to define their images. They had a precedent. After 1896 the Atchison, Topeka and Santa Fe

Santa Fe Railroad Station, 1907
Kingman, Arizona

The Santa Fe station at Kingman was very plain by Santa Fe standards. Designers modeled the stepped bell-cote, which marks the entrance to the tracks, on the bell-cote of a Spanish mission. Small scallops defined the banks of windows that flanked the entrance. Both details showed up in motels and gas stations the length of U.S. 66. Photograph by author, 1982.

Railway and the Fred Harvey chain of hotels defined Spanish Colonial as the architectural style for travel and used the style to promote tourism in the Southwest. The Santa Fe railroad built a series of Spanish Colonial stations, both large and imposing and small and utilitarian, across the Southwest between Las Vegas, New Mexico, and Los Angeles along the route that U.S. Highway 66 would follow thirty years later. Fred Harvey built handsome, Spanish Colonial hotels next door. There were, without doubt, many elegant and well-known architectural examples for the roadside entrepreneur to adapt to the motor court.[29]

In Waco, Texas, Lee Torrence discarded the rectangular layout common to early motel plans and created a Spanish village, or hacienda. Torrence developed the Alamo Plaza Hotel Courts with motels in Waco, across the Southeast, and on U.S. 66 at Oklahoma City. In 1928 he hired an architect to model the facade of his motor court on the Alamo, a Spanish mission revered in Texas and recognizable throughout the nation. Torrence broke the facade into

Chapel of San Antonio de Valero, the Alamo, 1724–1845
San Antonio, Texas

Spanish Franciscan missionaries founded the Mission of San Antonio de Valero on San Pedro Creek west of the San Antonio River in 1718. The Franciscans moved the site of the mission several times before settling on the present location in 1724. The king of Spain secularized the mission in 1793 and sold its land. In 1801 it became a military post. When the mission became the site of the battle of the Alamo thirty-five years later, the chapel was already a roofless ruin surrounded by a three-foot rock wall. After Texas entered the Union in 1845, the Catholic Church restored the facade of the chapel to its present appearance. It is the upper portion of this facade that served as the model for the Alamo Plaza Courts and the Park Plaza Courts.[30] Photograph courtesy of the San Antonio Convention and Visitors Bureau.

three elements: At the center he erected a long, two-story wall that imitated the facade of the Alamo and tapered to a single story at the sides; at either side he built a single-story, scalloped wall that could be repeated if the motel grew. Behind the facades, he laid out his hacienda—blocks of rooms that braced the walls and were perpendicular to them and a long block across the rear of the complex. He housed the office and owner-manager's residence in the two-story center. Guests entered the complex through flat arches cut in the center element on either side of the office.[31]

RATES FROM $1.50 UP
THE SOUTH'S FINEST TOURIST APARTMENTS
A SEALY MATTRESS ON EVERY BED
A BATH WITH EVERY APARTMENT

ALAMO PLAZA, 900 BLOCK ELM STREET, WACO, TEXAS

Alamo Plaza Tourist Apartments, 1928
Waco, Texas

In 1928 Lee Torrence hired a Waco architect to design a facade for an auto court. This court, modeled on the Alamo, would be the first of a chain that had several branches. The two-story center building and the single-story side elements provided a flexible plan that could be used for any size motor court. Over the next twenty years motel builders on 66 mimicked Torrence's plan and his Alamo facade in motor courts between St. Louis and Flagstaff. Torrence himself built only one Alamo Plaza on U.S. 66, in Oklahoma City in 1937.[32] Reproduction of the postcard of the Alamo Plaza, Waco, from the Texas Collection, Baylor University.

Torrence's 1928 Alamo facade—a flat, wood-frame wall covered with stucco swirled over chicken-wire lath to give it texture—was so cheap and easy to build, and was such an compelling architectural form, that over the next twenty years it found numerous imitators on U.S. 66. Torrence never pursued the folks who copied his design and, in at least one case, gave it away.[33] Jack Sibley mimicked the Alamo facade when he built El Sueno in Claremore, Oklahoma, in 1938. The Lakeview Courts west of Oklahoma City also mimicked the design. In 1942 Torrence gave Milton and Lemuel Stroud of Waco the use of his architect and his design when they developed the Park Plaza Courts, a chain with motels in St. Louis, Tulsa, Amarillo, and Flagstaff. Finally, Abe Schwartz copied the Park Plaza Courts at St. Louis when he built the New Grande Courts at Sullivan, Missouri, in 1949.[34]

As the pioneer years along Route 66 ended with the beginning of World War II, urban motel builders between Chicago and Amarillo abandoned the vernacular architectures of the Ozarks and the Southwest for the Streamline Moderne, a progressive style that assured their customers the best in indoor plumbing and cleanliness. Glazed brick and glass block became their materials of choice, but the construction techniques and the general plan—café, gas station, and office facing the highway and cabins along a curved drive or U-shaped interior court—remained the same. In 1941, St. Louisan John Carr hired architect Adolph L. Strubig to design the Coral Court. Strubig presented Carr with a series of Streamline Moderne cabins constructed of hollow clay tile faced with yellow-ochre glazed tiles, or "soaps." Stepped triangular windows in glass block filled the rounded corners of each cabin. Only in the St. Louis region did builders use ochre soaps, of the kind found in public bathrooms of the day. Elsewhere, they found they could build the smooth curved walls demanded by the style as easily and more cheaply in structural tile and stucco. In the Southwest, motel builders rejected the Streamline Moderne and continued to use variations on the Spanish Colonial and Spanish Pueblo well into the 1950s, when standardized designs began to take hold in motel building.

Gas rationing during World War II cut travel along America's highways considerably—and with it the demand for overnight housing in all regions along the road, except those near military bases. Along 66 near Fort Leonard Wood in the Missouri Ozarks, the demand for housing was so great that farmers converted their chicken coops to sleeping rooms for people. Some added a cabin or two along the roadside and rented it first to construction workers at the base and then to army personnel and their families, who were desperate for housing. The same phenomenon happened near army air force bases at Amarillo and Albuquerque and a gunnery school near Kingman, Arizona.[35]

With the end of World War II, traffic on Route 66 boomed as Americans took to the road and increased the demand for motel rooms. Motel owners abandoned individual cabins when they found that attached rooms laid out in an L or a U around a parking court made more economical use of their land. At the same time they discovered the ease and economy of building with concrete block and finishing it in stucco. They added overhangs to these long barrackslike buildings, giving them the appearance of the ranch houses that were sprouting across the countryside as Americans, funded by the GI bill and Federal Housing Administration loans, abandoned their cities and moved to the suburbs. In 1943, Lyle and Ruby Overman prophesied the American passion for the postwar suburban ranch house when they squeezed the Carlyle Court onto a tight urban lot in Oklahoma City. They wrapped an oval drive around the ranch-style office and owner's residence. The building's broad hipped roof extended out from the office as a canopy. Around the drive and at a forty-five-degree angle to it, they set six little ranch houses of three rooms each.

The ranch house itself was a derivative of the eighteenth-century California Casa. Reinforcing the allusion to ranch houses, the most popular names for postwar motels were El Rancho, Ranchito, and Ranchero, particularly in Texas, New Mexico, and Arizona.

In California, where one would expect the Streamline Moderne or the ranch house to blossom, roadside builders stayed with the domestic styles that had proliferated in the Los Angeles suburbs in the years following World War I—the Spanish Colonial and the Craftsman Bungalow—but used more efficient plans.

The passage of the Federal Aid Highway Act in 1956 and the advent of franchise chains such as Holiday Inn made the survival of family-owned motels in small towns along 66 tenuous. The biggest threat to small motels was the interstate bypass around town. But that did

Casa of Mission San Gabriel Archangel, 1768
San Gabriel, California

The Mission Adobe house, adjacent to the bell tower at Mission San Gabriel, was the perfect house for the mild southern California climate. Deep porches that were extensions of the shingled tile roof and open windows and doors on either side of the house allowed for the free circulation of air. In the courtyards the porches allowed for passage from one room to another where there were no interior halls. This design and others like it were the model for the American ranch house. And it was the perfect model for motel builders when they abandoned detached cabins and began building blocks of attached rooms after World War II.[36] Photograph by author, 1998.

not come until the mid-sixties and early seventies. The last town to be bypassed on 66 was Williams, Arizona, in 1985. In the meantime, the architectural competition for attention along Main Street was tremendous as motel owners went for the International Style characterized by glassed-in offices and huge signs with imperative arrows directing travelers off the street and into the office.[37] Older motel owners, like Pete and Jessie Hudson at the Munger Moss in Lebanon, Missouri, replaced their cozy offices with large, transparent, brightly lit lobbies dominated by a huge neon sign. The Hudsons' sign was a frank imitation of the Holiday Inn arrow.[38] Out in the Mojave Desert, where he was the sole proprietor of the town of Amboy, California, wrecker and tow-master Buster Burris erected a wedge-shaped neon sign over a huge glass office with a soaring roof and his line of tiny stucco cabins.[39]

As the interstate highways neared completion, the franchise chains bought up the land near the interchanges, where they had first crack at the traveler coming off the road. Mom and Pop with their sparkling offices and their huge signs could not compete and had to wait until the chains filled up for the night before customers came their way. Out in the Mojave, Buster Burris, who had employed ninety full-time employees in his garage/gas station/café/motel, watched helplessly as the traffic past his complex stopped when I-40 between Needles and Ludlow opened, carrying customers a dozen miles to the north.

For a long time the old motor courts and motels could survive on transients staying at weekly rates and an occasional traveler, and many continue to do so in small towns along 66. In the big cities, however, the suburban land they occupied became too valuable. Their owners sold them to builders of subdivisions and shopping centers. Such was the fate of the Coral Court in St. Louis. When the motel, architecturally the finest on 66, was razed in May 1995, one cabin was salvaged as a museum piece by the National Museum of Transport in St. Louis. The rest met the same fate as the 66 Auto Court, the 66 Park In Theatre, and the other architectural icons of Route 66 in St. Louis—razed to make way for more economically viable developments.

Cafés and Food Stands

It was not until the 1930s that American auto tourists warmed to roadside food cooked by others. When Americans took to the road in the first decade of the twentieth century, they took their food with them and picnicked on the roadside, or they ate in city lunchrooms or hotel and railroad station dining rooms. They found city lunchrooms dirty and filled with local workingmen; they found hotel and railroad dining rooms too expensive and time-consuming for a family in a hurry. On the edge of town they might find a ladies' tearoom that served tiny portions of dainty food. Occasionally they came across wayside inns or resort hotels, which, like urban hotels, were expensive and time-consuming. Roadside food for the most part remained tied to the cities. Until the fourth decade of the twentieth century, travelers figured it was easier, cheaper, faster, and healthier to carry their food with them.[40]

In the mid-twenties in the Southwest, however, railroad station restaurants began to experience an influx of auto tourists. In New Mexico, Arizona, and California where Main Street became 66 and often ran next to the Santa Fe line, auto tourists stopped at the Fred Harvey restaurants in the local railroad station. By the 1930s in Gallup, New Mexico, Harvey's business from the road had grown so large the restaurant cut a new door onto Main Street to make it more inviting to travelers on 66.[41]

At the same time, pioneer campground proprietors began providing kitchens so travelers could cook a hot meal in the evening. They maintained the kitchens even as they began building cabins. But as they continued to modernize their facilities, and as travelers came to accept roadside food cooked by others, motel owners ripped out the kitchens and built cafés designed to appeal to their guests, to noontime passersby, and to locals. The café offered them another source of income, and a family member could always be found to run it. Hence Lois and Emis Spears built the café at Camp Joy in Lebanon, Missouri, that was run by Lois's mother, Lida. By 1939 half of the better motor courts ran cafés.[42] Rural motels had a captive clientele at dinner and breakfast, and travelers were happy to find a rural café that offered wholesome food at noon.

Running a café was hard work. Ann Little served three meals a day and cleaned rooms at the Littles' motel, café, and gas station at Hinton Junction, Oklahoma. In 1939 when a movie company was filming *The Grapes of Wrath* not far from the Littles' complex, husband Leon suggested they go watch. Ann was too busy.[43] When Sidney Gottlieb and Wallace and Mary Gunn expanded their trading post in 1937 and built a motel and café on U.S. 66 in Cubero, New Mexico, the Gunns operated the motel and Gottlieb's sister the café. She found it hard going and quit. Mary added the café to her duties.[44]

Architecturally, the motor-court cafés were built in the same style as the cabins. Thus the Spearses' café was housed in a frame-and-clapboard building like the cabins at Camp Joy in Lebanon, Missouri; the Littles' café in the same kind of simple structural-clay-tile-and-stucco building as the gas station and motel units; and Mary Gunn's café in a small adobe-like building very similar to the small cabins that surrounded the office and gas station.

Few roadside entrepreneurs on U.S. 66 built cafés in the 1920s. Most of what remains from that decade were businesses that predated U.S. 66 but were located on heavily traveled roads that were incorporated into 66 when that road was laid out. Illinois had a tradition of roadside taverns. Many dot the road between Chicago and St. Louis, and, like so much of the roadside architecture along 66 in Illinois, they were wood-frame buildings covered in clapboard or asphalt shingles. The Blue Mill in Lincoln, a tavern that looked like a Dutch windmill, used its architecture to attract local diners and began catering to auto tourists.

During the depression, if you could cook and keep things clean, you could open a café or a food stand, the precursor to the fast-food franchise. If you were handy, you could build your own frame-and-stucco building from materials in the local lumberyard, or you could convert an existing building. Gus Belt did just that in Normal, Illinois, where he converted a Shell station into a roadside tavern, which he then converted to a drive-in hamburger stand when Normal went dry in 1934. He was so successful with hamburgers and milkshakes that he expanded the food stand into a well-known regional chain called Steak 'n' Shake.

Running a café was a good way to make a living in remote places along the road west of Tulsa. Elizabeth Threatt, one of the few African-American entrepreneurs on the roadside, supplemented her income as a schoolteacher in Luther, Oklahoma, by serving breakfast and dinner in her café adjacent to her husband's gas station on the edge of their farm.[45] Just west of the Oklahoma border, Shamrock, Texas, sat on the intersection of U.S. 66 and U.S. 83 where Marie Taylor opened the Kansas City Steak House across the highway from John and Bebe Nunn's U-Drop-Inn. In Santa Rosa, New Mexico, two boyhood buddies, Phil Craig and Floyd Shaw, recently migrated from Texas to work on grading and paving New Mexico 6, opened the Club Cafe in 1934. Phil ran the café while Floyd continued working on the road. West of Santa Rosa on the lonely 120-mile stretch to Albuquerque at the intersection of 66 and U.S. 285, the Cline family supplemented the income from their gas station with a small tin café at a place they called Clines Corners.

Most of the cafés built along 66 in the 1930s were basic frame-and-clapboard or block-and-stucco buildings. They went up quickly and served their purpose well until they burned or were abandoned for a larger, fancier building. When the Kansas City Steak House burned, Marie Taylor moved across the road and opened up in the Western Motel. The fledgling

Club Cafe grew with Santa Rosa into a huge roadside institution housed in a large International Style glass-front building on Santa Rosa's Main Street.

Of the remaining cafés built in the thirties only the U-Drop-Inn, located in the Art Deco Tower Station in Shamrock, Texas, stands out architecturally. John Nunn designed the building when he drew the flared tower of the gas station in the dust of U.S. 66. Two canopies, one facing 66 and the other U.S. 83, fronted the office of the gas station and embraced the tower. To the rear, under a shorter tower facing 66, John and his wife, Bebe, installed their restaurant. Otherwise, depression-era cafés followed the same local vernacular styles that motels did in the 1930s: wood frame and clapboard or brick on the Illinois prairie, flat sandstone in the Missouri Ozarks and eastern Oklahoma, Western Bungalow in western Oklahoma and the Texas Panhandle, adobe in New Mexico, western ranch in Arizona, and California Bungalow in California.

While few cafés opened during World War II—wartime rationing made it difficult—GIs returning from service found that feeding people was still an easy business to get into. Like their depression-era colleagues, they converted old buildings or built simple stucco structures. Ex-GI Red Chaney converted a gas station and motel to a hamburger stand on the western edge of Springfield, Missouri. Chaney tried to manage the few cabins that came with the gas station but decided to concentrate on hamburgers and tore the cabins down. Marvin Porter, on the other hand, added a motel to the gas station he converted to a café in Weatherford, Oklahoma. Army cook Jesse Fincher returned to his hometown of Adrian, Texas, opened a café on 66, then later moved it to Wildorado and added a motel. Albert Wong limited himself to cooking food when he returned to the Grand Canyon Cafe on Santa Fe Avenue in Flagstaff.

Café owners were far more willing to build in new styles of architecture—particularly the Streamline Moderne and later the International Style—than were motel owners, who stayed with the local vernacular well into the 1940s and early 1950s. In the years just before and just after World War II, restaurant owners began building in the Streamline Moderne style. In urban regions, they embraced it wholeheartedly. The style reassured travelers that the restaurant was clean, the food healthful, and the service efficient. Louis Eckelkamp lured families into the Gardenway at Gray Summit, Missouri, with an American Colonial motel built in 1945 but assured those same families of the efficiency and cleanliness of the Diamonds Restaurant and Truck Stop with a Streamline Moderne café built three years later at Villa Ridge, a few miles west of the Gardenway.

After the war, the Streamline Moderne use of colored tiles, combined with the International Style use of huge windows and soaring rooflines, produced a look that might be called Food-Stand Moderne. It became the vehicle by which food stands established their images as fast-food enterprises. In the 1950s food-stand operators simplified and standardized their menus and invented the fast-food chain. With the standardization of food came the standardization of architecture. In Normal, Illinois, Gus Belt replaced the gas station that housed his first Steak 'n' Shake with a white-and-black-tile Streamline Moderne building that had a cornice along which running lights framed his menu—"Tru-Flavor Shakes and Steakburgers." His carhops, an invention of the 1920s, took orders from and delivered food to customers who ate from stainless steel trays hitched to their car windows. Belt also offered table service and counter service inside and takeout—"Takhomasak." He standardized the layout of the stainless steel cooking facilities, the counter, and the table seating as well as the menu and the size of the portions. To demonstrate his slogan, "In Sight, It Must Be Right," he ripped out the walls of the kitchen and opened it up so diners seated at the counter could watch the kitchen theatrics, where grill cooks slapped burgers flat and fried them paper-thin. From this beginning, Belt built a chain of Steak 'n' Shakes, expanding first to Bloomington and then across Illinois, Missouri, Indiana, and south into Florida.[46]

Belt was not the only man to turn a food stand into a chain. In 1948 in San Bernardino, California, brothers Maurice and Richard McDonald fired the carhops who had been serving customers at their hamburger stand. They threw out the crockery and pared down the menu to hamburgers, french fries, and milkshakes, all served in containers made of paper. They adapted a model that had proliferated on the streets of Los Angeles since the 1930s—the open-air, walk-up food stand—and opened walk-up windows through which customers ordered and were served their meals, which they ate in their cars. By 1952 the McDonalds were serving a million burgers a year from their stand. Like Gus Belt, the brothers wanted to open additional stands in nearby towns in California and Arizona. They hired architect Stanley C. Merston in 1953 to design a food stand they could reproduce over and over every time they expanded into a new city. Merston produced a Streamline Moderne pavilion in red-and-white-striped tile. Richard McDonald improved upon it. He raised the roof and slanted it backwards, hinting at the coming International Style. Under his soaring roof, he slanted large expanses of plate glass inward to deflect glare and reveal a factory that produced burgers, fries, and shakes. Then McDonald invented the most enduring icon of the fast-food industry—the Golden Arches that seemingly supported the roof. Outlined in neon, they were the first thing hungry motorists spotted as they sailed down the highway at forty miles an hour.[47]

Two years later, a Lily Cup salesman, Ray Kroc, persuaded the McDonalds to let him franchise their hamburger stand nationwide. He opened his first pair of Golden Arches in a red-and-white-striped building in Des Plaines, Illinois, in 1955. Until the 1980s, McDonald's was a suburban phenomenon found along the commercial strips like Watson Road, U.S. 66, in St. Louis, where William Wyatt and Don Kuell opened the first red-and-white-striped McDonald's in 1958.[48] The chain did not proliferate on the rural roadside until the interstate highway system neared completion in the 1980s when the mansarded buildings, which replaced the pavilions, began popping up on interchanges.[49] Ironically, McDonald's led the way in the mansarding of the American roadside in the early sixties when the company applied a rough-shingled mansard roof to the existing soaring roofline of the original pavilion and covered the candy-striped tile with brick.[50]

With the completion of the interstates, cafés, particularly those that stood alone in the center of town, survived better than did motels. They could depend on local business to keep the doors open. But cafés in small towns struggled to compete with the huge restaurant/truck stop/gas station/gift shop or the chains like Denny's, Stuckey's, and Nickerson's Farm that opened up on the interchanges. Cafés tied to motels, particularly those in rural areas, did less well with the opening of the interstate when the traffic outside the front door simply stopped. There was no more business. The Littles at Hinton Junction, Oklahoma, closed down soon after the interstate opened in 1962.

Finally, the advent of restaurant chains and fast-food franchises and the standardization of menus brought an end to the era of roadside cafés serving regional food. Like the highways, which are safe, predictable, and boring, so is the food along America's interstates, which carry the bulk of auto traffic today. A Big Mac is a Big Mac is a Big Mac whether you eat it in Lincoln, Illinois, where the Huffmans once served pork and veal with a special sauce at the Blue Mill; or in Groom, Texas, where Ruby Denton whipped up chicken and dumplings according to her grandmother's recipe at the Golden Spread Grill; or in Grants, New Mexico, where Eskie Mazon offered chilies rellenos at the Monte Carlo.[51] Like the motels—a Super 8, after all, is not that much different from a Holiday Inn—the chain restaurants are safe and predictable, and they all look alike.

Roadside architecture is an ephemeral art. Times change; architectural fashions change. What looked sharp, up-to-date, sleek, and clean in the 1930s looked a little tawdry in the 1940s and downright shabby and tasteless by the 1950s. By the 1960s, all roadside architecture was in disrepute. The motel and restaurant chains that began to dominate the roadside in the 1960s and 1970s used a corporate architecture repeated over and over across the country to define their images in the same way the oil companies had been doing since the teens. And they all changed their architectural clothing periodically, making their old buildings look outdated. These constantly renewed images of the chains made Mom and Pop's homemade buildings look crude and unsafe. In fact, many were. While many folks in small towns continue to build without the benefit of architects and building codes, that is no longer possible for a roadside business serving the public. Fire safety and access for the disabled are too important.

It is ironic that of the three major building types on U.S. 66, restaurants, which reached for the most up-to-date architecture, have survived best, and many continue to do business today in buildings that date to the 1926–56 period. If a restaurant like the Ariston in Litchfield, Illinois, could survive fire and explosions, the routing and rerouting of 66, the I-55 bypass around town, the migration of roadside business to the I-55 interchange, the decline of Main Street, the change of generations, and the mansarding of roadside buildings, and, if it could maintain the level of professionalism demanded by the traveling public and serve good food, it could cash in on the myth of Route 66 in the 1990s. The Ariston did. Its handsome facade, somewhere between Spanish Colonial and Streamline Moderne, still welcomes travelers to its Art Deco dining room, where Nick and DeDe Adam follow the tradition of good food started by his father and mother in 1924, two years before U.S. 66 was routed past their front door.

Illinois

Illinois 66 started at the intersection of Michigan Avenue and Jackson Boulevard in Chicago, followed the Pontiac Trail south through Joliet and Wilmington, crossed the Kankakee River, and traveled southwest across the glaciated prairie to St. Louis.

Assuming it went smoothly, the trip between the urban centers of Chicago and St. Louis was never more than a day. There was little need for motels. A 1994 survey of the buildings along Route 66 in Illinois found only fifty-two motels between Joliet and St. Louis. Most were built after World War II.[1] However, there was a need for gas stations and restaurants and, if the trip went poorly, a garage. Illinois was a wonderful place to look at the simple vernacular gas stations of the pioneer years when owners built with clapboard or shingled walls and projected canopies over their service areas to protect people from the elements.

Illinois had a long tradition of roadside taverns built in a variety of vernacular styles, but it was also a good place to watch the evolution of the Streamline Moderne style from the Spanish Colonial style. In Cicero, Bloomington, and Springfield small food-stand operators with big ambitions relied on the Streamline Moderne to convey a message of cleanliness.

Illinois had "hard" roads years before the rest of the states along 66. Follow old, old 66 near Auburn, and you will find a road paved with brick. Before 1931 Illinois 4 carried U.S. 66 between Springfield and Staunton. First it was a hard road, then a brick road, then a hard road. Three layers of paving. The surface of the road depended on the financial interests of the current governor. After 1931 the road out of Springfield ran through Litchfield to Staunton.[2]

Jackson Boulevard at Michigan Avenue
Chicago

Roads follow roads. Route 66 began at the corner of Jackson and Michigan in Chicago. With the end of the 1933 World's Fair, Jackson was extended to Lake Michigan on land reclaimed from the lake for the fair. It is both fitting and ironic that turning west from Lake Michigan the first building the traveler sees is the Atchison, Topeka and Santa Fe Railway building at Jackson and Michigan Avenue. Fitting because in the early years of the twentieth century, the Santa Fe railroad used the Spanish Colonial architecture of its stations in New Mexico and Arizona to promote travel in the Southwest. Ironic because in 1926 Route 66 followed the Santa Fe railroad between Albuquerque, New Mexico, and Los Angeles, running parallel and often adjacent to the Santa Fe tracks. The automobile gave Americans the freedom to go anywhere, and U.S. Highway 66 and the other federal highways laid out in 1926 gave them the means, spelling the end of long-distance passenger trains.[3] Photograph by author, 1983.

Henry's Hot Dog, 1950, ceramic-tile stripes added 1960
Cicero

"Ray Kroc was his idol," Bob Henry says of his father. Bill Henry did not change American eating habits in the same way Ray Kroc and the McDonald brothers did—he lived, after all, in Chicago, where folks preferred hot dogs to hamburgers—but he did have a food stand that mimicked their red-and-white-striped hamburger stand.

In 1946 Bill Henry was a shipping clerk for the Crane Company, a manufacturer of plumbing fixtures in Chicago. That summer he hauled a wooden trailer to the corner of Ogden and Austen in suburban Cicero, outfitted it with a kitchen, and started hawking kosher hot dogs on evenings after work. The family helped: His wife blanched the fries and sliced the pickles at home, and his young sons toted them several blocks to the trailer. Henry had a good location: Ogden, U.S. 66, carried commuters out of Chicago to the south-western suburbs in the years before urban freeways. By 1950 his hot dogs were so successful that Henry quit his job at Crane and expanded. He built a six-stool, red-brick diner with two walk-up windows a half block up Ogden.

When Ray Kroc opened a red-and-white-striped McDonald's a mile down Ogden from Henry's Hot Dog, Bill Henry decided he wanted a building just like it. So he overlaid the brick with blue and white ceramic-tile stripes, mounted a sign of his own design—a giant hot dog and fries with an arrow pointing to the stand—and admonished passersby to come in and enjoy his hot dogs and french fries in portions so large that, as the sign said, "It's a meal in itself."[4] Photograph by author, 1980.

Peter Rossi's Service Station, 1939
Braidwood

Peter Rossi's father, uncles, and brothers worked the Coal City Mine and manufactured macaroni in Braidwood. But "Petey" was a builder. In his fifty years on U.S. 66 in Braidwood, he built a dance hall, two gas stations, and a motel. Each time, starting with the dance hall in the late '20s, he reached for a modern image, using the latest designs and best materials. In his two Braidwood service stations, he swung between the Spanish Colonial and Streamline Moderne styles. His first gas station had a curved false front that read Spanish Colonial. Adjacent to it he built cabins and the dance hall. After the complex burned, he built a new gas station, veneered in white glazed tile, a favorite material of the Streamline Moderne, but he retained Spanish forms in the black-tiled parapets and the white-tiled brackets on the garage openings.[5] Photograph by author, 1983.

Riviera Roadhouse, 1926
Gardner

In 1926 Jim Girot quit the coal mine in South Wilmington and opened the Riviera, a roadhouse on U.S. 66 two miles north of Gardner. It was rumored that Jim offered gambling at the Riviera. Actually, he offered a little bit of everything: a little bit of gambling, a little bit of booze, and a little bit of prostitution. He cobbled it together from a little bit of everything: part of a church, part of a school, part of a tin store, and part of the payroll office from the mine where he had dug coal. The final assemblage was several typical Illinois buildings patched together, similar to the late-nineteenth-century or early-twentieth-century houses that lined the streets of towns served by 66 in Illinois.[6] Photograph by author, 1997.

Bus Stop, ca. 1930
Gardner

A group of investors from Chicago built a stucco bus station and restaurant of indeterminate style at the south end of Gardner in the 1930s. They started with the one-story gas station and bus stop on the right, which they rented to a man named Brushingham. Then they added a restaurant in a two-story section in the center. They hired a woman to run the restaurant but had to replace her when she went to prison for murder. They finished the building with a tavern in the one-story section on the left. They reserved the second story for living quarters or, perhaps, rented the rooms to passing travelers. Mini–false fronts capped by shingled roofs were raised over the gas station and the tavern.[7] Photograph by author, 1980.

Gas Station, 1932
Odell

Patrick O'Connell built the shingle-style gas station and garage at Odell instead of buying a prefabricated building. He leased it out to a succession of oil companies, starting with Standard Oil of Indiana, followed by Phillips 66, and finally by Sinclair Oil. He installed broad windows overlooking the service area under the canopy and painted all but the roof white. There, green asphalt shingles on a grey background announced to oncoming cars that "Standard" gas was sold here.[8] Photograph by author, 1980.

Rodino Square, 1926, razed 1989
Pontiac

Carmen Rodino could neither read nor write, but he could figure in his head and sign his name. An Italian immigrant, he followed his father and uncle to Dwight, Illinois, in 1907 and went to work for the railroad. On the side he grew vegetables that he sold, first from a pushcart, then from a horse-drawn wagon, and finally from a truck. He moved his young family to Pontiac in 1919 and opened a grocery. In 1926 Carmen built Rodino Square, a plain brick Main Street block of the kind found in railroad towns the length of the highway. It faced both the railroad and 66. Rodino rented space to enterprises that served both. On the south side he leased a restaurant and the hotel upstairs to Eli Bromley. Out front he leased the gas station to Robert Kay. He installed his grocery on the north side of the first floor for travelers who picnicked on the roadside.[9] Photograph by author, 1980.

Go-Kart Track, ca. 1950
Bloomington

The construction of entertainment complexes on the outskirts of both large and small cities allowed the owners to build a more fanciful architecture designed to attract customers—hence this crude replica of the Arc de Triomphe as the ticket booth for a Go-Kart track. Next door, in the same complex, stood the Eiffel Tower at the center of a miniature golf course. Photograph by author, 1980.

O-W Root Beer, ca. 1950, formerly A & W Root Beer
Bloomington

Early franchise restaurants such as A & W and Steak 'n' Shake developed standardized buildings that were recognizable to any customer anywhere. The customer saw the building and associated it with Steak 'n' Shake's unique grilled steakburger or A & W's foamy root beer. It was an architecture capable of making the mouth water. Patrons of A & W root beer stands, founded by Roy Allen in 1919, parked under canopies on the sides of the stands and had their orders delivered to their cars by "tray girls." A & W adapted an International Style design that came to roadside food stands after the Streamline Moderne fell out of favor.[10] Photograph by author, 1980.

Steak 'n' Shake, ca. 1950
Bloomington

As soon as Gus Belt opened a roadside tavern in a converted gas station in 1934, Normal went dry. Gus then converted his tavern to a hamburger stand, hired carhops to deliver customers' food to their cars—but continued to offer dining inside—and named it Steak 'n' Shake. As the business grew into a chain with stands in cities in Illinois, Missouri, Indiana, and Florida, Gus developed a standardized restaurant based on a Streamline Moderne prototype, building one in Bloomington. He tore out the walls of the kitchen and exposed its stainless steel interior so that diners seated at the counter could watch the kitchen theatrics where the grill cooks smashed the patties flat, sizzled them to perfection, and slung "chili three ways"—chili with spaghetti, extra beans, extra beef, all with special sauce. The black-and-white-tile building, with the deep cornice on which Gus advertised "Steakburgers" and "Tru-Flavor Shakes" between running lights was as much a symbol of his steakburger as the Golden Arches were of the Big Mac.[11] Photograph by author, 1980.

Dixie Truckers Home, 1965
McLean

In 1928 oil distributors J. P. Walters and his son-in-law, John Geske, leased an old gas station in Shirley, just north of McLean, to house a retail outlet for their products. To increase their business, they stayed open twenty-four hours a day. The only travelers at night were truckers, so they began to cater to truckers and developed the Dixie, fueling the trucks at the pumps and the drivers at a food stand. In 1965, when a fire swept through the original Dixie, Geske replaced it with a long, low International Style supermarket and restaurant for truckers. He built the new Dixie large enough to accommodate tourists, for whom he added a separate seating area in the restaurant.[12] Photograph by author, 1983.

The Blue Mill, 1929
Lincoln

By the end of the nineteenth century nearly every town on the Illinois prairie had a little brick steam mill along the railroad tracks. But none looked like the Blue Mill located at the southern end of Lincoln. The Blue Mill was a tavern designed to draw travelers off the road at mealtime. At the Blue Mill the Huffman family, who pur- chased the building in 1945, specialized in serving schnitzel, either in a quick sandwich served at the long bar or with a leisurely meal served at a table in the dimly lit dining room.[13] Photograph by author, 1980.

Pig Hip Restaurant, 1937
Broadwell

Ernie and Frances Edwards named their restaurant after a sandwich of thinly sliced ham slathered in Pig Hip Sauce—a blend of egg, oil, catsup, Worcestershire, sugar, and salt. The Pig Hip was typical of the family restaurants that lined the roadside. Ernie and Frances served their sandwich in a nondescript board-and-batten building with picture windows.

Unlike the Huffmans at Lincoln, who used their building itself to attract customers, the Edwards employed a fat chef mounted on the top of a sign to get motorists speeding through Broadwell to pay attention and stop and enjoy "Breakfast, Lunch, or Dinner."[14] Photograph by author, 1980.

Elkhart Oil Co., 1948
Elkhart

Fenton Craner complained that pumping gas had always been a penny business, but he returned from the World War II, married his sweetheart, gave up a career in engineering, and opened a gas station in Elkhart. In 1948 he and his partner built a gas station on the corner of U.S. 66 and Main Street. While he was affiliated with Texaco, he chose not to house his business in Walter Dorwin Teague's standard Texaco design but rather in a Streamline Moderne facade constructed with structural glazed tile. The sweeping curve of the building drew the traveler from U.S. 66 onto Elkhart's Main Street and into the station.[15] Photograph by author, 1980.

Jack Robinson System, No. 7, 1948
Springfield

Manuel Suarez was sixteen when he started cooking at Jack Robinson's barbecue joint in 1924. He continued to cook for Jack when Jack opened his first hamburger stand ten years later. Jack built a chain, a small one with three stands in Springfield and two in Decatur. He numbered his restaurants 1 through 7. In 1948 he built No. 7 on South Grand East, a half block off U.S. 66 in Springfield, and made Manuel manager. Like so many food-stand operators who sold their burgers and hot dogs out of stands built in the latest architectural fashion—Bill Henry in Cicero and Gus Belt in Bloomington,

for instance—Jack Robinson encased No. 7 in a Streamline Moderne building clad in white-and-black-striped porcelain-enameled steel. Inside, everything was white and black except the slick, stainless steel kitchen. Manuel served diners at a curved white counter where they sat on white stools trimmed in black. Black-and-white-tile hexagons covered the floor. When Jack died in 1966, he willed the chain to Manuel, who continued to operate No. 7 until he retired in 1982.[16] Photograph by author, 1981.

Art's Restaurant and Motel, 1952
Farmersville

In 1932 Montgomery County, Illinois, was wide open. Art McAnarney, and Marty Gorman kept a speakeasy on Main Street in Farmersville. They went legit with the repeal of Prohibition and moved to the edge of town, where they leased the tavern in John Fromme's gas station at the corner of Main and U.S. Highway 66. They built an addition to house a dance hall and casino. Art took care of the tavern, Marty the dance hall and casino. In time, Art decided he wanted out of the gambling business, broke up the partnership, picked up the new addition, and moved it to the west side of 66, where he opened a bar and restaurant. In 1937 Art sold the addition back to Marty, who moved it back to the east side of 66. Art leased the two-story Hendricks Brothers' Cafe and Gas Station and settled in for the long haul on the west side of 66, where he grilled steaks, pumped gas, and rented out the six cabins that came with the building.

On a Saturday night in 1952, when the joint was jumping and a thunderstorm raged outside, the neon tubing, which outlined the steep roof of the building, arced, setting fire to the second story. All but the dining room burned to the ground. Art rebuilt, setting a single-story café and gas station on the original foundation next to the old dining room. He joined the new to the old with a sheathing of manufactured stone. Art died in 1957, but his sons, Elmer and Joe, continued the business, adding a thirteen-room ranch-style motel in 1960.[17] Photograph by author, 1995.

Ariston Cafe, 1935
Litchfield

In the early days of auto tourism politicians and celebrities traveled the road, particularly between the urban centers of Chicago and St. Louis. Jimmy Dorsey, Henry Wallace, and Hubert Humphrey all stopped at the Ariston Cafe. Clara Bow, her chauffeur, and her horse stayed at the Belvedere, a restaurant and motel, also in Litchfield. Contractor Austen Henry Vasel built both restaurants using identical plans and only slightly varied facades.

Pete Adam opened the Ariston on the courthouse square in Carlinville, Illinois, in 1924. He served food inside and pumped gas outside. In 1926 the Illinois Highway Department designated the road through Carlinville U.S. 66. When the highway department moved the road east to Litchfield in 1931, Pete followed. In 1935 he hired contractor Vasel to build a forty-by-sixty ochre, yellow, and ochre-tweed brick building that seated a hundred people. Pete advertised it as the most up-to-date restaurant between Chicago and St. Louis; Vasel chose the most up-to-date architectural style— Streamline Moderne. While the walls of the Ariston were ochre-tweed brick—a favorite Streamline Moderne material—the building itself, with its bowed false front and its corner caps accented in white tiles, could be identified as either Streamline Moderne or Spanish Colonial. Over the years the Adam family shifted the front door of the restaurant to the rear of the building and back again, as 66 shifted its alignment front to back. After 66 finally abandoned the Ariston altogether, the family welcomed their guests through the door at the front of the building.[18] Photograph by author, 1995.

Belvedere Cafe and Motel, 1935
Litchfield

Lester and Edith Kranich owned the Belvedere, built in the years following the 1933 Chicago World's Fair. The café was of the same ochre-tweed brick as the Ariston and in a style that was somewhere between Streamline Moderne and Spanish Colonial. By contrast, the motel was a plain white clapboard building housing a series of attached units, unusual in an era when motel owners generally built individual cabins.[19] Photograph by author, 1995.

Soulsby's Shell Station, 1926
Mount Olive

Henry Soulsby, a coal miner, and Russell, his sixteen-year-old son, laid the concrete-block foundation for their twelve-by-thirty-foot gas station as soon as they learned Illinois 16 would come through Mount Olive. They built a simple clapboard office to which they attached a canopy. Shell Oil provided the shell-shaped globes on the canopy lights. The Soulsbys opened for business in July 1926. With the help of his children—son Russell and daughter Ola—Henry ran the gas station as a sideline while he continued working the Hoosier Mine near Mount Olive. In 1931 the Illinois Highway Department designated Illinois 16 as U.S. 66. In 1944, however, U.S. 66 moved several blocks west to a newly constructed, dual-lane highway, taking with it the Soulsbys' tourist business. Some years later, Russell added twelve more feet to the office section of the station and set up a television repair shop. Ola continued to work the pumps, as she had from the start. Thus Russell stayed out of the mine and continued to make a living in the little yellow clapboard building where he pumped gas, fixed televisions, and—in his old age—entertained 66 groupies until the station, which actually belonged to Ola, was auctioned off in July 1997, a year after her death.[20] Photograph by author, 1979.

The Coliseum, 1924
Benld

Russell Soulsby liked to dance. And why not? The best bands of his youth played at the Coliseum in neighboring Benld, located on the Illinois 4 version of U.S. 66. Four coal mines provided the economic base for Benld, but during Prohibition it was a little Las Vegas. Dominic and Ben Tarro, brothers who were butchers and grocers in Benld, kept gaming tables—craps and blackjack—and slot machines at the Coliseum; but then every tavern in Benld offered some form of gambling. Al Capone kept a distillery on the outskirts of town and shipped hooch north, up U.S. 66 to Chicago. It was live and let live in Benld until 1930 when the Illinois state's attorney called Dominic to Springfield to testify about the fifty thousand dollars' worth of sugar he sold to the still. Persons unknown intercepted Dominic on his way to Springfield. His body was found in the Sangamon River four months later.

But the music, the music and the dances are what people remember in Benld. Guy Lombardo, Sammy Kaye, Tommy Dorsey, Count Basie, Duke Ellington, Lionel Hampton: They all played the Coliseum. Chuck Berry got his start in Benld; so did Tina Turner. Russell Soulsby danced to them all.

Dominic and Ben, who financed the Coliseum with the proceeds from their butcher shops, had hired an architect from Edwardsville to design the roller rink/dance hall in 1924. The architect spanned the ten-thousand-square-foot space with a curved truss and enclosed the building in brick. The facade followed the arc of the truss. The brothers seated four hundred people on the main floor and four hundred in the balcony.[21] Photograph by author, 1998.

66 Terminal, 1940, razed ca. 1982
Staunton

Joe Roseman discovered there were many ways to earn a living on 66. He started with a gas station the year before the beginning of World War II and enlarged it to a truck stop. He added a restaurant for truckers, and then cabins—a row of simple glazed cubes—and a central bathhouse. Joe chose a clean, modern image to appeal to the truckers who were his customers. He built a low building of yellow glazed block, a favorite Streamline Moderne material in the St. Louis region, with large corner windows that looked out on the cornfields across the road. He inspected his building constantly, driving back and forth in front of the terminal, trying to figure how he could make it more attractive to passing customers. He eventually added a tower that supported a big sign.[22] Photograph by author, 1979.

Schlechte's Service Station, 1937
Worden

Fred Schlechte was a coal miner who worked the Livingston Mine while his sons ran the family farm. In 1937 he hired a carpenter to build a simple hipped-roof, clapboard station with large picture windows that monitored the service area. Next door son Harry built the Worden Y, which he leased to Flick Urick who ran it as a nightclub, bringing in bands on the weekends. Russell Soulsby may have danced at the Coliseum, but he played the Worden Y as the clarinetist for the Melodeons, his dance band.

In 1954 the Illinois Highway Department took over the Schlechtes' site in order to widen 66, putting them out of business. Fred quit; Harry didn't. Instead, he picked up both buildings and moved them a short distance to a site on old, old 66, which proved to be the Worden interchange on I-55. Still, Harry felt he needed to repair cars as well as pump gas, and he added two service bays to the rear of his father's station.[23] Photograph by author, 1979.

Tourist Haven, 1930
Hamel

In 1918 George Cassens settled in Hamel—a crossroads town that would become the intersection of U.S. 66 and Illinois 140—married Louise Wilkening, the daughter of a town father, and purchased all four corners of the intersection. On one corner he located a gas station; on the second an automobile showroom; on the third an office building; and on the fourth the Tourist Haven, which he built for Louise. Constructed in yellow-and-brown-tweed brick with a massive pitched roof with clipped gables, the restaurant was of an inde-terminate vernacular style. George and his brother Louis went on to open a Chrysler-Plymouth dealership in Edwardsville in 1933. At the same time the Cassens brothers and their sons, Arnold and Albert, formed a partnership and purchased their first auto transport carrier. The red "portable parking lots" hauled new cars from auto factories in the Midwest to dealerships up and down U.S. 66.[24] Photograph by author, 1995.

Site Service Station, 1940
Edwardsville

Phil Siteman built a chain of gas stations along U.S. 66 and other highways radiating out of St. Louis, Missouri. Each station was different. Each reflected Siteman's affinity for the Streamline Moderne. The Edwardsville station was a simple brick box with picture windows on either side of the entrance. SITE in red, yellow, and black letters declared the brand of gas on the false front raised above the box.

This particular form of the Streamline Moderne sign with its graduated rounded corners was also associated with the Spanish Colonial–style false front. What read as Streamline Moderne in Illinois in the 1940s read as Spanish Colonial in New Mexico in the 1920s, '30s, and '40s. Photograph by author, 1979.

Luna Tavern, 1927
Mitchell

On leaving Edwardsville, 66 dropped from the prairie into the American Bottom, the vast Mississippi floodplain that extends to the east bank of the river. The Luna billed itself as the oldest building on Route 66. Not so. Lots of buildings on 66 were older than the Luna. The church of San José de Laguna, built in new Mexico in 1699, is probably the oldest. Closer to home, the Tarro brothers had built the Coliseum in Benld three years before the Luna went up in Mitchell. With its tall false front, the Luna just looked old when Irma Rafalala built it in 1927. Two stories high, it was a clapboard building covered first in wood, then in asbestos shingles, and finally in metal. The false front acted as a signboard carrying the word LUNA in neon over a crescent moon with a profile of the man-in-the-moon. From the Luna, U.S. 66 took a left turn and went through Granite City, Madison, and Venice to the McKinley Bridge, where it crossed the Mississippi to St. Louis. In 1929 John and Tom Scott would try to change all that.[25] Photograph by author, 1995.

Chain of Rocks Bridge, 1929
Mississippi River

In 1929 John R. Scott and Tom J. Scott, brothers, completed four miles of roadway from Mitchell to the east bank of the Mississippi, where they had constructed a most eccentric toll bridge. It was narrow, only twenty-four feet wide, and it had a right turn in the middle. It also had remarkable views of the Chain of Rocks, a major obstruction to shipping in the Mississippi, and of the little castles that housed the pumps for the St. Louis waterworks.

The Scott brothers and a group of investors had begun planning this bridge in 1924, two years before U.S. 66 was designated. They wanted to provide a way into St. Louis that bypassed Granite City, Madison, and Venice, Illinois, and the McKinley Bridge—old 66 into St. Louis—and cut eight to ten miles off the trip between Chicago and St. Louis. A bridge at the northern extreme of St. Louis would do that.

The brothers started construction on the Missouri side before they had found the bedrock anchor for the pier on the Illinois bank.

They never did find bedrock, at least not in the place they needed it if they were to build a straight bridge. So the Scotts' engineers poked around along the Illinois shore until they found bedrock two hundred yards up stream and then designed a turn in the bridge.

When the Scotts opened the bridge on July 20, 1929, Missouri and Illinois failed to mark it on their official maps. After the initial publicity, traffic dwindled and so did income from tolls. The bridge went into foreclosure. The Scotts reorganized, laid an additional six hundred feet of road from the west end of the bridge to connect with Lindbergh Boulevard, which became the 66 bypass around St. Louis, and renewed their efforts to encourage drivers to use the bridge. Discouraged, they sold the bridge in 1939 to the City of Madison, Illinois, which managed to turn it into a "golden goose." The I-270 bridge eventually replaced the narrow, two-lane bridge with the right angle in the middle where two trucks, going in opposite directions, could not pass.[26] Photograph by author, 1979.

St. Louis

The Chain of Rocks Bridge dumped travelers at the northern reaches of the city of St. Louis. From there they could take the 66 bypass around the city. Or they could take City 66, which wrapped around the city and crossed every major north-south and east-west thoroughfare before heading west along the Old State Road, a ridge road that wound through the Ozark foothills to Villa Ridge. There 66 picked up the Old Wire Road and set out for Rolla and Springfield. In 1933 the Missouri Highway Department moved the road from the ridge to the Meramec Valley, where it went west to Villa Ridge.

After the day's drive from Chicago, travelers found St. Louis a good place to spend the night. Tired folks, ready to stop at the first available place, checked in at one of the several small motels at the east end of the Chain of Rocks Bridge. Eager folks, wishing to get an early start west, discovered more and better motels just west of St. Louis. In a city where there were plenty of restaurants and gas stations, motels offered sleeping accommodations only. St. Louis had food stands—White Castle, Steak 'n' Shake, and Ted Drewes' Frozen Custard. The architecture on the roadside covered the spectrum from simple bungalow courts to a fine Spanish Colonial garage to the finest Streamline Moderne motel anywhere. The simple bungalows, frequently with decorative gables over the doors, mimicked the Tudor houses in the surrounding neighborhoods. The St. Louis region was the only place along 66 where builders employed the ochre glazed tile that gave those Streamline Moderne motels their St. Louis character.

For a big city, where the turnover in small commercial buildings is usually quite fast, St. Louis and its environs had, until the early 1990s, a remarkable treasure of roadside architecture from the 1926–56 period.

Nelson's Garage, 1931
West Florissant near Taylor

Nimrod J. Nelson had a filling station on West Florissant in the late 1920s. In 1931 he moved across the street, expanded his business, and adapted the Spanish Colonial style to an auto repair shop. He sold the business a year later to Clarence Settlage, who kept Nelson's name and his sign. In 1936 the Missouri Highway Department designated West Florissant City 66.

In reality, the building was a long stucco garage with Spanish Colonial details to give it its character: a bell-cote over the center office and arched entries into the four service bays. Between the bays at either end of the building, large black letters advertised the shop's services: BODY and MECH.[1] Photograph by author, 1980.

White Castle, 1937, razed 1983
Chippewa and Hampton

Not all food stands were Streamline Moderne ceramic-tile boxes. Some were steel castles. Edgar W. Ingram, an insurance man, and Walter L. Anderson, a short-order cook, started the White Castle system in 1921 in Wichita, Kansas. They sold a standardized, easily cooked hamburger in a standardized prefabricated building of easily assembled porcelain-enameled steel. White Castle started with a rusticated concrete-block box with a small turret over a corner to make look it like a castle. In 1926 the company switched to smooth block covered in stucco. A short time later they switched to white glazed brick with black trim. In 1928 L. W. Ray, White Castle's con-

struction manager, developed the steel building. He set the prototype on a parking lot in Wichita to see if it could survive the blistering Kansas summers and the freezing Kansas winters. It did. In 1934 the company established a subsidiary to manufacture the building, which became the standard for the next twenty years. In St. Louis, White Castle set its building down on the corners of busy intersections, three on City 66, where aficionados could purchase "belly-bombers"—small hamburgers with five holes punched in them, steamed over chopped onions on a grill, served on tiny buns, and packaged in cardboard castles.[2] Photograph by author, 1979.

Ted Drewes' Frozen Custard Stand, 1941
6726 Chippewa

In 1929 Ted Drewes, Sr., mounted a frozen-custard machine on the back of a ten-year-old Cadillac truck and began selling frozen custard. His first batch was terrible, but he tinkered with the recipe, substituting fresh milk for powdered, adding cream, and stirring in eggs until he had created ambrosia. For six years he spent his summers traveling with the All-American Carnival, making and selling custard. In the winter, he and his family headed for the Florida beaches, where they soaked up the sun and sold custard. But his wife hated the travel. So Drewes built a permanent stand in St. Louis in 1935. Six years later he opened a second stand on Chippewa, City 66.

Ted Drewes' Frozen Custard became a St. Louis institution. It was the type of business that could do well on a transcontinental highway and thrive on the myth of Route 66. No Streamline Moderne for this food stand. Ted Drewes, Sr., built a clapboard cottage and hung icicles from the roofline to attract sticky summer travelers along U.S. 66 to the cool, rich taste of his frozen custard. Like Gus Belt at Steak 'n' Shake, Drewes left his food preparation open to view, where the mix machine oozed the golden-white custard into a large vat from which his helpers scooped it up for cones, sundaes, and concretes.[3] Photograph by author, 1980.

Coral Court, 1941, razed 1995
Watson Road

In 1940 John Carr purchased twenty-nine residential lots along U.S. 66 in St. Louis and hired Adolph L. Strubig to design the Coral Court. Strubig laid out twenty-five two-unit buildings with attached garages. Guests entered their rooms from the garages. In later years, when the motel developed its reputation as a "hot-sheet joint," where chambermaids serviced the rooms night and day, the garages allowed for discreet arrivals and departures.

Constructed of structural clay tile or concrete block and sheathed in ochre-glazed-tile soaps with brown lintels and stringcourses, the motel's architecture was Streamline Moderne at its best. The rounded corners of each unit were filled with glass blocks stacked up in a stepped pyramid. Strubig placed the office building at the center of the complex; it was constructed of the same materials as the rest of the motel but had a semicircular bay of glass block. Nothing

at the Coral Court was left to chance. A low limestone wall landscaped in evergreens set the property off from the road. On either side of the office, the wall curved up and supported a neon sign that heralded, ENTRANCE. The post that finished the wall supported a lantern with the initials CC arranged in a monogram. The whole property was landscaped in pin oaks that eventually towered over the buildings. There was nothing else like it the length of U.S. 66.

The Coral Court was razed in May 1995, though the National Museum of Transport rescued one unit and moved it to its grounds in St. Louis County. When they bulldozed the buildings, the wreckers mounted a sign on the site, proclaiming, "It's checkout time at the Coral Court. No more one night stands."[4] Photograph by author, 1980.

Crystal Court, 1946, razed 1988
Watson Road

The Rischbieter family opened a service station on U.S. 66 in 1941. With the end of World War II and the boom in tourist travel, they purchased a lot across 66 from the Coral Court and constructed a frank imitation of it, using the same triangular glass-block windows but substituting yellow ochre brick for the tile soaps. The Rischbieters squeezed their motel onto a smaller site than the Coral Court, erecting four buildings containing four units each and attached garages. In the sixties, as Streamline Moderne lost its architectural respectability, the Rischbieters felt the need to modernize the Crystal Court and added mansard roofs to the buildings.[5] Photograph by author, 1980.

66 Auto Court, ca. 1945, razed 1980s
Watson Road

In contrast to the Coral Court, the 66 Auto Court was more typical of the motor courts of its era. It was a series of two-unit stucco bungalows set in a semicircle around a driveway. The units were laid out using an open site plan based on that of the bungalow courts that proliferated in the suburbs of Los Angeles in the teens. Each unit of the 66 had a front and a rear entrance. The front opened onto the driveway, the rear onto a grassy courtyard typical of the open plan. Each unit offered hot water, heat, insulated rooms, and free radio. A decorative gable over each entrance gave the bungalows their homey character. Reflecting the little brick-and-stone Tudor houses in the surrounding neighborhoods, it might be called the St. Louis–style cabin.[6] Photograph by author, 1978.

66 Park In Theatre, 1948, razed 1996
Watson Road

Richard Hollingshead invented and patented the drive-in movie theater in 1933 and formed a company to franchise his concept and layout. But even though he had wedded the American passion for movies to our passion for cars, only fifty such theaters were built by the beginning of World War II. All that changed in 1946, as American servicemen returned home, married their sweethearts, started their families, piled everyone in their shiny new cars, and went to the movies. More than seventeen hundred drive-in theaters lined suburban roadsides by 1950.

With fourteen motels along the suburban stretch of 66 between the Coral Court and the road's intersection with the 66 bypass at Watson and Lindbergh, a drive-in movie offered cheap entertainment for the overnight traveler. The Flexor Corporation built the 66 Park In Theatre in 1948 and sold it to Paul Krueger the following year. To obtain the steel for the screen tower after the war, Flexor had to apply for a building permit for a billboard. To attract business from the busy suburban strip, Flexor used the screen tower itself as the sign, outlining 66 PARK IN THEATRE in neon tubing. Krueger added a glass-block ticket booth and the signboard in the modernistic vernacular of the 1950s.[7] Photograph by author, 1980, from *Route 66: The Highway and Its People,* photographs by Quinta Scott, text by Susan Croce Kelly (University of Oklahoma Press, 1988).

Big Chief Hotel, 1928
Pond, Missouri

In 1928 William Clay Pierce of the Pierce-Pennant Oil Company in St. Louis went into the motel business with a plan to build a chain of motor courts along U.S. 66 between Springfield, Illinois, and Tulsa, Oklahoma—and with the intention of bringing first-class hotel services to the roadside. He built a court on old 66 at Rolla, Missouri, and a Spanish Colonial court on the old ridge road at Pond, west of St. Louis. It was a U-shaped motor court with attached rooms and garages. Across the front of the property Pierce housed the office, the restaurant, and the gas station in three separate buildings. A porte cochere, fronting a two-story restaurant with a tile roof and small scalloped parapet, gave it the look of a large Spanish Colonial house. Shaped parapets over the smaller buildings reinforced the look.

The chain was an ambitious project that tied the motor courts to the chain of Pierce-Pennant gas stations in St. Louis and restaurants in St. Louis; Springfield, Missouri; and Tulsa. In 1930 Pierce abandoned his plans and sold the chain to Henry Sinclair of the Sinclair Refining Company, who planned to extend it south into Mexico. In 1933 the Missouri Highway Department moved 66 to the flat Meramec Valley, turning the Big Chief into a white elephant. Sinclair sold it.[8] Photograph by author, 1980.

Red Cedar Inn, 1934
Pacific, Missouri

The year 1933 was a critical one for the Smith brothers of Villa Ridge, Missouri. Prohibition ended, and the Missouri Highway Department moved U.S. 66 to the Meramec Valley. James and Bill Smith, who had bootlegged hooch from the family farm at Villa Ridge, opened legal taverns—Bill at Fenton and James a tavern and pool hall at Eureka. And they built a restaurant on new 66 at Pacific. They cut long, straight red cedar trees on the farm and hauled them to the edge of the new road. They hired Dutch Wehrle—who worked on Saturday, partied on Sunday, and took Monday off—to construct a sprawling log building with a low front gable, incorporating a cedar tree on the site into the structure. George and Otto Manetzke chinked the logs, filling the gaps with cement. Wehrle hung a broad porch on the front of the brown-and-white-striped restaurant.

When James and Bill finished the building, they named it the Red Cedar Inn, turned its management over to James II, and went back to the pool hall in Eureka and the tavern in Fenton.

James II was twenty-four when he took over the restaurant in 1934. Katherine Brinkman was twenty when she started waiting tables the following year. They married in 1940. By 1959 the Smiths were working from dawn to dark and had two teenagers, Ginger and James III. They moved into the restaurant, running a knotty-pine wall down the center of the dining room and setting up housekeeping in one half. James II and Katherine closed the Red Cedar in 1973, but Ginger and James III reopened it in 1987 and cashed in on the myth of Route 66.[9] Photograph by author, 1997.

Gardenway Motel, 1945
Gray Summit, Missouri

In 1937 the Missouri Botanical Garden, in association with the National Park Service and the Missouri State Highway Commission, landscaped thirty miles of new 66 with native flowers, shrubs, and trees between the St. Louis city limits and the Botanical Garden's arboretum at Gray Summit. They named it the Henry Shaw Gardenway, after the founder of the Missouri Botanical Garden. When Louis B. Eckelkamp built a motel not far from the family home on property adjacent to the arboretum, he named his motel after the Gardenway and reached for an American Colonial design.

Attempts at American Colonial architecture were rare along U.S. 66, where the architectural influences moved west to east rather than east to west; where the Spanish Colonial filtered up the road from Los Angeles and Santa Fe; and where the Streamline Moderne, a style that originated in Los Angeles, appeared in cities east to Chicago. Eckelkamp's forty-one-unit motel was a combination of red brick and white clapboard topped with several cupolas. It was a linear Mount Vernon plunked down on the eastern edge of the Ozarks and amended by a frankly Streamline Moderne sign, an imperative arrow supported by a stone base filled with glass brick and backlit with colored lights. Once 66 was abandoned to the interstate that cut through the hill below, Eckelkamp added the long GARDENWAY sign on the roof to notify travelers on I-44 of accommodations up on the ridge.[10] Photograph by author, 1980.

The Diamonds, 1948–73
Villa Ridge, Missouri

Spencer Groff housed the first Diamonds in a wooden building at the Y where U.S. 66 split from the Old State Road, picked up the Old Wire Road, and headed west. After the original building burned in 1948, Groff teamed up with Louis Eckelkamp to build a second Diamonds. While Eckelkamp lured families into the Gardenway Motel with a homey American Colonial architecture, Groff and Eckelkamp projected an aura of efficiency to travelers and truckers with a Streamline Moderne architecture at the Diamonds. The great curved front of the beige-brick restaurant overlooked the intersection of Old State Road and Old Wire Road. While families were welcome at the Diamonds, Groff and Eckelkamp isolated them from the truckers in a separate dining room. They provided truckers with sleeping rooms and showers on the second floor, while they directed civilians to the Gardenway.

The Diamonds was one of the rare businesses to survive the coming of the interstate. When I-44 replaced 66 in 1973, Groff and Eckelkamp took their sign in the shape of a diamond, moved to the interchange at Gray Summit, and built a motel and restaurant that catered to tourists. The Tri-County Truck Stop, which had lost its building to I-44 in Sullivan, twenty miles west of Villa Ridge, took over the abandoned building and mounted a sign that stretched the length of the roofline.[11] Photograph by author, 1980.

Sunset Motel, ca. 1945
Villa Ridge, Missouri

Devices such as the decorative gables over the entrances to the units at the 66 Auto Court in St. Louis, here at the Sunset Motel in Villa Ridge, and at the Shamrock Motel twenty miles west in Sullivan sometimes proliferate in a region. They indicate that the three motels may have had the same architect or the same owner or builder. The attached beige-brick units of the Sunset were laid out in a V overlooking a broad green space. Like the units at the 66 Auto Court, each unit at the Sunset had two entrances—one from the driveway and the other from the lawn. Photograph by author, 1980.

Harty's Dine-O-Tel, 1937
St. Clair, Missouri

Not as liberal as the folks in Illinois, Missourians built few roadside taverns. Roger Harty housed his Dine-O-Tel in a simple two-story clapboard building, sold packaged liquor at one end, offered "Chicken-in-the-Hay" in the dining room, and provided sleeping rooms upstairs. Some things did not change when Harty's became the Surf Lounge. The new owners continued to sell packaged liquor from its bar in the east end of the building.[12] Photograph by author, 1980.

Skylark Motel, ca. 1955
St. Clair, Missouri

St. Clair represents the western limit of the St. Louis Streamline Moderne influence. West of here, business owners built in a regional vernacular using materials characteristic of the Ozarks—bungalows built of logs or a rusted Ozark stone.

Sometime around 1940 Charlie and Liza Johnson built their first motel in St. Clair. It had a stone office and St. Louis–style cabins. In the mid-1950s Charlie and son Robert built the Streamline Moderne Skylark. Perched on the crown of a hill, the two-story white stucco building sported a tall glass-block tower filled with colored lights that could be seen from a fair distance to the east or the west. The Johnsons housed additional guests under the broad roof of a low, stucco ranch house with eight units and garages.[13] Photograph by author, 1980.

Missouri

The Indians called it the Moon Road and the Buffalo Road. The white man called it the Kickapoo Trail, the Osage Trace, and the Spanish Trace. Then he called it the Springfield Road. Then, when they had that battle down at Pea Ridge, Arkansas, in 1862, he called it the Military Road. Then, when the telegraph came through, he called it the Wire Road.

—Larry Baggett[1]

At Villa Ridge, Missouri 66 split from the Old State Road, connected with the Old Wire Road—and headed west. At Springfield, it connected with the Ozark Trail, a road established by the Ozark Trails Association in 1915, which took it to Santa Rosa, New Mexico. Occasionally the influence of the Streamline Moderne and the St. Louis–style Tudor, so pervasive in St. Louis, popped up in the small towns like Cuba and Sullivan.

West of Rolla, 66 plunged into the Ozarks and into a vernacular architecture that was unique to the region. Here proprietors built stone cottages and log cabins using the local materials—oak logs cut from the forests and warm, rusty Ozark sandstone cut from the hills. Slabstone, or "giraffe stone," construction was developed in the teens and the twenties in Thayer, Missouri, near the Arkansas border, and carried north to Rolla. "Rock men" set flat slabs of sandstone on a concrete foundation and laid up stone as a veneer over a wood frame or concrete wall. In Ozark lingo, they "rocked" the building.[2]

With the beginning of World War II, small rental cabins proliferated along 66 from Rolla to Springfield when Ozark hill people, many of whom earned their living selling local crafts to travelers, turned their skills to building wood-and-rock cabins along the roadside. Their primary customers were army families who found inadequate housing at newly completed Fort Leonard Wood at St. Robert and would rent anything with a roof and reasonable access to the fort.

Missouri is known as the cave state. The Ozark hills are underlain with limestone and dolomite, which are soluable in acid. Water, made acidic by the oak forests that cover the hills, percolates down and dissolves the rock, creating channels that become the courses of underground springs and river systems and grow into caverns. Water flowing through the caverns enlarges the chambers, forming rooms. When the water flows out and fresh air fills the chambers, groundwater rich in minerals leached from the rocks drips down creating stalactites and stalagmites made of colorful cave onyx, also called dripstone.

In the late thirties and early forties, auto tourists motoring down U.S. 66 could turn themselves momentarily into spelunkers and explore Missouri's commercial caves, including three handsome caves south of Leasburg. For forty cents they could view the immense cavern of Cathedral Cave where the stalagmites and stalactites were whiter than white. Fifty-five cents admitted visitors to Missouri Caverns where indirect lighting dazzled them with the dramatic shapes and colors of the rock formations. And it cost forty cents to float through the winding channel of the Lost River in Onondaga Cave.

But before travelers even got to Leasburg, Lester Dill made sure they stopped at Meramec Caverns, his four-story gem at Stanton, a few miles east. For a mere thirty-five cents Dill guided them through his cave, where he projected an American Flag on the Natural Stage—a curtain of rock sixty-eight feet high—while Kate Smith moved his visitors with her recorded version of Irving Berlin's "God Bless America."[3]

Meramec Caverns, 1933
Stanton (barn in Bourbon)

If you'd have asked Lester Dill where Route 66 really began, he'd have told you west of St. Louis, near Meramec Caverns. Dill grew up exploring caves in Meramec State Park where his father was the superintendent. In the 1930s Dill purchased Meramec Caverns, located three miles off U.S. 66 at Stanton, and turned the cave into a first-class tourist trap, offering tours of his gussied-up cave. He provided a restaurant and a souvenir shop inside the cave and a motel outside. He lured travelers on 66 to his cave with signs—all painted in white letters on a black ground—on the sides and roofs of barns from Ohio to Texas. It was a win-win deal: The farmer gave Dill free advertising space; Dill painted the whole barn for free and added MERAMEC CAVERNS, 66, MO. By the time Mom and Dad and a carload of kids neared Stanton, the clamor to visit Meramec Caverns was overwhelming. In time Dill also purchased Onondaga Cave, several miles west of Meramec Caverns, and advertised it on his barns.[4] Photograph by author, 1979.

Shamrock Motel and Cafe, 1945
Sullivan

The U-shaped plan of the Shamrock Motel and Cafe at Sullivan was almost identical to the V-shaped plan of the Sunset Motel at Villa Ridge. Both housed eleven attached rooms and an office; both had St. Louis–style decorative gables over each door. But there were differences: The Sunset, with front and back entrances, framed a lawn; the Shamrock framed a parking court. The Sunset was brick; the Shamrock was stone.

Grandpa Berti, an Italian stonemason, built the Shamrock for F. E. Dobbs. Berti selected large chucks of warm, hard sandstone from the Sulky Quarry near Sullivan and took them to the site, where he cut them to fit the building. He ordered smooth, dressed stone to frame doors and windows. He laid up a chimney next to the entrance to the office to mark the dining room fireplace. Finally, between each opening in the facade, he set his signature, a sunburst, a round stone surrounded by flat rays of rusty stone.[5] Photograph by author, 1997.

Esther White's Gas Station, ca. 1926
Cuba

With their gas station located on a lonely stretch of 66 between Bourbon and Cuba, the White family saw no need to impress their customers with a large building. Anyone low on gas would be grateful to find them. So they built a small structure, covered it in cement-asbestos siding, and added a bit of rickrack trim along the roofline. It looked more like a child's playhouse than a place of business. Photograph by author, 1979.

Circle Inn, ca. 1955
Cuba

The owners of the Circle Inn wanted simple, straightforward food-stand architecture made homey by curtains in the windows. They built a concrete-block box with broad windows and entrances on the sides. Dozens like it lined the streets of towns the length of 66.

The proprietors attached their menu to the corners of the building and above the windows and mounted numerous signs on the roof to draw customers in for a burger and fries.[6] Photograph by author, 1979.

Wagon Wheel Motel, 1934
Cuba

Cuba advertised itself as the Gateway to the Ozarks, and the Wagon Wheel represented the first use of "colorful Ozark stone." However, the Wagon Wheel looked east to St. Louis rather than west to Rolla for its design. Robert and Margaret Martin hired local stonemason Leo Friesenhan to design and build the Wagon Wheel Motel, Gas Station, and Restaurant. A German immigrant, Friesenhan had been a mason in St. Louis until he settled on a farm in Bourbon, Missouri, in the teens. Once settled, he continued to commute to St. Louis, where he worked with a contractor who built some of the five-room Tudor bungalows that line the streets of south St. Louis. Friesenhan was familiar with the St. Louis Tudor bungalow, built generally of red brick with stone trim around the windows and doors and a decorative gable marking the front door. In Cuba, where Ozark stone was readily available, Friesenhan built stone cottages with brick trim around the windows and over the arched porches. Six units were housed in each cottage, making them larger than any St. Louis bungalow.[7] Photograph by author, 1997.

Lierman and Jaques Gas Station and Tire Shop, ca. 1933
Rolla

Boyhood friends C. T. Lierman and William Jaques, the sons of coal miners, grew up in Lexington, Missouri, and followed their fathers into the mines. In 1928 they migrated to Rolla, where they opened an ice and wood yard in a wooden shack on U.S. 66. When they needed something bigger and wanted something fancier, the partners hired their neighbor Vernon Prewett to "rock" them a building. Prewett gave them Streamline Moderne with teeth. He designed the three-part facade and veneered it with large, irregular slabs of sandstone mortared together with beaded joints. Along the curved roofline, Prewett set sharp, pointed rocks—teeth. At one time there were numerous examples of this variation on the Ozark slabstone building between Rolla and Devils Elbow. All are gone now.

As the thirties drew to a close, Lierman and Jaques gave up ice and wood, installed gas pumps, and went into the wholesale tire business, selling tires to the U.S. Army at Fort Leonard Wood. In 1973 Lierman and Jaques sold the business to Lee Lutz, who whitewashed the whole and painted the teeth red.[8] Photograph by author, 1981.

Aaron's Radiator Shop and Service Station, 1929
Rolla

In 1929 Billy and Lynna Aaron returned from St. Louis to her family's homestead on 66 just west of Rolla. There they opened the only radiator repair shop between Cuba and Springfield. Aaron Miles, a professor of mechanical engineering at the Rolla School of Mines, designed a two-story garage built of flat slabs of rusty Ozark sandstone. Billy and his sons quarried the sandstone from the hollows along the creeks that ran through the homestead. Using wedges and sledge hammers, the crew split the rocks into manageable but irregular, flat-sided building blocks, which a mason fitted together into a flat, vertical plane in the typical Ozark vernacular.

When it was all done, Billy put the operation of the radiator shop in the hands of an associate and returned to his job as a railroad engineer.[9] Photograph by author, 1979.

John's Modern Cabins, ca. 1932
Doolittle

Occasionally the Ozark folk cut oak logs from the surrounding hills to build their tourist cabins. Bill and Bessie, last name long forgotten, built John's Modern Cabins in the early 1930s and sold the complex to John Dausch after World War II. It included a dance hall/beer hall/café, a service station, a souvenir shop, and cabins, all built in stages. Bill and Bessie had started with the dance hall/beer hall/café housed in a stucco box. Then they strung four log cabins along the highway. They chinked the logs with cement and lined the inside walls with fiberboard. Standard barn windows in three walls provided ventilation. Young Bill Aaron, he who had harvested sandstone for his father's radiator shop, visited Bill and Bessie's as a teenager in the later 1930s and found a pair of girl's panties tacked to the door of a cabin. Years later he noted that "It was no place for that country kid."

After John Dausch took possession of the complex and renamed it, he built four closely spaced frame cabins that measured twelve feet square. These he sided in cement-asbestos shingles and installed large double windows in three walls of each cabin. John must have provided curtains or shades, because the side windows all lined up. A person seated on a bed in the first cabin could see clear to the end of the line if all the curtains were open and all the shades pulled up.[10] Photograph by author, 1979.

Munger-Moss Sandwich Shop, 1936
Devils Elbow

Devils Elbow was a logging and fishing camp at a sharp bend in the Big Piney River. The lumberjacks who stripped the Ozarks of trees and floated them down the river called the bend where their logs jammed up "one devil of an elbow."

In 1936 Nelle Munger, a widow, married Emmett Moss. They built a barbecue and sandwich shop adjacent to the bridge that crossed the river. A wood structure with clipped gables and wide-plank siding housed their café. During World War II they added a few cabins to accommodate army personnel from Fort Leonard Wood. One army wife who lived at the Munger-Moss drove a taxi between the fort and St. Louis. She made the trip in two hours flat, no mean feat on the narrow, twisting highway.[11] Photograph by author, 1980.

The Hillbilly Store, 1947
Hooker Cutoff

Once U.S. 66 came through their region, local craftspeople along the road discovered the commercial value of their artifacts. In Missouri, Ozark hill people hung white-oak baskets and chairs on wires strung up along the roadside at Clementine, which was no more than a strip of houses just east of Devils Elbow. In New Mexico, Acoma potters laid out their pots, and Navajo weavers set up their looms. After World War II, souvenir stands began to take over the sale of local crafts. Sterling Wells saw opportunity in the Hooker Cutoff, a new four-lane divided highway that cut through the Ozark hills, bypass-ing Devils Elbow. He built a big barn of a store that housed a sou-venir stand and a café. He designed it to look like a hillbilly cabin and set a neon-lit hillbilly with rotating arms on top to beckon folks off the road. Inside he sold hamburgers, Ozark white-oak baskets, and other crafts made by the artisans in the region. And he sold junk, the kind that kids find irresistible and parents hate. When the Hooker Cutoff was bypassed by I-44, Wells moved the Hillbilly Store up to a nearby interchange. Photograph by author, 1982.

Gascozark Cafe and Gas Station, 1931
Gascozark

Frank A. Jones, who made his living from the Gasconade River and the Ozark hills, coined the name "Gascozark." He operated a resort down on the river and the Gascozark Cafe and Gas Station up on the hill above the river. In 1931 he bought a small building on the hill and added on to it. When he finished, he had several simple stucco buildings knitted together with an uneven roofline. Four years later he hired Mr. Lillard, a rock man, to rock the building. Lillard wrapped a veneer of large, flat Ozark stones around the front and the sides of the building, using small stones to fill the gaps between the large stones. To even out the roofline, he shaped an arch that spanned the facade and finished it with round cobbles rolled smooth by the river. At the corners he piled up columns of rubble and mounted lanterns on top. Like that of the Ariston in Litchfield, Illinois, the architectural effect was somewhere between Spanish Colonial and Streamline Moderne, with, of course, an Ozark twist.[12] Photograph by author, 1998.

Walker Brothers Resort, 1916
Hazelgreen

Long and low, the Hazelgreen Trading Post was an early form of rural roadside architecture. Between Gascozark and Hazelgreen, 66 skirted the northern edge of the Mark Twain National Forest. Here the Gasconade River cut north through the hills, providing a recreation area. In 1916 Elmer and John Walker built a hunting and fishing resort that ten years later served 66 with the basics of a roadside enterprise—a gas station, a café, and cabins. Short columns set on tall stone bases supported a porch that shaded the entrance. The false front and the porch columns provided surfaces for painted signs that notified travelers of the goods and services offered inside.[13] Photograph by author, 1979.

4 Acre Court, 1949
Lebanon

Ray Coleman and Blackie Walters provided both cabins and a camp-ground at the 4 Acre Court several miles east of Lebanon. They set little slabstone cabins, some with two rooms and short chimneys, back from the roadside and built a two-story stone building out front to house the gas station, office, and owner's residence.[14] Photograph by author, 1997.

Camp Joy, 1926
Lebanon

Emis and Lois Spears left Nebraska City, Nebraska, on their honeymoon and toured the West and Southwest with his parents, looking for a place to build a tourist camp. They would pick a town, sit on the roadside, and count the passing cars. After spending several days tallying up the traffic through Lebanon, they bought a block of land on the edge of town, opened a campground, built bath and cooking facilities, and started renting tents for fifty cents a night. They were so successful that Emis and his father began building cabins right away. At first they built no garages, but later they added lean-tos to the cabins which they developed into garages and then turned into more rooms. This progression from garage to cabin was typical in early motels. It was cheaper to turn garages into cabins than it was to buy more land.

Spears and his father built front-gable cabins of wood with a door and a window. They covered the frame buildings in clapboard and painted them white. They housed the gas station and café in a two-story building at the front of the property. As competition stiffened, the Spearses tore out the gas station and changed the name from Camp Joy to the Joy Motel.[15] Photograph by author, 1979.

Munger Moss Motel, 1946–73
Lebanon

In 1945 Pete and Jessie Hudson sold their saloon in St. Louis and purchased the Munger-Moss Sandwich Shop at Devils Elbow. As soon as they had settled in, the Missouri Highway Department started construction on the Hooker Cutoff, the four-lane divided highway that bypassed Devils Elbow, leaving Pete and Jessie stranded down by the river. They sold the sandwich shop, kept the name Munger-Moss (but dropped the hyphen), and moved to Lebanon. There they purchased the Chicken Shanty Cafe and an adjacent lot, renamed it the Munger Moss Barbecue, and set about building a motel. They built seven stucco cottages with rooms on each end and garages in the middle. They added a little gable over each door, ran neon tubing around it, and fixed a neon number in the center. They laid out the units along a semicircular drive in an open plan based on the Los Angeles bungalow courts. They left a green space in the middle for a garden and seating. They added eleven more buildings along the drive. Like the Spearses did at Camp Joy, to create more units they converted the garages to rooms, then filled in the gaps between the buildings, and later built blocks of rooms on the opposite side of the drive and in the green space. By the time they quit, they had seventy-one rooms.

Everything the Hudsons did was designed to bring in business. When the demand became apparent, they added air conditioning, television, and a swimming pool. As architectural styles changed, they covered the stucco with brick and extended the roofline out to cover a walkway in a style that echoed the suburban ranch house, which was increasing in popularity across the nation. The addition of small cupolas on the roof gave the motel added respectability and a faintly colonial look. The motel took its final form in the late fifties when the Hudsons added a fancy office and a sign sporting a giant yellow arrow that swept over the name of the motel. Taller than the office, it was a frank imitation of the familiar Holiday Inn sign that was appearing along the highways.[16] Photograph by author, 1998.

Lenz Homotel, 1932
Lebanon

In 1932 William Otto August Lenz and his wife, Ethel, converted their three-story, fourteen-room house into a tourist home. They supplied linens and home-cooked meals at a time when campgrounds supplied tents and early cabin courts supplied bare mattresses and communal kitchens. As auto camps became upscale motels and tourist homes fell out of favor with the traveling public, William and Ethel put out a sign advertising their tourist home as the LENZ HOMOTEL.[17] Photograph by author, 1979.

Campbell 66 Express, n.d.
Lebanon

Trucker Frank Campbell named his trucking company Campbell 66 Express, using his own name and the name of an entity he purchased, the 66 Transit Company. Campbell, who pronounced his name "camel," pirated a standing camel for his logo from a cigarette package and painted it on the side of his trucks. One day when he was taking his usual morning coffee at Big Alice's café near his office, Alice asked him, "When are you going to get the camel running?" Campbell returned to the garage and asked his sign painter if he could make the camel run. The sign painter came back two days later with a running camel, but Campbell noted that if the camel was running a long way, its tongue would be hanging out and its breath coming in puffs from its nose. The painter added a tongue and breath, Campbell added 66 to the hump, named the camel Snortin' Norton, and advertised that he was HUMPIN' TO PLEASE.[18] Photograph by author, 1981.

Abby Lee Court, ca. 1942
Conway

During World War II the population of the Ozarks between Lebanon and Springfield swelled with the wives and children of army personnel looking for housing. Motels, mostly simple frame-and-clapboard bungalows built by locals, proliferated. In some cases a farmer built a few cabins near his house, but other proprietors built tourist courts that survived the war and served the horde of travelers who flocked down 66 in the years following. One such court, the Abby Lee, continued in business after the war, offering the public eight large cabins with attached garages and a café.[19] Photograph by author, 1981.

Flying Red Horse Sign, 1932
Marshfield

As important to oil companies as the design of their stations was the symbol on their signs. The symbols, developed in the 1930s, became instantly recognizable and expanded brand loyalty. Phillips Petroleum adopted an orange and black highway shield with "66" on it, Texaco put its "T" in a red star, and Shell chose the scallop shell. In 1932 SOCONY Oil Company, known today as Mobil, replaced its gargoyle symbol with the flying red horse.[20] Photograph by author, 1979.

Trail's End Motel, 1938
Springfield

In Springfield the use of Ozark sandstone reached a crescendo. One after another, motels and cafés were built using the flat slabs laid up in the giraffelike pattern. West of Springfield clear to Shamrock, Texas, roadside entrepreneurs used stone veneers on their garages, cafés, and motels, but never with the skill or the elegance found in the Springfield model. Only in Springfield did rock men use alternating courses of yellow and red brick to sharpen the edges around windows and doors and as quoins on the corners.

That Springfield, like St. Louis, developed a style of motel that was distinctive to the area is due to the talents of rock man Ed Waddell. Waddell worked with "Mac" MacCandless, a developer, to build the Trail's End Motel in 1938 and then the Rock Village Court and the Rock Fountain Court, both in 1947. They built the same little front-gabled cabin with a built-in porch and one or two bedrooms at all three sites. They used the bungalow-court site plan, laying out their cabins around a semicircular drive.

Rock Fountain Court, 1947
Springfield

MacCandless and Waddell used red and yellow brick around the doors and windows of the Trail's End, but dropped its use at the Rock Fountain Court and veneered only the front of the cabins. All these devices also show up in the private homes MacCandless and Waddell built in Springfield and Lebanon.[21] Photographs by author, 1981.

Rest Haven Court, 1947
Springfield

In 1937 Hillary Brightwell abandoned his "starvation place" on West 66 in Springfield and rented a gas station on East 66. Seven years later he and his bride, Mary, bought the gas station, remodeled it, and began building the Rest Haven. They followed the same pattern as the Hudsons had at the Munger Moss, starting small and growing large: eight rooms in four cabins in 1947, ten more rooms in 1952, and another ten in 1955. They added a swimming pool when the public demanded it and, finally, a huge sign with an arrow lit by nine hundred flickering bulbs.

When Hillary designed the first four cabins, he prepared simple frame two-unit buildings for a sandstone veneer. At the same time, he selected rocks from a farmer's pasture along Turnback Creek near Halltown and hired a local rock man named Bench. Bench carefully laid the veneer, shaving a piece from a large rock here, adding a small rock there, building the pattern. To sharpen the edges, Bench laid alternating layers of red and yellow brick around the windows and doors and on the corners. In the early 1960s, the Brightwells filled in the gaps between the original four cabins, adding more rooms. Finally they added a porch and large cupolas and transformed the Rest Haven into a ranch-style motel.[22] Photograph by author, 1997.

Red's Hamburg, ca. 1930
Springfield

Not everyone in Springfield conducted business in a rock building. Red Chaney served hamburgers in an old clapboard gas station. With World War II over, Chaney packed up his business degree and his bride and left Chicago to find a business on U.S. 66. He found Wayne Lillard's gas station and cabins on the western edge of Springfield. He added a hamburger stand. When he found himself wearing too many hats, he quit pumping gas and renting cabins. He converted the office and garage to a restaurant and concentrated on hamburgers, luring customers off the road by unconventional means. First he erected a tall sign in the form of a Latin cross, painting GIANT on the arm of the cross and HAMBURG on the leg. Actually, he had started to paint HAMBURGER but ran out of room.

Unlike so many food-stand operators, Chaney never replaced his gas station with a Streamline Moderne café or a concrete-block box. The only streamlined object on Chaney's property was the white Buick parked next to the sign. On the roof of the Buick, Chaney mounted a washing machine motor to whose twirling metal arms he attached used milk bottles—"anything," as he said, "to attract attention."[23] Photograph by author, 1979.

Rainey's Wrecker Service, 1945
West of Springfield

When sixty-five miles of old 66 were bypassed by I-44 between Springfield and Carthage in 1964, the old road became a veritable museum of roadside artifacts. In the heyday of 66 there were six gas stations in Halltown competing fiercely for the customers coming down 66 from Springfield. Some earned no more than two dollars a day selling a hundred gallons at a two-cent profit. Presumably, gas station owners west of Halltown did no better. Whatever their profit margin, they built simply, using Ozark sandstone. As the road neared Carthage, occasionally they piled up a wall with chunks of fieldstone, a departure from the carefully cut and fitted sandstone finishes that were so familiar to the east.

When World War II gas rationing forced Bert and Ina Rainey out of their gas station at Millbrae, California, they returned to her parents' farm outside Springfield. With the war over, they left the farm, purchased a "rocked" gas station just west of Springfield and bought a wrecker. They added a second story to their gas station for their living quarters and continued the rock veneer to the roofline. When they added a garage for the wreckers, they used concrete block, a material that came into general use after World War II.

Ina Rainey was delighted when I-44 siphoned the traffic off 66. It did not hurt their towing business, and she was tired of rising every morning to a driveway full of broken-down cars.[24] Photograph by author, 1982.

Las Vegas Hotel and Cafe, ca. 1930
Halltown

Hometown boy Charlie Dammer grew up and went to California before returning to Halltown to build a hotel with four rooms upstairs and a café below. A barber by trade, he installed his barbershop in a tiny tin building next door. In a town where Ozark sandstone, brick, and wood siding were the materials of choice, Charlie showed the influence of his California sojourn by finishing his hotel in stucco. To the front he added a curved false front with two small finials on the corners and a balcony on the second floor, giving the building a hint of the Spanish Colonial style.[25] Photograph by author, 1981.

House and Motel, ca. 1930
Halltown

The owner of a two-story bungalow added a line of stucco cabins with covered garages to the rear of his property. The pyramidal roof that covered each motel room and garage gave his buildings the look of the Western Bungalow that spread across Kansas and Oklahoma in the late nineteenth century. Photograph by author, 1981.

Bill's Station, ca. 1930
Phelps

Further west along 66, Bill Tiller also finished his gas station in stucco and added a wooden lean-to at the rear. Bill may have had a canopy over service area that met a bad end. The little mansard roof supported by steel poles must have been added to the front later. A few steps to the east Bill built a small wooden garage. Photograph by author, 1980.

Log City Camp, 1926
Avilla

At Avilla, Carl Stansbury and Messrs. Whitson and Hammond competed for the overnight traveler along this isolated stretch of 66 where other accommodations were basic at best. Carl Stansbury began clearing trees from the site of Log City in 1926 and used them to build fourteen log cabins. Out front he built a café of rough fieldstone and a gas station with a rock base and a vertical siding top. Whitson and Hammond arrived across the road two years later to build ten rock cabins the size of suburban houses and added front porches. Stansbury promptly added four rock cabins. Whitson and Hammond added a café, Stansbury a coffee shop. Stansbury added a dining room, Whitson and Hammond a tavern and dance hall.

The rivalry went on for years; as one topped the other, the other undercut and undersold the first. What was good for the customer must have been hard on Stansbury, Whitson, and Hammond.[26] Photographs by author, 1981.

Forest Park Camp, 1928
Avilla

Boots' Court, 1939
Carthage

In Carthage, at the intersection of U.S. 66 and U.S. 71, there was more money for architecture than at Phelps or Avilla—and more competition for business. In 1939 Arthur G. Boots built the first section of his Streamline Moderne motel in stucco and rounded all the edges. Boots defined the roofline of the office with neon and a line of black glass tile. He ran additional stripes of black glass above and below the windows and emphasized the roundness of the corners with verticals of black glass. He added new rooms in the back section in 1945, bringing the total to fourteen.

Boots offered all the modern amenities—tile showers, radiant heat in the floor, air conditioning, and garages. In 1946 he added a Streamline Moderne drive-in across the road. Two years later he sold the motel to Rachel Asplin and her husband, who had left the cold of Minnesota for the milder climate of southwestern Missouri. When the Streamline Moderne lost its architectural respectability in the 1960s, the Asplins plunked down a gabled roof over the office.[27] Photograph by author, 1981.

Park Motel, ca. 1935
Joplin

Joplin, the last urban center before the Kansas line, served the lead and zinc mines that surrounded it and extended west through Kansas into northeastern Oklahoma. Roadside proprietors in Joplin abandoned the vernacular architecture of the Ozarks and reached for the common architectural styles of the big cities—in the twenties, the Spanish Colonial; in the thirties and forties, the Streamline Moderne; and in the fifties, the ranch house. Motel owners took fancy names that alluded to the big St. Louis hotels—the Park and the Koronado. While their aspirations were greater than those of their Ozark brethren to the east, their building methods were the same. Both the Park and the Koronado were low, frame-and-stucco structures with attached rooms and no garages. To give his motel a Spanish Colonial flavor, the owner of the Park added scalloped false fronts finished with hexagonal shingles over the room entrances. Photograph by author, 1979.

Koronado Hotel Courts, 1938
Joplin

Harry M. Bennett laid out a Spanish village of fifty frame-and-stucco cottages with red tile roofs in a U. The office faced the street on one end of the U and the café on the other. Bennett maintained a full-service gas station next door.

As the burgeoning motel industry changed its mind about what to call a motel, Bennett—and later owners—changed the name of the Koronado: It was at one time the Koronado Hotel Kourts, then the Koronado Kourts, and finally the Koronado Motel. In the last variation the owners erected a red sign with white letters that was taller than the building itself and consisted of two elements. On the horizontal bottom element KORONADO was outlined in neon and an arrow pointed to the office. Neon wrapped around the vertical upper element, which announced that the Koronado was now a motel.[28] Photograph by author, 1979.

Kansas and Oklahoma

The Old Wire Road, which carried U.S. 66 through Missouri, ended at the Kansas border. U.S. 66 took no more than eleven and a half miles to make a left turn from Missouri through Kansas into Oklahoma, where it continued along the Ozark Trail, which carried it through Oklahoma, Texas, and New Mexico.

John Steinbeck, Woody Guthrie, Dorothea Lange, and conventional wisdom suggested that Oklahomans fled their state during the dust bowl, escaping down U.S. 66 to a better life in California. Steinbeck did caricature an occasional roadside shopkeeper in *The Grapes of Wrath,* but he and his fellow artists who documented the dust bowl failed to note that many rural Oklahomans escaped their foreclosed farms to settle on 66. There they pumped gas and served food to those Oklahomans, Missourians, Kansans, and Nebraskans trekking west.[1] Nor did conventional wisdom take into account the fact that 1934 was the first really good tourist year after the stock market crash of 1929, and tourists as well as migrants were supporting roadside businesses.

Oklahoma abounded in buildings from the period, mostly simple, vernacular buildings erected quickly in frame and clapboard, frame and stucco, or structural clay tile and stucco. Although Oklahomans occasionally used sandstone, they did not develop the strong, varied vernacular found in the Missouri Ozarks. They did use variations on the little Russian-German bungalow in their motels of the thirties and forties. Introduced to the Midwest by Russian-German Mennonites who settled in central Kansas in the 1870s, the tiny house with a pyramidal roof developed into the Western Bungalow that spread across the plains. Sooners carried it south into Oklahoma with the opening of the territory to settlement after 1889.[2]

Oklahomans used other domestic styles—Tudor and ranch. Two of the best ranch-style motels, those that most closely resembled the houses of the postwar suburbs, appeared along the roadside in Tulsa and Oklahoma City. Finally, Oklahomans produced gas stations with heavy canopies, often supported by a single elaborate pier.

Gas Station, n.d.
Galena, Kansas

As U.S. 66 traveled west, gas station canopies became heavier and heavier. As the sun grew hotter and the air drier, the need to supply shade at the pumps grew imperative. Missourians built nothing like this gas station with its heavy canopy supported by tapered columns and heavy brackets. This was a city gas station, brick below and stucco above, set diagonally on its corner lot so it could be approached from either U.S. 66 or the side street. Photograph by author, 1979.

Bank Building, ca. 1900
Baxter Springs, Kansas

The Missouri-Kansas-Oklahoma region was known as the Big Business Corner. It is a region scattered with small white mountains, tailings from the local zinc and lead mines that dominated the region's economy until the late 1940s.[3] In Illinois and Missouri, U.S. 66 seldom went through the center of town. Rather, it tended to stick to the budding commercial strip on the outskirts. But once the road entered Kansas and Oklahoma, it truly became the Main Street of America, following Main Street through most cities and towns clear to California. In 1926, the turn-of-the-century towns along 66 in the Big Business Corner were still fairly new and exciting, and business was booming in the lead and zinc mines between Galena and Miami. The short, massive granite column supporting the arched entrance to the bank building housing the Baxter Springs Chamber of Commerce was very impressive—and was repeated over and over in towns throughout the region. Photograph by author, 1979.

Spencer's Diner, 1944
Baxter Springs, Kansas

Spencer's Diner was laid to rest just west of the Kansas-Oklahoma line after first seeing service on the KATY Railroad as a passenger coach and then as a diner in Baxter Springs. For the most part, American diners were manufactured buildings designed to be carted on a truck from the railroad depot to the site. When A. T. Spencer, who ran gas stations on 66, purchased a passenger coach from William Lea of Chetopa, Kansas, in 1944, he hitched it to a truck and hauled it to Baxter Springs. The truck's axle broke under the strain, but once Spencer got the coach to his site, he set it on a foundation, added a kitchen, and began serving burgers, hot dogs, and chili—the staples of roadside food. In 1962 he sold the diner to new owners who hauled it to its final resting place outside of Commerce, Oklahoma.[4] Photograph by author, 1979.

Sooner State Kourt, 1950, razed 1981
Miami, Oklahoma

The nineteen-unit Sooner State was a medley of styles. The basic building material for the motel was the slab-cut sandstone that was so familiar in western Missouri. The builder applied Tudor half-timbers to the stucco gable of each unit and to the dormer over each door. Inside the rooms, the Sooner State offered tile baths, carpeting, and free radio. In 1956 the motel charged extra for television and air conditioning.

At odds with the homey appearance of the motel building was the large Streamline Moderne sign supporting a Conestoga wagon and team. It was installed a decade after the motel proper was built. A base constructed of the ledgestone made popular by Frank Lloyd Wright and other prairie school architects supported the sign.[5] Photograph by author, 1979.

Cherokee Motel, 1952
Miami, Oklahoma

The Cherokee was a frankly ranch-style motel with a wide, flat Wrightian chimney of coursed stone that supported the sign on one side while a neon arrow supported it on the street side. Depicted on the sign was a clownish American Indian welcoming the traveler.

The Cherokee also provided a marriage parlor with a minister on call. It was one of several such parlors in Miami, where it was possible to marry without a three-day wait for a blood test.[6] Photograph by author, 1979.

The Coleman Theater Beautiful, 1929
Miami, Oklahoma

Carl and Robert Boller, brothers, designed the Coleman Theater for George L. Coleman, Sr., who built it at a cost of $590,000. The sixteen-hundred-seat theater opened to a full house on April 18, 1929. The Bollers incorporated both a movie house and a vaudeville theater into a commercial block. Their first design called for an Italianate facade. They changed it in midconstruction, however, creating a spectacular Spanish Colonial addition to Miami's Main Street. They carried the Spanish motif the length of the commercial block but saved the most elaborate decorations for the theater and movie house. Over each marquee the designers molded an ornamental surround to the window that was drawn straight from the decorations over the doors of the Spanish mission churches scattered throughout Texas, Arizona, and California. They continued the allusion to a Spanish mission by adding corner towers to the facade of the theater and finials the length of the commercial block.[7] Photograph by author, 1997.

Buffalo Ranch, 1953
Afton, Oklahoma

Russell and Alleene Kay sold their hotel at Greensburg, Kansas, and spent two years touring the West looking for a road with traffic, lots of traffic, where they could build a tourist stop. They found it at Afton, where four federal highways—U.S. 59, 60, 66, and 69—came together. They settled there in 1953 and spent the next three years building the Buffalo Ranch, where the opportunity to view seven head of buffalo was the come-on. The Kays erected signs on the four highways offering a free look at "America's first animals." Folks stopped, looked, and bought—ice cream at the dairy ranch, burgers at the barbecue, and moccasins at the trading post, all housed in a series of low, nondescript buildings. Out back, behind the stores, was the pen for the buffalo. The herd grew to number forty, not counting the plywood cutout of a buffalo in the parking lot.[8] Photograph by author, 1997.

Main Street, ca. 1900
Afton, Oklahoma

On the corner of Main Street and 66, Smith's Store occupied the ground floor of an office block similar to the building that housed the Baxter Springs (Kansas) Chamber of Commerce. Washed white, with black signs, Smith's Store offered SUNDRIES and FOUNTAIN SERVICE to travelers eager for a rest and a soda or a shake. Photograph by author, 1981.

D-X Service Station, ca. 1940
Afton, Oklahoma

That Oklahomans built heavy-duty gas stations is probably a reflection of the amount of oil they pumped out of the ground and the intensity of their sun. In Afton they built three stations in four blocks, all along 66. All had medium-sized offices and large canopies that extended over the pumping area. The roofing material of choice was tin, which was shaped like Spanish tiles, giving each station a faintly Spanish flavor in spite of the frankly modern forms such as the irregularly hexagonal office and the run of lights on the underside of the support beams in the D-X station. Photograph by author, 1981.

Cities Service Station, ca. 1933
Afton, Oklahoma

Down the street from the D-X station, Cities Service built a station that was more clearly Spanish in design, with its rough stucco finish, heavy arched porte cochere, and green-painted tin-tile roof. A canopy must have been attached to the flat surface on the front of the porte cochere. Under the porte cochere, two storefronts— enough room for a café and a gas station office—monitored the service area. Tiny square rest rooms with overscaled hipped roofs were added in adjacent buildings. Cities Service provided living quarters in the rear for the agent, Doc Story, who operated the station.[9] Photograph by author, 1998.

Will Rogers Hotel, 1930
Claremore, Oklahoma

Partners Louis Abraham, Walter Krumrei, and Morton Harrison had two reasons for building a large hotel in the center of Claremore. First, medicinal waters were discovered in Claremore in 1903, and for a while the town flourished as a health spa. Second, U.S. 66 was routed through the center of town in 1926. Combine these two factors in 1930, name the establishment after Will Rogers, Claremore's most famous son, and the city could support a hotel offering sixty-eight rooms and seven apartments. It was Krumrei, a construction engineer, who decided the hotel should resemble Rogers's Spanish Colonial house in Santa Monica, California. So he covered the building in terra-cotta details applied to the windows and doors and topped one corner of the six-story building with a Spanish mission bell tower. After Rogers's death in 1935, the construction of the Will Rogers Memorial provided additional business for the hotel, which unlike so many large hotels in small cities continued to thrive into the 1980s.[10] Photograph by author, 1998.

El Sueno Tourist Court, 1938
Claremore, Oklahoma

In 1938 Jack Sibley quit his job as a state tax commissioner, a position in which he inspected gas stations for their octane ratings, and settled his wife, Margaret, and their toddler in the two-bedroom owner's residence over the office of El Sueno—The Dream, his dream.

A year earlier, Jack had traveled west along U.S. 66 looking for architectural ideas for his tourist court. The family legend has it that he saw an Alamo look-alike somewhere on 66 in northwestern Arizona. In fact, he needed to look no further than Oklahoma City, where Lee Torrence had just opened an Alamo Plaza Hotel Court.

When Jack built El Sueno, he followed the Alamo Plaza plan and elevation closely.

The scalloped center of the tourist court housed the office on the first floor and the Sibleys' apartment on the second floor. The facade dropped off over the two entrances into an interior courtyard, where duplex cabins, set perpendicular to the street, lined both sides of a U-shaped drive. A pair of smaller scalloped buildings flanked the main building and housed additional units.[11] Photograph by author, 1981.

Star Motel, 1945
Claremore, Oklahoma

At one time the center unit of each of the low brick buildings was a pair of garages for the rooms on the ends. Little brick porches marked the entrances of each of the original units. Like the Hudsons at the Munger Moss in Lebanon, Missouri, the owner of the Star filled in the garages as the demand for rooms grew, the demand for garages slackened, and the cost of additional land increased. Like the sign at the Munger Moss, the Star's sign, which advertised the availability of TV, dwarfed and outshone the individual units. Photograph by author, 1981.

Chief Wolf Robe's Trading Post, 1952
Catoosa, Oklahoma

Wolf Robe Hunt, an Acoma Indian, and his wife, Glenal, started their business with sixty dollars in borrowed money in 1936. They rented space from Skelly Oil in a Spanish Colonial building at Eleventh and Harvard on U.S. 66 in Tulsa. Glenal's brother, Hugh Davis, built the Hunts a beautiful wooden showcase, which they filled with Osage beadwork. When the beadwork sold immediately, they bought more. They added Navajo jewelry supplied by Wolf Robe's brother, Blue Sky, who had a shop in Albuquerque, and Acoma pottery supplied by Wolf Robe's cousin, Juana Leno, a potter at Acoma Pueblo in New Mexico. They expanded into the shop next door, and Hugh built more showcases.

As traffic grew and the store became crowded, the Hunts opened a second store at Catoosa and put its management in the hands of their sister-in-law, Zelda Davis. During the summer Zelda rose at 3 A.M. and prepared for the onslaught of tourists who traveled in the cool of the night. She always did her best business before 10 A.M.

In 1952, when the Will Rogers Turnpike opened and the tourist business in Tulsa dried up, the Hunts packed up their wooden cases, now numbered 1 through 6, and moved to the large concrete-block building at Catoosa, where traffic continued to flow. A colonnade across the front supported a narrow porch below the stepped parapet that was typical of block buildings. Wrought iron grills done in American Indian designs protected the windows.[12] Photograph by author, 1982.

Zelda Davis's Alligator Farm, 1960
Catoosa, Oklahoma

Zelda Davis managed the trading post for her in-laws, Wolf Robe and Glenal Hunt, but she wanted her own tourist business. She loved alligators, so her husband, Hugh, the director of the Tulsa Zoo, who knew animals and was handy with tools, built her an ark, peopled it with Noah, his wife, and a full menagerie, and located it across 66 from the Hunts' trading post. Zelda started with a few small alliga-tors. As they grew, so did her business. Next door, Hugh built himself the Blue Whale Swimming Hole, which he peopled with cartoon characters he had sculpted in plaster and a giant blue whale that served as a slide into the swimming hole. Because his customers included local kids, his business survived long after traffic on 66 stopped.[13] Photograph by author, 1981.

Tulsa

Until this point we have motored west along Route 66, town by town, building by building. In Tulsa and West Tulsa, we come to a good place to look at the chronological progression of architectural styles. Therefore we will cruise the early motels along Southwest Boulevard in West Tulsa before returning to Eleventh Street in Tulsa to look at a restaurant built by West Tulsa motel owners and a fine ranch-style motel.

Gone from Tulsa is Cyrus Avery's Old English Inn. In 1921, before he routed a federal highway through his hometown, before he had it numbered U.S. 66, before he founded the U.S. Highway 66 Association to promote his road, Cy Avery built a gas station, twenty-five tourist cabins, and the Old English Inn on the eastern outskirts of Tulsa at the corner of Admiral and Mingo. When U.S. 66 came to town five years later, it was routed straight down Admiral right past the Old English Inn. In time, Eleventh Street replaced Admiral as 66, and in 1943 the Old English Inn was razed to make room for a traffic circle, proving that not even Cyrus Avery was immune to shifts in the highway's alignment.[14]

Shady Rest Cottage Camp, 1936
West Tulsa, Oklahoma

Maurice Colpitts, a plumbing inspector for the city of Tulsa, hired a contractor to build the Shady Rest in 1936. The contractor may have built the little ten-by-twelve-foot, nine-inch clapboard shacks at the Shady Rest from a prefabricated kit purchased at the local lumber store or from a design published in *Popular Mechanics* in 1935. That article had laid out a set of plans and specifications for a ten-by-twelve-foot frame cabin, finished with sheathing of the owner's choice—clapboard, log siding, or stucco—on the outside and fiberboard on the inside. It was a front-gable cabin constructed with a seven-foot-high frame of two-by-four-inch studs set on a four-by-

four-inch sill plate. The gable was three feet to the ridge. The roof could be roll tar paper or shingles. Standardized barn windows in the walls provided cross ventilation. Each room was big enough to accommodate two people in a standard double bed. Colpitts's contractor finished the cabins in clapboard and constructed carports in the space between the shacks. When the Shady Rest was completed, Colpitts moved his family to the auto camp, where they all had a hand in maintaining the site while he continued to inspect plumbing for the city of Tulsa.[15] Photograph by author, 1997.

El Reposo Tourist Camp, aka 66 Motel, 1939
West Tulsa, Oklahoma

The site of El Reposo Tourist Camp made it more difficult to construct than the Shady Rest had been. Isaac Burnaman purchased his lot from Thomas Hardwick, a junk dealer. He wedged a gas station, café, and ten tiny rooms—probably no larger than the ten-by-twelve rooms at the Shady Rest—and their garages around the perimeter of a triangular lot that dipped into the floodplain of the Arkansas River. Guests entered their rooms through the garages, assuring privacy and protection from the weather. Burnaman installed glass-block windows around the office door, giving El Reposo a Streamline Moderne look even though it had an ersatz Spanish name.[16] Photograph by author, 1998.

Park Plaza Courts, 1942
West Tulsa, Oklahoma

As newlyweds, Mickey and Milton Stroud, Jr., left their home in Waco, Texas, and traveled U.S. 66, working as substitute managers at the Park Plaza Courts, a small chain with motels in St. Louis; West Tulsa and Amarillo, Texas; Raton, New Mexico; and Flagstaff, Arizona. In 1950 they pulled up in their green and white two-toned Cadillac to their first assignment, the Park Plaza Courts in West Tulsa, where they monitored the desk, worked the switchboard, fixed the plumbing, and cleaned the rooms while the resident managers took a two-week vacation.

Milton's father, Milton, Sr., and his uncle, Lemuel, had started Park Plaza Courts at the suggestion of Lee Torrence, owner of the Alamo Plaza chain. Torrence had given them the use of his architect and his design for the Alamo Plaza and had helped them learn the business. When they started building their motels, Lemuel supervised construction at each site, while Milton stayed in Waco and managed the business. They built their first Park Plaza Court in West Tulsa in 1942. When they finished it, first Lemuel, then Milton, Sr., managed the motel in order to learn the business. And they continued to build motels—in Amarillo, Raton, Flagstaff, and finally, in 1948, St. Louis. All but the Raton motel were located on U.S. 66. A salesman taking the four-day drive from St. Louis to Flagstaff via Raton could stay in Park Plaza Courts all the way.

Dorothy Harrison, who owned the Park Plaza in West Tulsa long after the Strouds pulled out, described it as "a little Spanish village" set in a grove of pecans and oaks on the floodplain of the Arkansas River, three miles south of downtown Tulsa. The facade of the Park Plaza was an elaborate variation on Jack Sibley's El Sueno at Claremore. As Torrence and Sibley had done, the Strouds broke the facade into three elements, a long, two-story center element that tapered to a single story at the sides and two single-story facades on either side. Behind the facades, they laid out a hacienda, blocks of rooms set at different angles along the drive and a long block across the rear of the complex. They housed the office and owner-manager's residence in the two-story center. Guests entered the complex through flat arches cut in the center element on either side of the office. At some point the arch was cut away and the facade broken into five sections. The Strouds repeated the same design from site to site. In the quality of architecture, including the master plan, the Park Plaza Courts, and by extension the Alamo Plaza Hotel Courts, were to the Spanish Mission design what the Coral Court was to the Streamline Moderne.[17] Photograph by author, 1981.

Golden Drumstick, 1948
Tulsa, Oklahoma

In 1948 the Stroud brothers built restaurants in St. Louis and Tulsa, both from the same design. In St. Louis they located the restaurant next to their Park Plaza Court. In Tulsa they located the Golden Drumstick at Eleventh and Yale rather than next to the Park Plaza Court in West Tulsa. Their stucco building was a good example of the confusion that could exist between the Spanish Colonial style of the 1920s and '30s and the Streamline Moderne style of the '30s and '40s. While a parapet crowned the building and red-tile awnings shaded the windows in the Spanish style, the corners were rounded and the building smooth in the Streamline Moderne style.[18] Photograph by author, 1981.

Manor Motel, 1958
Tulsa, Oklahoma

As the fifties wore on, Americans climbed in their cars, escaped the aging cities, and settled in suburban ranch houses in countrylike settings. To the eye of the late-fifties traveler, the little cabins of the Shady Rest looked quaint and dirty, the Streamline Moderne of El Reposo unfashionable, and the Park Plaza Courts like an aging dowager. James Norcom's Manor Motel, however, looked clean and fashionable and imitated the ideal home of the era. The Manor was one of several motels Norcom owned in Tulsa. Its architecture—a series of attached ranch cottages constructed in coursed stone with arched porches supporting low rooflines—echoed the postwar suburban dream. It was as sophisticated an application of the ranch style to motel building as the Coral Court in St. Louis was of the Streamline Moderne style.[19] Photograph by author, 1982.

Rock Cafe, 1939
Stroud, Oklahoma

As 66 approached Oklahoma City, it passed through the eastern border of the Sandstone Hills, which extend to the western edge of the state. The soft red sandstone, buried under the rolling hills, is what gives Oklahoma soil, and an occasional roadside building, its distinctive color.

When highway engineers cut U.S. 66 through a layer of sandstone near Kellyville, they sold the discarded rock to Roy Rieves for five dollars. Rieves carted it to a site on the eastern outskirts of Stroud and constructed the Rock Cafe, a one-story building with very tall ceilings. Unlike the "rock folk" in Missouri who laid up slabs of sandstone as a veneer against a frame building, Rieves used masonry construction, laying his hunks of rock, varying from light yellow through red to almost black, on a concrete foundation. At the corners of the building, Rieves carefully set horizontal stones to build columns that projected through the roof. He took the same care with the fireplace and chimney. In between, he laid the stones every which way. When he finished, he topped the building with a hatlike tin roof pulled down low. He painted the roof green, and on it he advertised the café's speciality—BAR-B-QUE—punctuating the word with the round face of a fat pig.[20] Photograph by author, 1997.

Gas Station, ca. 1940
Davenport, Oklahoma

Located on a curve in the road on the eastern edge of Davenport, this gas station, constructed of concrete block formed to look like stone, snagged travelers low on gas before they entered town. The customers kept cool under a heavy canopy lined with stamped tin and supported by a massive brick pier in the Oklahoma fashion. Photograph by author, 1981.

Lincoln Court, 1939
Chandler, Oklahoma

Joe Gibson first catered to salesmen at Gibson's Court, located near the railroad station in Chandler. In 1939 he decided to cater to tourists and built the Lincoln on 66 on the eastern edge of the city, where he could catch travelers on their way into town. Protected from the highway by a tall hedge, descendants of the Russian-German bungalow lined the driveways of the Lincoln Court. Gibson sheathed each wood-frame bungalow, which housed two rooms, in vertical boards stained brown.[21] Photograph by author, 1997.

J & J Eat Shop Sign, ca. 1950
Wellston, Oklahoma

Jack Abraham, who served THICK STEAKS at the J & J Eat Shop in Bristow, erected a sign forty miles west in Wellston. He also served fried chicken, fried shrimp, a Syrian salad bowl, and icebox pies.[22] Photograph by author, 1981.

Pioneer Tourist Court, 1921
Wellston, Oklahoma

The Pioneer Tourist Court was one of the earliest motels on U.S. 66. As in the design of so many early roadside buildings along 66, a false front raised over the center gave bulk to this low, one-story building, which looked more like a western bunkhouse than a motel. Photograph by author, 1981.

Threatt's Grocery and Gas Station, 1926
Luther, Oklahoma

When the Unassigned Lands in central Oklahoma opened for settlement with the "run" of 1889, the Threatts, one of a number of African-American families to settle east of Guthrie and Edmond, claimed a section near what would become Luther eight years later. They farmed cotton and corn, ran cattle, and quarried red and pink sandstone on their 160 acres. In 1926, when U.S. 66 was charted along the edge of their farm, Alan Threatt worked on the road and then with his son, Ulysses, built a slabstone—Oklahomans called it giraffe stone—gas station with rock from their quarry. They added a grocery in 1935.

In 1937 Ulysses Threatt married Elizabeth, a schoolteacher. She opened a café on the site. She called it "The Junior" after her brother-in-law's Oklahoma City restaurant, the Brown Bomber Cafe, named in honor of Joe Louis. Elizabeth rose a 4:30 each morning to serve an early breakfast at her café, taught school all day, then returned to cook dinner in the early evening. She also kept a garden, bringing in fresh tomatoes and collards to serve in the summer.[23] Photograph by author, 1998.

Prokupt's Gas Station and Bus Stop, ca. 1926
Luther, Oklahoma

Prokupt's Gas Station and Bus Stop, Threatt's Grocery and Gas Station, and a third gas station west of Threatt's used red and pink sandstone quarried from the Threatt farm in their construction. None of buildings could be called "Giraffe Stone Moderne" in the Missouri Ozark sense. Rather, each was a simple vernacular building constructed by people who needed a place to do business.

Edna Prokupt and her husband purchased the pink-sandstone Greyhound station at Luther from Preacher Spinks in 1945. The small, three-room station with a canopy out front was built as a gas station. The Prokupts had an apartment in the basement. Edna worked the bus station, while her husband worked on the Rock Island Railroad. The bus companies paid Edna 10 percent of each bus ticket she sold. To supplement her income from tickets, she sold a little bit of everything—cigarettes, candy, gum, and sandwiches.[24] Photograph by author, 1981.

Main Street, 1927
Arcadia, Oklahoma

The folks in Arcadia did a booming business during the heyday of 66. Then the town shrank, leaving the old gas station, an old grocery, the round barn, and a few houses.

Sooners had established the town after the 1889 land rush, and W. H. Odor had built the round barn out of burr oak nine years later. In 1927 Carter Holbrook built a simple vernacular gas station out of which he pumped Rose Gas. He framed up a simple office, covered it in cement-asbestos siding, and extended the roof out over the pumping area, shading the office. He attached a small house on the east side of the station and added a garage in a separate building to the west. In between he built a small icehouse.[25] Photograph by author, 1981.

Skyview Drive-in, 1948
Oklahoma City, Oklahoma

Sam Kapriolotis landed in New York with his father and brother at the turn of the century. For two years, the family made their living selling fruit and gum from a pushcart on New York streets. Then, when Sam's father and brother returned to their native Greece, nine-year-old Sam stayed. He raised himself, became a citizen, and took a new name—Caporal, the name of his favorite smoke. Young Sam Caporal drifted to St. Louis, where he learned to be a movie projectionist, and then to Oklahoma City, where he opened his first movie house in 1916. In 1948, Sam and his sons—George, Chris, and Pete—built the Skyview Drive-in.

A drive-in movie screen needed to be no more than an extra-large billboard, and many screens in rural areas were just that. In the big cities, however, it was necessary to use architecture to draw customers to the outskirts of town. The Caporals understood that when they hired architect David Baldwin to design the Skyview, located on Northeast Twenty-third Street, two and a half miles from the capitol and U.S. 66. Baldwin gave them a reinforced-concrete, Spanish Colonial screen tower. The contractor used slip-form construction to build the tower. The process, the same that had been used in the construction of grain elevators since the turn of the century, took six days. The workers started on the ground, filled the forms with concrete, let it set, moved the forms up a bit, and poured more concrete. It was a twenty-four-hour-a-day operation. As the tower moved upward, workers installed prefabricated windows, shaped like quatrefoils and glazed with opaque glass, in the center section of the screen tower. The Caporals painted the piers white and the center royal blue and outlined the whole in neon. They installed lights behind the quatrefoil windows so that at night they glowed like large golden stars. They set SKYVIEW on top in giant neon letters and proudly placed their name, CAPORAL, at the top of the left pier.[26] Photograph by author, 1981.

Carlyle Courts, 1943
Oklahoma City, Oklahoma

Lyle and Ruby Overman did a lot of traveling in the days when tourists hauled the comforts of home—linens, food, and cooking and eating utensils—with them. Hence, when they built their first motor court in the 1930s, they met the public's demands for the latest in comfort and continued to do so with each new motel.

Lyle and Ruby started in the motel business in St. Louis after 1933, when the Missouri Highway Department moved U.S. 66 from the ridge road to the Meramec Valley. They built the Trav-o-Tel Deluxe, the only motel in St. Louis recommended by Duncan Hines in 1938. It was sixteen brick cottages set on a pretty site down by the Meramec River. But every time the river rose, it swamped the pretty site. So the Overmans sold the cottages in 1940 and moved to Oklahoma City, where they could stay dry and where they built two motels along Thirty-ninth Street, U.S. 66, at the western edge of Oklahoma City. The first was the Major Court, which they operated through World War II.

During the war, Lyle and Ruby continued their building program, anticipating the American passion for the suburban ranch house. Unlike suburban homeowners who set their dream house on a fairly large lot, the Overmans squeezed the Carlyle Court on a tight urban lot. They eliminated the garages and placed the office and manager's residence and a small green space in the center of the site. They wrapped an oval drive around the office and built six little ranch houses of three rooms each, setting them at a forty-five-degree angle to the drive. Across the rear of the property, they added a four-unit house. Steel-casement corner windows, new to motels, provided cross ventilation—a necessity on hot summer nights in Oklahoma. Duncan Hines noted in 1946 that the Carlyle also offered carpeted floors with radiant heat and tile bathrooms. By 1956, the Overmans had added air conditioning and had sunk a swimming pool in the green space.[27] Photograph by author, 1997.

Sauer's Red Rock Gas Station, 1941
El Reno, Oklahoma

With the depression easing in the early forties, a fellow by the name of Sauer experimented with new forms using old materials and built the Red Rock gas station. He used old materials, wood frame covered in stucco, for his building. However, he shaped a rounded false front that could have drawn its inspiration either from the new Streamline Moderne forms that proliferated in Oklahoma City in the forties or from the old Spanish Colonial forms that had been so popular in the thirties.[28] Photograph by author, 1981.

Hamburger Inn, 1926
El Reno, Oklahoma

John Steinbeck described the food stand circa 1937: "Along 66 the hamburger stands—Al and Susy's Place—Carl's Lunch—Joe and Minnie—Will's Eats. Board-and-bat shacks. Two gasoline pumps in front, a screen door, a long bar, stools and a foot rail." He went on to describe how Al cooked an onion-fried hamburger at his café: "He presses down a hissing hamburger with his spatula. He lays the split buns on the plate to toast and heat. He gathers up stray onions from the plate and heaps them on the meat and presses them in with the spatula. He puts half the bun on top of the meat, paints the other half with melted butter, with thin pickle relish. Holding the bun on the meat, he slips the spatula under the thin pad of meat, flips it over, lays the the buttered half on top and drops the hamburger on a small plate."[29]

"No, No, No! No butter on the bun, just pickle relish and mus-

tard," laughs Ross Davis whose father, Henry Wesly Davis, plagiarized the onion-fried hamburger from White Castle in Wichita. The senior Davis built the Hamburger Inn, a clay-tile cube covered in stucco, in El Reno in 1925 and opened with a counter and ten stools in 1926. Davis wanted to have a chain of hamburger stands like White Castle's, and he built several of the little cubes in cities across Oklahoma. Later he bought a portable concrete building from a firm in Tulsa. When he sold the business in 1939, he had eight outlets for his onion-fried burger. Henry's son, Ross, bought back the business in 1942, built a larger stand on the eastern edge of El Reno, and sold the original building to Lawrence Hendy, who added the neon Streamline Moderne sign in 1956, giving the little stucco cube a fast-food image.[30] Photograph by author, 1982.

Tavern, ca. 1934
West of El Reno, Oklahoma

West of El Reno, U.S. 66 entered the plains where the towns were spread farther apart. When the road was laid out in 1926, it turned north a few miles west of El Reno and passed through Calumet and Geary before dipping south to cross the South Canadian River via the Swinging Bridge, a delicate suspension bridge, at Bridgeport. Then it continued west through Hydro to Weatherford and on to Texas. In 1934 the Oklahoma Highway Department built a solid steel truss and concrete bridge across the river south of Bridgeport, necessitating thirty-five miles of new pavement between El Reno and Weatherford and bypassing Calumet, Geary, Bridgeport, and Hydro. A lot of folks found opportunity along this lonely stretch of highway and opened a restaurant, a tavern, a gas station, or a motel. They built using a simple, functional architecture that drew on the vernacular of the western Oklahoma plains—variations on the Western Bungalow. This tavern at the top of a hill was larger than a bungalow but its broad clipped roof made it seem to squat low to the ground.[31] Photograph by author, 1981.

Leon Little's Gas Station and Café, 1940
West of Hinton Junction, Oklahoma

Ann and Leon Little made a good living on this stretch of highway west of El Reno. When they married in 1932, they bought an old gas station next to the Swinging Bridge on 66 at Bridgeport. In 1934, when the Oklahoma Highway Department bypassed Bridgeport and rerouted 66 to a new bridge over the South Canadian, the Littles built a new station at the west end of the bridge at the intersection of U.S. 66 and U.S. 281. Six years later they expanded their business and built a third station, a café, and a motel west of the junction. Little laid up walls of structural clay tile, which he protected with stucco. He whitewashed the imposing two-story gas station and residence—razed before 1981—and the boxy café, but Oklahoma dust soon turned the buildings pink. The eight-room motel was a long, low ranch-style bungalow set on the back of the property.

When Leon was drafted in 1943, he got a six-month deferment in order to organize his affairs. He leased the business to E. B. Enze, who closed down Leon's complex and opened his own business in a new stucco building at the intersection of 66 and 281. By the time Leon's deferment was up, the army had set age thirty as the upper limit of draft eligibility. Since Leon was thirty-two, he didn't go into the army, but he honored the lease to Enze and sat out the war in Borger, Texas, towing cars. When the lease on the business was up in 1945, he and Ann returned to their complex and started over.[32] Photograph by author, 1987.

Enze's Cafe, 1945
Hinton Junction, Oklahoma

Where the Littles' buildings looked backwards to the thirties, Enze's building looked forward to the fifties and a crude International Style architecture. Rather than using rounded Streamline forms to attract business, Enze sculpted a heavy cornice dominated by large squares over the picture windows. Over the central square, which was hol- lowed to hold a light, he mounted an arrow whose legend, EAT, invited the traveler on 66 to stop in. Enze added four motel rooms and garages in a low, stucco, flat-roofed building at the back of his property.[33] Photograph by author, 1981.

Harvey House, 1934
Bridgeport, Oklahoma

The Harvey House Court drew its famous name from the Fred Harvey hotels and restaurants that served the Santa Fe railroad's Spanish Colonial stations across the Southwest; it drew its architecture from the western plains—a low stucco building with a hipped roof and a low, overhanging tin canopy supported by posts.

Before 1934 Harvey Wornstaff ran a gas station at the east end of the Swinging Bridge at Bridgeport. When the Oklahoma Highway Department rerouted 66 across the new bridge—five miles east of Bridgeport and a half-mile south—the citizens of Bridgeport got into a dispute about the future of their town. As it turned out, Bridgeport had no future. The fight ended in a draw: Half the town moved to Hinton, the other half to new 66 where they established a roadside stringtown for which they reused the name Bridgeport. It

stretched for a mile along 66, all little gas stations, motels, cafés, food stands, and a dance hall. Dale Lee had a gas station and repair shop, Jack Hind a gas station and hamburger stand, Velma and Ray Yount a gas station and lunch room, Nancy Rose a grocery with pumps, Happy Jack the dance hall, and so on, all competing for the dollars that came down 66. Harvey Wornstaff had a gas station, restaurant, and motel. He named it after himself and housed the restaurant, the gas station, and his living quarters in the low stucco building. To the east, he built little square cabins for overnight guests.

What was left of old Bridgeport? A grocery, an old hotel converted to apartments, the post office, and the telephone office. That was it. The rest just disappeared—as did the new Bridgeport after the interstate replaced 66 in 1962.[34] Photograph by author, 1981.

Hamons' Gas Station and Court, 1934
Hydro, Oklahoma

Lucille Hamons married the son of a homesteader two months before the beginning of World War II. They settled in the second-floor apartment that served as the canopy for his Conoco station, located on new 66 one-half mile south of Hydro. Supported over the pumps by stuccoed columns, the apartment was covered in black asphalt shingles. The first-floor office of the frame building was clapboard. While her husband drove a truck, Lucille pumped gas fifteen hours a day and sometimes at night. After the war, when travel boomed, she built five cabins behind the station, and for thirty years she rented them. When the fence along I-44, built adjacent to old 66, cut her off from her customers, she decided to stay put to spite the interstate. And she continued to sell gas, beer, cigarettes, and homemade pickles.[35] Photograph by author, 1981.

Cliffhouse Diner, 1941
Weatherford, Oklahoma

Marvin Porter had a motto: "Don't ever set a diner on the south side of the road." If you were driving west, and most travelers were, he reasoned that it was easier to turn right into and out of a diner on the north side of the road than to turn left into and out of a diner on the south side of the road. Porter was right: In the road's heyday, traffic along 66 was so heavy that a left turn was nigh on to impossible.

Marvin Porter went into the diner business in 1941 when he inherited five hundred dollars from his uncle. With the money in hand, he gave up his job at the local auto supply store, made a down payment on a lot and a house on the western edge of Weatherford, and purchased a diner from the Valentine Systems of Wichita. When Valentine delivered the prefabricated diner to the site—on the north side of 66—all Porter needed to do was to open the door and start cooking. The exterior of the building had a white enamel finish with red stripes. The interior came outfitted with cooking facilities clad in stainless steel and a counter with stools, all set on a tile floor. The diner was immaculate and was easy to keep that way. To the wall next to the door the manufacturer fixed a metal label with the company's trademark and a slot. It was the piggy bank into which Porter deposited 10 percent of his daily gross until he had paid for the building, which he outlined with the first neon lights to go up in Weatherford.

When Porter enlarged the café, he simply bought another diner and knitted the two together. Then he built a gas station next door. He purchased other diners from Valentine and had them delivered to El Reno and Elk City, Oklahoma, and to Shamrock and Vernon, Texas. Once he had these businesses going, he sold them.[36] Photograph by author, 1981.

R Boy Drive-in, ca. 1956
Weatherford, Oklahoma

The R Boy, offering "Char-burgers, Hot Dogs, Malts," departed from the Streamline Moderne style of the traditional food stand and embraced the International Style with its soaring roof and huge areas of plate glass that displayed the inside to the outside. This food stand offered both window service and eat-in-your-car service, and, like many food stands, it posted its menu on the outside walls. Photograph by author, 1981.

Rio Siesta Motel, ca. 1955
Clinton, Oklahoma

On west, in Clinton, the owners of the Rio Siesta responded to the competitive pressures of a booming highway and erected a tall sign out on the edge of the road. The sign towered over a semicircle of four-unit bunkhouses with decorative gables, and the big arrow with moving lights enticed travelers to stay the night. The man in the sombrero asleep against a cactus appeared with increasing frequency on signs and other motel ornaments as 66 traveled west. Photograph by author, 1981.

Ideal Trailer Park, ca. 1946
Clinton, Oklahoma

To boost their income, the owners of the Ideal Trailer Park added a fireworks stand to the front of their property. The stand was a simple wooden structure sided with old venetian blinds. Like Red Chaney in Springfield, Missouri, the owners assembled their sign from uncommon objects to attract attention to their business—a bomb casing that supported a colonial lamp that supported a small rocket. Finally, they edged the roadside with smaller bombs. Photograph by author, 1981.

Granot Lodge, 1927
Clinton, Oklahoma

Weatherford and Clinton abounded in motels. It was thirty miles or more to Elk City from Clinton, and the next big town after that was Shamrock, Texas, fifty-five miles west of Elk City. Frank Granot, who owned a local lumberyard, built the first motel in Clinton, a long line of white clapboard cabins, and named it after himself. He marked the entry of each unit with a small porch.[37] Photograph by author, 1981.

Pop Hicks's Restaurant and the Glancy Motor Hotel, 1936–48
Main Street
Clinton, Oklahoma

Along 66 west of Oklahoma City, competition for business grew stiff on Main Street. As land along the roadside became crowded and expensive, restaurant owners like Ethan "Pop" Hicks—who started with a three-booth, seven-stool diner and lean-to kitchen in 1936—built right up against the street. Next door to Hicks, motel owners Chester and Gladys Glancy jammed as many units as possible on a narrow site.

The Glancys had married in 1925, farmed for a year down the road at Foss, and then moved to Clinton, where they ran a carnival, a restaurant, a fruit stand, a grocery, and a filling station. When Chester realized that local motel owners took in more cash in one night than he could earn in a week with all his businesses, the Glancys rented the Clinton Courts south of town.

Then, in 1939, Chester and Gladys built the Glancy, choosing the site because it was next door to Pop Hicks. When they enlarged the motel in 1948, they responded to mounting competition with an imperative arrow on a bigger, taller, gaudier sign that hung out over the street. By the time they retired, the Glancys had built a small regional chain in western Oklahoma, with motels in Oklahoma City, Weatherford, and Elk City.[38]

A sad note: On the morning of August 2, 1999, a fire, probably electrical, broke out in the back room of Pop Hicks, a restaurant that had been thriving on the myth of Route 66. That afternoon, page one of the Clinton *Daily News* reported that what started as a small fire, quickly grew into a big fire, and Pop Hicks burned to the ground. Next door, the Glancy fared well, suffering only minor smoke and water damage in the wing closest to the restaurant. Photograph by author, 1997.

Neptune Court and Tavern, 1934
Clinton, Oklahoma

In March in Oklahoma the baby wheat is so green against the red dirt that it makes your eyes ache. But when Albert "A. P." Sights left his native Clinton to visit California, he was so impressed by the blue Pacific that he carried its color home in his mind's eye. In 1927, he purchased a quarter-section, forty acres, of green Oklahoma prairie southwest of Clinton, subdivided it into sixteen lots, and named his project Neptune Park after the Greek god of the sea. Then, in 1934,

Ralph Kobel built the Neptune Court—a motel, filling station, and tavern—on lot 14 at the Y where U.S. 183 split from 66 and went south. In the late 1990s only the two-story filling station and tavern remained of Kobel's stucco-covered Spanish Colonial complex with brown-tiled awnings over the first-floor doors and windows.[39] Photograph by author, 1997.

Cotton Boll Motel, ca. 1955
Canute, Oklahoma

Motel names did not vary much from place to place. Owners named them after themselves or their children. They named them after the road—the 66 Court—or after some fancy hotel in the big city—the Plaza or the Park Plaza—or after the time of day—the Sunrise or the Sunset. Very popular were variations on "ranch"—Ranchito or El Rancho or Ranchero. Occasionally, owners looked around their regions and drew a name from nearby mountains or rivers—the Ozark or the Rio Grande.

The owner of this motel in Canute looked across the cotton fields that spread out through western Oklahoma and called his establishment the Cotton Boll. It was a ranch-style building with a soaring canopy and large plate-glass office windows canted outward to prevent glare. It was straight out of the International Style of the 1950s. To the travelers who had passed up Clinton or, worse, had found Clinton full, or who could find nothing appealing in the tiny towns of Stafford and Foss and were too tired to make it to Elk City, the brightly lit office of the Cotton Boll beckoned them to stop and stay the night. Photograph by author, 1981.

Star Courts, 1940
Elk City, Oklahoma

Roadside architecture was not too different from modern stage set design. Often only a hint of decoration gave a motel a Spanish Colonial flavor or a Streamline Moderne flavor. Built in a coarse pink brick, the tile-capped parapet on the tiny Star Courts—only six units—alluded to Spanish Colonial architecture. With or without the tile, the Star Courts was early postwar in the rhythm of its units—garage, cabin, garage, cabin. When Dr. Walter Andrewkowski and his wife purchased the Star in 1951, they added a boomerang moderne sign advertising AC and TV—two 1950s amenities.[40] Photograph by author, 1981.

Queenan Indian Trading Post, 1948
Elk City, Oklahoma

Most of the trading posts that dotted the western reaches of U.S. 66 were like the Hillbilly Store in Devils Elbow, Missouri, or the Buffalo Ranch at Afton, Oklahoma: They sold some serious arts and crafts, but mostly they sold junk, what Wanda Queenan—pronounced "Queen Ann"—politely called "little souvenirs." Wanda and her husband, Reese, known as the Moccasin Man because he wore a braid and looked like an American Indian, sold the good stuff, including beadwork—moccasins, medallion necklaces, bags, and vests—made by local Cheyenne and Arapaho Indians. Several times a year they left their business in the hands of her parents and traveled to Gallup, New Mexico, where they traded their local beadwork for Acoma pottery, Navajo jewelry and rugs, and the crafts of other southwestern Indians.

The Queenans started in business in downtown Elk City in 1942. Six years later, with World War II over and tourism booming, they realized they were losing business because their customers could not find parking. They moved to the western edge of town, where they built a frame-and-stucco building. They supported the roof with vigas, large, round wooden logs that jutted through the walls. The Queenans worked and lived in the store with only a curtain separating the salesroom from their living room. By 1962 when the stucco finish had cracked and deteriorated, Reese sealed the building with manufactured stone.

The star attractions of the Queenans' trading post were two giant kachina dolls that guarded opposite ends of the drive. Reese and Johnny Grayfish, a Delaware Indian with a welding shop in Sayre, constructed the dolls from oil tanks, water tanks, galvanized water pipes, and whatever else they could find in Johnny's shop. Johnny and Wanda then polychromed the dolls, who raised their arms to greet the customers they lured into the trading post.[41] Photograph by author, 1981.

Sunset Motel, ca. 1950
Sayre, Oklahoma

Sayre, the last town of any substance in western Oklahoma, offered only one or two motels. The Sunset was typical of motels in western Oklahoma—a big sign dwarfing small, ranch-style buildings. Amenities in each of the sixteen rooms of the Sunset included carpeting and picture windows that overlooked the parking lot.

Although Duncan Hines noted in 1956 that the Sunset was a "modern" brick motel, it still offered garages, an amenity that had become too expensive to be a feature in other motels by 1950.[42] Photograph by author, 1982.

Café, n.d.
Texola, Oklahoma

Texola, on the Oklahoma-Texas border, was a Route 66 town where most of the business was geared to the road. When I-40 replaced 66, roadside business in Texola dried up. Photograph by author, 1981.

Texas

Cross the Texas line at Texola, and the landscape changes. The red dirt of Oklahoma fades to pink. Trees disappear, even those that, blown by a steady wind, lean to the northeast as they do in Oklahoma. The horizon expands; low clumps of mesquite hug the ground. Towering black thunderheads rise over the landscape in the west and announce the advent of a storm. After it passes, pelting down rain and hail, the storm's backside shimmers pure white in the sun.

Texas 66 had diverse architectures. In the small trading centers—Groom, Conway, and Adrian—it was the vernacular of the plains with an occasional bow to fashion. The construction materials of choice were wood frame and stucco, cheap and easily purchased at the local lumber supply store.

Like St. Louis, Amarillo was surprisingly rich in 66 artifacts. In the 1930s and 1940s when Amarillo Boulevard (aka Gasoline Alley) was booming, Amarillo was the first place the traveler from the east could see motels built to look like Pueblos. And, even though they may only have been constructed of clay tile and finished in stucco to imitate adobe, these motels were the first taste of western architecture for wide-eyed easterners. And then there was Shamrock.

Shamrock, the first town west of the border, was the breaking point for truckers coming from Oklahoma and heading across Texas. Oklahoma law allowed truckers to carry fourteen thousand pounds per axle. Texas law allowed only seven thousand pounds. Trucking companies maintained terminals in Shamrock where they divided a large load in one truck coming from Oklahoma into small loads in two trucks to go through Texas. Maybe this is why the architecture of Shamrock was special.[1]

Or maybe Shamrock was special because it was at the intersection of two major transcontinental highways—66 from Chicago to Los Angeles and 83 from Canada to Mexico.

Or maybe it was because Shamrock gas jockeys pumped "drip." Shamrock sits atop the Panhandle's natural-gas field, the largest in the world in the 1930s. Texas natural-gas companies transported their product to market through huge underground pipelines. In places where the gas cooled and condensed, it formed "drip gasoline," which slowed transmission and was not worth refining. The pipeline companies were happy to allow farmers and retail gasoline dealers to tap their lines and drain off the drip—free. Shamrock dealers pumped "drip" unrefined in the winter but mixed it with refined gasoline in summer because it tended to evaporate and cause vapor lock. Either way it was pure profit.[2]

Or maybe it was because someone was playing with the decorative possibilities of concrete block, or because R. C. Lewis had a thought: "Just a plain square building is, well, just plain. You make it a little more attractive if you dress it up a little."[3]

Tower Station and Cafe, 1936
Intersection of U.S. 66 and U.S. 83
Shamrock

J. M. Tindall arrived in Shamrock in 1911 with eleven cents in his pocket and a roll of barber's tools. He opened a six-chair barber-shop; married Mamie, his cashier; and operated the shop until 1927. Then he quit, bought a cotton gin, and built a cottonseed oil mill, which ran on drip siphoned—thousands of gallons at a time—off the pipeline that ran through his "sandy-land" farm.

In 1936 Tindall built the Tower Station and Cafe. They were two buildings really, which as a pair became the centerpiece of Shamrock's roadside architecture. Tindall's partners in the venture were R. C. Lewis, the local Conoco dealer and the first tenant in the gas station, and John and Bebe Nunn, the first tenants in the café. As the four stood in the driveway of the Cross Roads Motor Court, owned by Bebe's parents and located across the road from the site

of the Tower Station, John scratched a fantasy in the dust. The investors hired an architect from Amarillo to make the fantasy real—a flared tower outlined in neon and raised over two canopies, one facing 83, the other facing 66. To the 66 facade, they added the annex that would hold the café. The builders sheathed the station and the café in tile glazed in green and gold and arranged in a jazzy pattern over the windows. They molded stucco over the wood frames that supported the tower—there was enough lumber in the tower to build a house—and molded stucco as well in decorative rolls on the canopies. The cost of the entire complex was twenty-nine thousand dollars.[4] Photograph by author, 1981, from *Route 66: The Highway and Its People,* photographs by Quinta Scott, text by Susan Croce Kelly (University of Oklahoma Press, 1988).

U-Drop-Inn, 1936
Shamrock

During the post–World War II boom years, buses stopped at the corner of 66 and 83. Their passengers spread out to the twenty cafés, restaurants, and food stands in Shamrock. Many stopped at John and Bebe Nunn's U-Drop-Inn, right there on the corner and known as the best place to eat between Oklahoma City and Amarillo.

When John Nunn sketched the annex that would hold his café, he added a second, shorter tower, supporting a ball, over the entrance to the business that started as a drugstore. John loved children, and having none of his own, he wanted a business that would attract youngsters and teenagers. He installed a drugstore with a soda fountain in the annex to the Tower Station. The soda fountain did well, but the drugstore was too far from the center of town to be successful. So Nunn converted his business to a restaurant, held a contest to name it, and attracted the most important people in town—the high school football players. Their parents soon followed, and so did the tourists.[5] Photograph by author, 1998.

P. B. Wooldridge Gas Station, 1938
Shamrock

P. B. Wooldridge pumped drip. During World War II drip was not rationed; refined gasoline was. Wooldridge and other pump jockeys in Shamrock sold gasoline for ration stamps and drip for cash. They operated from stations that complemented the Tower Station without mimicking its architecture. All followed the same architectural themes—broad overhangs above wide picture windows, sur-mounted by parapets built into step pyramids of concrete block at the corners with a larger, heavier, decorative element in the center. Route 66 through Shamrock was unintentionally baroque in its planning, with similar buildings at the east and west gates of town and the grand Tower Station at its center.[6] Photograph by author, 1981.

Whiting Bros. Gas Station, 1938
Shamrock

Like P. B. Wooldridge, the Whiting brothers sold drip. The brothers—Eddie, Ralph, Ernest, and Art—bought one of the fancy stations in Shamrock, erected their signature sign, painted it yellow with red lettering, anchored it with the family crest, and lighted it with neon.

In 1926 the Whitings had started with a small gas station on the National Old Trails Highway at St. Johns, Arizona. When they realized that U.S. 66 across Arizona would bypass St. Johns, they moved the business north to meet the highway at Holbrook. Then in the 1930s they began to expand west along 66, first to Winslow, then Flagstaff, and finally, clear into Los Angeles. Then they came east to Texas, to Shamrock. To draw attention to their chain, they erected signs along the roadside, just like this one at Shamrock, but longer and taller—three hundred feet long and sixty feet tall.[7] Photograph by author, 1981.

Panhandle Gas and Garage, 1926
McLean

West of Shamrock, the architecture of Texas 66 slipped back into the rhythms of the plains, drawing its style from the folk vernacular and repeating forms that appeared on the Oklahoma roadside. The massive pier with its curved brackets supporting the canopy of Panhandle Gas came straight out of Oklahoma.

Gas station owners devised several ways to set their stations on a corner to allow access from both streets. Some, like the owner of the station at Galena, Kansas, set the building at the rear of the lot, and at a forty-five-degree angle to both streets, and projected the canopy out over the service area. This solution required only one set of pumps. Or, like J. M. Tindall at the Tower Station, they set the building at the rear of the lot, but square with the corner, and projected canopies out to each street, requiring two sets of pumps. Or,

like the owners of Panhandle Gas, they set the building at the edge of the street and square with the corner, then chopped off the corner of the building and projected a canopy out over the resulting service area, requiring only one set of pumps.

The Panhandle Gas building started out as an automobile showroom and garage. Then in the 1940s the Panhandle Gas Company took it over and made it the office for a service station. The original builders had used yellow brick on the portions of the building that faced the public and used concrete block for the garage. They had covered the roof of the canopy over the service area in Spanish tiles made of tin. Sometime later, someone stuccoed over the yellow brick on the facade and the lower half of the column, adding to the Spanish character to the building.[8] Photograph by author, 1997.

Gift Shop and Gas Station, 1936
McLean

George Graham built a café and beer joint in the days when beer was legal in McLean. When McLean went dry during World War II, he converted the building to a grocery store and filling station. Sometimes when builders reached for fashion, they missed the mark and produced a vernacular variation on the real thing. Graham reached for the Streamline Moderne style when he rounded the end of the large windows that overlooked the service area. Then he painted the clapboard building white and trimmed it in red. It all lay in the shade of a tall canopy. Edith Smith Bybee purchased the building in 1957 and converted the grocery to a gift shop.[9] Photograph by author, 1981.

Regal Reptile Ranch, n.d.
Alanreed

Lyman Riley hated those little zoos and reptile gardens that went into business along the highway. As president of the Missouri Highway 66 Association, he spent a year traveling the highway checking on their legitimacy. But to a kid who had never seen a rattler, the Regal Reptile Ranch was irresistible, and Adie Alred made sure it was hard to miss. When Adie and her brother built the Regal Reptile Ranch on the outskirts of tiny Alanreed, they designed every detail to draw customers off the highway. They raised the height of their small frame cube with a false front on which they painted REGAL REPTILE RANCH, and they stretched the sides of the building with fences on which they listed the inhabitants of their herpetorium. They painted everything yellow and trimmed it in red. In the parking lot, a tin cobra, fabricated from stovepipes, rose over a sign inscribed, LIVE POISON RATTLESNAKES SHOWN TODAY. Inside the dark, cramped cube, the Alreds maintained dozing snakes and lizards stacked in cages, one on top of another. These they showed to the customers with the aid of a flashlight.[10] Photograph by author, 1982.

"66" Super Service Station, 1930
Alanreed

Bradley Kiser built a small gas station at Alanreed using the same yellow brick as was used for Panhandle Gas at McLean, leading one to believe the brick was common to the region. The station was elegant in its details, with its tiny office facing on the two service areas and its coffered canopies roofed in green Spanish tiles made of tin. A brick pier and heavy curved brackets supported each canopy. Kiser maintained a two-bay garage for car repair in an adjacent building constructed of the same materials.[11] Photograph by author, 1997.

66 Courts, 1947
Groom

In Groom, where monarch butterflies drift across the road in August and saucer-sized tarantulas amble across in October, the 66 Courts and the Golden Spread Motel reflect different eras on 66. Both were squeezed onto tight urban-sized lots—surprising, considering the emptiness of the landscape. The 66 Courts, built just after World War II, combined motel, gas station, garage, and café into a single complex. The gas station faced the street, and the motel rooms, with their adjacent garages, wrapped around the station along a U-shaped driveway. Everything was whitewashed stucco with green wooden trim around the doors and windows. Photograph by author, 1998.

Golden Spread Motel, 1953
Groom

Pete Ford was a restless man, always looking for a new way to make a buck. He had a restaurant, a produce business, and a meat market. He was in farming, ranching, and oil. Then, in 1953, he discovered real estate and motels. He bought all the vacant property in Groom and hired an architect in Amarillo to design a motel with twenty-two attached rooms around the parking court. Ford himself designed the key element—the sign. He wrapped an arrow of moving lights around a two-story brick buttress on which he mounted GOLDEN SPREAD MOTEL in neon. The arrow pointed to the office. The circle in the arrow announced that the motel offered TV. The buttress braced the two-story section that housed the office and manager's apartment. A canopy, which was also a deck for the apartment above, covered the entrance to the office and protected guests from snow, rain, and hail. Where the 66 Courts was roadside vernacular, the Golden Spread was International Style spectacular, an architecture that responded to the intense competition of the booming 1950s—even in Groom.[12] Photograph by author, 1982.

Buddy's Grocery and Cabins, ca. 1935
Conway

Only twenty-five miles east of Amarillo, Conway never developed into a roadside center. In 1946 Jack Rittenhouse, author of *A Guide Book to Highway 66*, found a gas station and garage, a grocery, a café, and a motor court in Conway—not much, but enough to rescue the weary traveler who found Groom full and was too tired to go on to Amarillo. The motor court, a simple line of rooms in a long stucco building, invited motorists in with a row of Spanish Colonial scal-lops over each unit. The neon sign at the roadside said simply, CABINS. Next door was Buddy's Grocery, with gas pumps under a canopy and a now-collapsed stepped false front over the entrance. Buddy wasted no money on neon; he merely painted his name on the side of the grocery. On down the road a frame-and-stucco café and gas station, with a gable facing the intersection and a hipped roof at the rear, sat at the crossroads.[13] Photographs by author, 1998.

Café and Gas Station, ca. 1935
Conway

Amarillo

Between Shamrock and Amarillo, Route 66 crossed cattle country where four wire gates blocked auto traffic in the 1920s. Travelers had to stop, open each gate, pass through, and close the gate behind them. But as early as 1927 Amarillo was a tourist town with twenty-nine auto camps chasing the tourist's dollar. Four major highways—66, 60, 87, and 287—provided the tourists and the growth for Amarillo, much of it coming during World War II.

Amarillo produced two of the essentials for the war effort—carbon black and helium—and when the army located an air base on the east end of town, housing in Amarillo grew very tight with the influx of airmen and their families.[14]

B & B Gas and Oil, ca. 1955
Amarillo

They loaded bombs at the Pantex ordnance plant in Amarillo during World War II, and a souvenir bomb casing wound up on the roof of the B & B Gas and Oil. The Texaco station was the first thing the traveler encountered at the east gate of Amarillo. Like Fenton Craner in Elkhart, Illinois, the original owners of B & B Gas and Oil chose not to house their business in Walter Dorwin Teague's standardized Texaco design. Instead, they set a building of wraparound glass on a base of red glazed brick and topped it with a metal wraparound sign. Photograph by author, 1981.

Forest Hills Tourist Court, ca. 1940
Amarillo

Amarillo in the 1930s and 1940s had a wealth of Spanish and Pueblo style motels with names like Pueblo Court, Spanish Courts, Grande Tourist Court, Casa Mia. It was the first place along 66 where motel builders used Pueblo architecture extensively.

When P. M. Johnson, who had a grocery on Northeast Eighth in Amarillo, built the Forest Hills Tourist Court in 1940, he put up a twenty-five-unit structural clay tile building with garages and finished it in stucco. He applied false vigas to the front and real clay tile drains to the rear to give the motel its Pueblo flavor. He polished the Pueblo image with scallops that defined the rhythm of alternating rooms and garages. He wrapped the motel around a U-shaped courtyard planted with trees, a plus in treeless Texas. When the stucco finish cracked, Johnson easily updated his image from Pueblo to Streamline Moderne. He hacked off the vigas and applied a thin veneer of white brick to the stucco everywhere but the rear of the building. He replaced the trees in the courtyard with a glass-block office with rounded corners. From the street, the Forest Hills Court was Streamline Moderne, slick and up-to-date. From the rear, the Forest Hills was still Pueblo, all cracked stucco and clay tile drains.[15] Photograph by author, 1998.

Elk Court, 1946
Amarillo

Tom Shell worked for Texaco. In 1946 he came into some money and built the Elk Court on West Sixth Street in the Monterey style of Spanish Colonial architecture. This variation had developed in Monterey, California, where Anglo immigrants in the 1830s had introduced pitched, shingled roofs and second-story balconies to the traditional single-story, flat-roofed Casa. Shell enclosed a very narrow courtyard with a two-story stucco building having two wings. Second-story balconies acted as an outside hallway to the rooms. Guests in the west wing of the Elk Court pulled their cars into the first-story garages and climbed inside stairs to their rooms. The east wing offered back-to-back rooms on the first story, facing a side street and the courtyard. On the courtyard side of the wing there were first-floor garages and rooms and second-floor rooms accessed by a balcony with an outside stair. The connecting block offered two rooms with garages on the first story and additional rooms accessed by a balcony on the second.[16] Photograph by author, 1997.

English Court, ca. 1926
Amarillo

When the army air force built an air base at Amarillo in 1942, it created a housing shortage. Airmen stationed in Amarillo were desperate for housing. At first they found temporary housing in motels along 66. At the west end of town they found the old English Court—a courtyard of stucco cottages made Tudor by the application of half-timbers on the canopy over each door and arranged in a cabin, garage, cabin formation. Photograph by author, 1981.

Air-O-Tel, 1941
Amarillo

When the motels filled up during World War II, entrepreneurs went to work building more hotels and motels. There were forty-four hotels and thirty-six motels in Amarillo by the time Jack D. Rittenhouse wrote his *Guide Book to Highway 66* in 1946. At the east end of town, one wartime entrepreneur built the Air-O-Tel. It was a barracks veneered in a bricklike finish made either of stucco or asphalt shingles. It housed airmen's wives during World War II and tourists after the war. The complex included a two-story building surrounded by a one-story barracks.[17] Photograph by author, 1981.

Triangle Motel, 1948
Amarillo

When S. M. Clayton retired as mayor of Borger, Texas, in 1948, he and Cora, his wife, moved to Amarillo where they built a Streamline Moderne motel on a wedge of land between U.S. 66 and U.S. 60. The Claytons arranged their attached units in two buildings using a room, garage, garage, room plan. They set their motel of buff bricks on a narrow base of deep-red bricks. A streamlined curve framed each garage opening and door. A line of soldier bricks formed a parapet. In the center of the complex they planted trees in an oval green space. Next to the motel, the Claytons built a large restaurant using the same combination of red and buff brick. At the point of the wedge where 66 and 60 came together, the Claytons maintained a gas station and garage.[18] Photograph by author, 1997.

Trail Drive-in Theatre, ca. 1946
Amarillo

The awkward lines of the decorative woodwork on the roof and cornice of the ticket booth of the Trail Drive-in proved that the Streamline Moderne style was better fabricated in stucco over wire or in small units of brick or tile than in straight pieces of wood. Next to the concrete-block screen tower the smooth curve of the cornice of the stucco concession stand reinforced that observation. The whole—the screen tower, which acted as the sign; the ticket booth; and the concession stand—was painted in sea green with pink trim, excluding "Trail," which was painted in white outlined in black. Photograph by author, 1981.

Rice's Dining Salon, 1945
Amarillo

Homer Rice knew meat. He sold beef for a packing company in Lubbock. Amarillo restaurateur Harry G. Kindig knew fish. He offered a menu heavy in seafood at the Long Champs, a restaurant he converted from a gas station on Amarillo Boulevard in 1945. Within two years Harry found that Amarillans preferred meat to fish and sold the Long Champs to Homer and his wife, Auline. The Rices gave the restaurant the family name, mounted a giant sign—of five thousand bulbs—over the entrance, and offered a menu heavy in meat, "with the emphasis on very good T-bone steaks which have been making a traveling man happy for years and years." The sign was part of the major renovation to complete the conversion of the gas station to a dining salon. The Rices used every Streamline Moderne device they could think of: They faced the building with a veneer of faux stone and added a curve to the roofline; they built planters under the windows with the same faux stone and added awnings over the windows; they erected a canopy over the entrance and punched a bull's-eye window into the wall next to the entrance.[19] Photograph by author, 1981.

Pennant No. 2, ca. 1950
Amarillo

Unlike most fast-food stands, the Pennant No. 2 sold beer. But, like most fast-food stands, it housed its kitchen in a small building, in this case a board-and-batten structure with a wedge-shaped sign that wrapped around the roof and down the front of the building.

Customers ordered their food at walk-up windows and ate in their cars under a tent supported by steel columns and cables. Like most fast-food stands, the Pennant advertised its menu on signs on the corners of the building. Photograph by author, 1982.

Dale's Garage and Gas Station, 1938
Adrian Mercantile, ca. 1910
Adrian

West of Amarillo the landscape spreads out across the Staked Plains, a flat, featureless country where pioneers drove stakes into the ground to mark their trails and where the farm towns of Wildorado, Vega, and Adrian never attracted much roadside business—a café, a gas station, possibly a motel. Most roadside buildings of the pre-66 and post-66 eras, even the two-story Mercantile in Adrian, were con-structed in frame and stucco, simple materials easily obtained. When I-40 passed to the south, it took the tourist business with it. Wildorado, Vega, and Adrian returned to being the small trading centers they were before 1926 when the largest business in town was the Mercantile. Photograph by author, 1982.

Adrian Court, 1947
Adrian

Manual Loveless purchased the local saloon in Adrian in 1937, dismantled it, hauled the lumber to the edge of U.S. 66 on the outskirts of Adrian, and built the Kozy Kabin Kamp. It was a typical rural motel/gas station/café complex with five units in an oblong building on the back of the property and the gas station, office, and café in a single building out front. Both buildings were wood frame covered in stucco. When the gas station and café burned in 1947, Loveless purchased the Adrian Land Office building, hauled it to edge of U.S. 66, and used it as his office and home. He rebuilt the gas station, renamed the Kozy Kabin Kamp the Adrian Court, and leased the site for the café to Bobby Harris.[20] Photograph by author, 1981.

Bent Door Cafe, 1946
Adrian

Bobby Harris also procured a secondhand building—the control tower from Dalhart Air Base, which had been dismantled after World War II. He hauled the tower to Adrian and made it the centerpiece of his concrete-block building, where vigas supported the roof and protruded on the concrete-block exterior. Harris intended to open a café but never did. Instead, he departed town, leaving the new café in the hands of his mother. She leased it back to Loveless, who named it the Bent Door Cafe because the door had to conform to the slanted profile of the control tower.[21] Photograph by author, 1997.

Diner, ca. 1946
Glenrio

Glenrio, smack on the Texas–New Mexico line, was the last stop in Texas and/or the first stop in New Mexico. Both states acknowledge the town as their own and put it on their maps. The U.S. Postal Service officially puts Glenrio in New Mexico, has since 1916. In 1946, Jack Rittenhouse found most of the town's roadside businesses in New Mexico, but when I-40 came along and bypassed Glenrio, the only exit to town was from Texas. Old 66 west of the state line is a dead end. What little is left of Glenrio today is found in Texas.

Glenrio never was a trading center like Adrian but depended completely on highway business. While the hamlet thrived, it mim-

icked some of the best in early standardized roadside architecture. If success can be measured by imitators, the porcelain-enameled steel Valentine diner, like the Cliffhouse Diner at Weatherford, Oklahoma, was a success. But the Little Juarez Cafe was not delivered to Glenrio on a flatcar and carted to its site. A mason or possibly the owner constructed the little café of concrete block, added a few streamline details similar to those on the Valentine diners, and painted it white with Texaco green stripes to match the standardized Texaco station next door.[22] Photograph by author, 1982.

New Mexico

Cross the Texas–New Mexico line and the rivers run fast and shallow and hot pink, when they run at all. The land is flat; early explorers found it featureless and named it the Llano Estacado—the Staked Plains.

In the late teens and early twenties, auto tourists followed a circuitous route across northern New Mexico. The Ozark Trail delivered them to Santa Rosa. There they turned north to Las Vegas and Santa Fe, where they picked up the National Old Trails Road, which dropped south along the Rio Grande through Albuquerque, through Los Lunas to Socorro, and turned west across the Magdalena Mountains to Springerville, Arizona, and then north through St. Johns to Holbrook. There was a road between Los Lunas and Gallup, but it required the travelers to ford many streams, skirt numerous mud holes, and risk tearing up their tires crossing the razor-sharp lava fields just east of Grants. The route through Socorro, while lonely—it was without a railroad, a trading post, or even a ranch for 230 miles—was a good dirt-and-gravel road.[1]

By 1923 drivers had a choice: They could take the Socorro road, or they could bypass it and take the newly graded and graveled road between Los Lunas and Gallup, which carried them safely across the lava fields. When Cyrus Avery and the American Association of State Highway Officials Association published their map of the federal highway system in November 1926, it showed U.S. 66 across New Mexico following the road between Tucumcari and Santa Fe, then traveling south to Los Lunas and west to Gallup. Within weeks A. T. Hannett decided to change all that.

In December 1926, Hannett, the former mayor of Gallup, was about to become the former governor of New Mexico. Miffed at the political scene in Santa Fe, he resolved to bypass the capital and reroute the cross-state highway in a straight line from Santa Rosa through Moriarty and Tijeras Canyon to Albuquerque. He had sixty-nine days to do so before the new governor would take office. To get it done, the state engineer divided the work into two crews. Working west from Santa Rosa and east from Moriarty in the December cold and dark, the crews surveyed and graded a gravel road. On Inauguration Day the two ends were just short of meeting. The new governor ordered the work halted, but his messenger, held up by a nasty January storm, arrived too late to stop completion of Hannett's cutoff, which was numbered New Mexico 6. It lopped ninety miles from the trip across New Mexico. In 1937 the state officially bypassed Santa Fe and moved 66 south to Hannett's route.[2]

New Mexican roadside entrepreneurs embraced Pueblo Revival architecture, particularly in Albuquerque. It was a truly indigenous architecture based on adobe brick. Before the Spanish arrived in the Rio Grande Valley, Pueblo Indians "puddled" adobe in layers. The Spanish introduced the practice of molding adobe into blocks by compressing a muddy mix of sand, silt, clay, and water into wooden molds. The wet blocks were spread on the ground to dry in the sun. Then they were laid up in walls using a mortar of the same mix and sealed with that mix, which washed away, albeit slowly in the rain-starved desert, thus softening and rounding the edges of Pueblo buildings.[3]

The seventeenth-century Spanish in New Mexico developed the Pueblo variation on the Spanish Colonial style when they used laborers from the pueblos along the Rio Grande to do the work. The Spanish Pueblo building was characterized by the same flat-roofed, rectangular structure as were the pueblos themselves. It was built in adobe brick but sealed in stucco rather than mud. As at the pueblos, the roof beams, called vigas, protruded through the walls.[4]

Through the centuries, New Mexicans continued to build in the Spanish Pueblo style; in 1900 they considered making it the official style of the territory, calling it Pueblo Revival. In the 1920s and 1930s every town in New Mexico still had its "adobe man," who made adobe blocks at his "factory" on the edge of town. The adobe makers also did construction work, setting the blocks with wet mud and sealing the walls with an inch of stucco plastered directly on the adobe or over a chicken-wire lath held in place with nails. Because nails tended to slip out of adobe, builders used "gringo bricks," scraps of wood set in the wall to anchor the lath.[5]

To take 66 through New Mexico in the 1920s and 1930s was to travel through three cultures: American in the east and west, Spanish in Santa Fe, and Pueblo Indian—Santo Domingo, San Felipe, Laguna, and Acoma—in the central region and along the Rio Grande. All three cultures showed up in the architecture along the roadside, with Pueblo Revival the dominant style. In the east, motel owners continued to use the architecture of the Great Plains as had their counterparts in Texas. In Santa Fe and Albuquerque, where there were wonderful examples of Spanish Pueblo buildings from the seventeenth and eighteenth centuries, roadside builders put up variations on the Pueblo Revival. In the western railroad towns of Grants and Gallup, businessmen lined 66 with Main Street commercial blocks and ranch-style motels.

Tucumcari

In 1901 the Rock Island Railroad made the trading center of Six Shooter Siding a division point with the El Paso and Southwestern Railroad. The city fathers changed its name to Tucumcari after the small biscuit-shaped mountain west of town. Highways came to Tucumcari in the teens when the Ozark Trail came through town. In 1926 U.S. 66 and U.S. 54 followed the railroads to their intersection at Tucumcari and turned Tucumcari into a highway town. The action shifted from the railroad depot south to 66 as the auto tourist business increased. In the years after World War II, land values along 66 in Tucumcari shot up as motel owners purchased lots, built their motels, and turned Tucumcari into a town with two thousand rooms.[6]

TUCUMCARI TONITE! urged the signs. And the city found it had a need for those two thousand rooms, for as Duncan Hines reminded travelers who carried his *Lodging for a Night,* they were "in a city miles from anywhere." Amarillo was 120 miles behind them, and Santa Rosa 60 miles ahead of them.[7]

Coronado Court, ca. 1930
Tucumcari

One after another, motels lined Gaynell Street from east to west. The office of the Coronado Court reflected the Western Bungalow style that had descended directly from the ranchers and farmers who populated the region at the beginning of the century. The Kirkpatricks ran the Coronado, offering the traveler who made it to the western end of Gaynell Street twelve rooms, with garages, sheltered in a long bunkhouse. Photograph by author, 1982.

Cactus Court, 1938
Tucumcari

When Pat Perry built the first section of the Cactus Court in 1938, he took his style straight out of the pueblos of central New Mexico, right down to the adobe walls and the protruding vigas that supported the roof. When Perry added two new sections after World War II, he abandoned structural realism but kept the look. Stucco slathered over structural clay tile and fake vigas screwed into the facade made for quicker and easier construction. Perry added western touches: Each unit was two steps up to a heavy plank door. A man with a sombrero pulled down over his eyes dozed in the wrought iron railings. Guests checked in at a big, low ranch house under a huge overhanging roof that protected them from the elements. There, Perry kept his office, his residence, and the Cactus Club, a nightclub and gambling hall housed in the basement. Ranchers in town to spend the night or take a turn at roulette tied their horses to the hitching post out front.

Perry sold the Cactus in 1950 to Norman Wegner, a restaurateur recently arrived from Rockford, Illinois, who hired a man from Amarillo to spruce up the place and cover the cracking stucco with manufactured stone.[8] Photograph by author, 1998.

Blue Swallow Motel, 1941, sign 1960
Tucumcari

W. A. Higgins built the Blue Swallow in 1941. He laid out thirteen attached units, organized in a cabin, garage, garage, cabin rhythm in a U around a central office. Blue neon swallows flew over the posts between the garages. The plasterer who stuccoed the building molded a bit of whimsy into the finish—ladies' fans.

In 1958, Floyd Redman, who ran the Bonanza Court in Tucumcari, purchased the Blue Swallow and gave it to his fiancé, Lillian, who was also his bookkeeper and who knew the motel business.

Lillian enlarged the office, added two rooms for her parents, and painted all the exterior pink, which contrasted nicely with the little blue neon swallows. Then, in 1960, as the competition for customers in the town with two thousand rooms grew fierce, Lillian added a huge sign—a blue swallow soaring over the name of the motel—turning the Blue Swallow into an architectural icon along U.S. 66.[9] Photograph by author, 1998.

Plains Motel, 1943
Santa Rosa

Santa Rosa grew as a railroad town after 1901 and boomed as a highway town after 1926. Before I-40 bypassed it, there were sixty-three gas stations, twenty motels, and fifteen restaurants in Santa Rosa, all competing for the business that motored down 66. The Western Bungalow and the bunkhouse style of the Plains Motel reflected Santa Rosa's beginnings as a small trading center for farmers and ranchers. A widow lady, long since forgotten, built the Plains during World War II, recycling old lumber for the window frames and old tin from Mexico for the roof. The basic structure of the motel was stucco over structural tile, which later owners covered with clapboard and manufactured stone. Eleven rooms and four garages were arranged haphazardly in the long bunkhouse. A Western Bungalow at the roadside housed the office and a restaurant, a grocery store, and a gas station.[10] Photograph by author, 1982.

Club Cafe, ca. 1955
Santa Rosa

Floyd Shaw left Texas Tech and the family farm in Abernathy, Texas, in 1934 and headed for New Mexico, where he put his engineering skills to work as a surveyor on Governor A. T. Hannett's Santa Fe bypass. His boyhood friend Phil Craig joined him, and together they opened a café in Santa Rosa. Phil ran the café; Floyd continued work on the highway. The café was tiny, seating only twenty-four patrons. When the highway department redesignated the bypass U.S. 66, tourists began stopping at the friends' little cubbyhole of a restaurant. Shaw and Craig erected their first Fat Man sign on 66. Business boomed. The friends sold the cubbyhole and built a large, modern place in which they installed a café and trading post. Next they erected more billboards up and down 66, using the Fat Man, a caricature of Phil Craig, to advertise the café's specialties. By the time folks reached Santa Rosa, their taste buds were set for sourdough biscuits and pinto beans, even when they had no idea what pinto beans were. Craig nursed the sourdough starter in a crock that sat on a counter in the kitchen and expected all waiters, cooks, and dishwashers to give it a stir when they passed it.

In a town where there were fourteen other restaurants, the most important elements in the new Club Cafe building were those that attracted the customers: the cornice decorated with patterns from Navajo rugs; the canopy over the door; the parapet decorated with a narrow concrete-block screen; and the red-and-white neon sign mounted on the roof. But most important was the big round Fat Man sign over the east door, a reminder from the highway to stop—here—and eat. In 1992 Ron Chavez, the last owner of the Club Cafe, stopped soaking the pintos, killed off the sourdough, and closed the doors, done in by the Golden Arches.[11] Photograph by author, 1982.

Save 5 Cents, ca. 1935
Santa Rosa

Seventy-five percent of Santa Rosa's business came down U.S. 66. At one point the sixty-three gas stations competed for every gasoline nickel that came through town. As the cost of refining gasoline fell in the 1930s, state and federal taxes on gasoline increased. Prices at the pump fell as taxes rose. The profit margin for all dealers shrank. Name-brand dealers had to maintain brand loyalty and thus the quality of their gasoline. Independents did not. They were free to blend nontaxable fuels—drip, kerosene, naphtha, heating oil—with their gasoline to reduce the cost and thus the price of their gasoline. The Hedges Oil Company, an independent dealer with a string of stations across New Mexico, found the facade of this simple stucco box—covered with cement-asbestos shingles to hide the cracking stucco—offered the perfect surface on which to advertise cheap gas. Hedges triggered the gas wars that raged up and down Santa Fe Avenue in Santa Rosa, sometimes charging as little as nine cents a gallon, only a penny over the eight-cent gas tax in New Mexico.[12] Photograph by author, 1982, from *Route 66: The Highway and Its People,* photographs by Quinta Scott, text by Susan Croce Kelly (University of Oklahoma Press, 1988).

Clines Corners, 1934–63
Clines Corners

They never threw a building away at Clines Corners, not even Roy Cline's original tin shack that stands in the back lot of Clines Corners, next to one of the stucco apartments Lynn and Helen Smith built to house their staff. Instead of razing buildings, successive owners moved them around, made additions, and spruced them up with new finishes.

Once Hannett's bypass was completed, the 120 miles between Santa Rosa and Albuquerque was virgin territory for folks like Roy Cline. In 1934 he had left his Arkansas "tick farm," moved his family to the intersection of the bypass and New Mexico 2, halfway between Santa Rosa and Albuquerque, and built a gas station. When the bypass became U.S. 66, he moved the tin shack eleven miles west to the intersection of U.S. 66 and U.S. 285, added a café, and persuaded the Rand McNally Company to put Clines Corners in their Road Atlas. Roy, Jr., painted the building white and swore he doubled his father's business. In spite of all this success, Roy, Sr., sold Clines Corners in 1939, but the name stayed. The place was, after all, on the map.

After World Word II, the business passed into the hands of Lynn and Helen Smith. Helen and her brother, Joe, had grown up in two hostelries in Santa Rosa—their mother's hotel on Main Street and their father's adobe motel on 66. Their mother had catered to rail-road passengers, their father to auto tourists. Adjacent to the motel was their father's gas station where young Joe learned the gasoline business. When Joe returned from World War II, he went to work for Standard Oil of Texas, managing the Standard station in Santa Rosa. In the meantime, Helen married a New Mexico highway patrolman, Lynn Smith.

It was Patrolman Smith's duty to cruise the Llano Estacado, where Clines Corner had become an oasis in the miles between Santa Rosa and Albuquerque. He watched carloads of tourists, overwhelmed by the long haul between the towns, fill up at the gas station, eat at the café, and check in at the motel. He was so impressed by the volume of business done at Clines Corners that he bought it.

Lynn and Helen enlarged the business and added new services. Under their guardianship, it grew from a white tin, single-room gas station and café with a few motel rooms to a full-service tourist trap. When they finished, they raised a distinctive sign over the complex, a vertical dart piercing a horizontal element on which they outlined CLINES CORNERS in hollow metal letters filled with neon. They carried out the motif on highway billboards that lined New Mexico 66 east and west of Clines Corners—and that still line I-40.[13] Photograph by author, 1998.

Longhorn Ranch, 1950
Moriarty

There was so little competition between Santa Rosa and Albuquerque that places like Clines Corners and the Longhorn could start small and grow large. Captain "Eric" Erikson, a cop from the East, opened a small café near Moriarty, forty-five miles east of Albuquerque. He added a hotel and restaurant, a coffee shop, and a cocktail lounge, all housed in an ersatz western ghost town with a bank, a tonsorial parlor and museum, a saloon, an emporium, and a Wells Fargo station. Underneath all the western phoniness were hints of Streamline Moderne, a curved wall here, a broad plate-glass window there, and a line of little stucco motel units out back.[14] Photograph by author, 1982.

Pie House, ca. 1936
Zamora

At Zamora the Staked Plains ease into the Sandia Mountains, which formed a backdrop for the Pie House. Smaller than the Longhorn, it was an operation on the scale of Leon Little's Hinton Junction in Oklahoma. The small complex of low stucco-and-wooden buildings housed a gas station, a café, and a motel. While the owners of the Pie House went with fashion for the architecture of the Spanish Colonial–style motel at the rear of the property, they opted for a plain stucco café at the roadside, with a low front gable that carried the sign, PIE HOUSE in tall black letters.[15] Photograph by author, 1982.

Albuquerque

Tijeras Canyon through the Sandia Mountains was the pass between young New Mexico and ancient New Mexico. Once U.S. 66 bypassed Santa Fe in 1937, Albuquerque, founded in 1706, became the oldest city along the road. It was at the crossroads of the Santa Fe railroad and the Rio Grande River, at the crossroads between the "English" who settled along the railroad and the Spanish who settled along the river. Traveling west along Central Avenue, City 66 through Albuquerque, it was possible to read the architectural digression from the International Style suburban shopping centers and motels of the 1950s to Spanish Old Town. Gone from Albuquerque now is the great Spanish Colonial hotel of the rail era, Fred Harvey's Alvarado, owned by the Santa Fe railroad. Also gone from Central Avenue is the great Franciscan Hotel.

During World War II, Oxnard Air Base at Albuquerque grew into a huge military complex, and a housing shortage followed. Motels along Central Avenue installed kitchenettes and rented the rooms to army personnel on a weekly basis. Albuquerque grew, but the number of motels did not. There was a boom in motel building, however, at the end of the war to meet the pent-up demand for rooms. Motel builders in Albuquerque were surrounded by excellent variations on Pueblo, Spanish Pueblo, and Pueblo Revival architecture—locally in Spanish Old Town, to the north in Santa Fe, and at the pueblos in between. The builders used all these styles to sell a place to sleep up and down Central Avenue.[16]

El Vado Court, 1937
Albuquerque

Dan Murphy, who learned the hotel business at the Waldorf in New York and at the Franciscan in Albuquerque, opened the El Vado just west of the Rio Grande in 1937. An Irishman from the East, he nevertheless chose to build El Vado in the Pueblo Revival style. Murphy laid out thirty units, all with garages and baths, in an E, with the office in the center wing. He built irregularities into the structure to give it the ancient look of the pueblos. Some of the parapets over the rooms were curved; others were straight. Murphy played with shadow and light, setting the garages back from the rooms. He reinforced this play and the walls with buttresses of different sizes and shapes. The effect was a compelling example of Pueblo Revival architecture.[17] Photograph by author, 1997.

Enchanted Mesa Indian Arts, 1948
Albuquerque

Fred and Margaret Chase spent their lives trading American Indian crafts. Margaret had a shop in Old Town Albuquerque; Fred traveled, selling Zuni jewelry to other traders across the Southwest. In 1948, when Fred tired of the road and Margaret of Old Town, they purchased a piece of property out in the East Central business district, which a few months before had been a parking lot for junked bombers from Oxnard Air Base. There Fred and Margaret built a shop that was a handsome mix of Streamline Moderne and Pueblo Revival, what some called Pueblo Deco. Stepped vigas jutted from the smooth stucco walls while corner show windows wrapped the ends of the building. The Chases embedded colored tiles in the raised stucco surround of the entrance. Finally, they crowned the building with a hollow Spanish Pueblo tower, similar to those found on seventeenth- and eighteenth-century Spanish Pueblo churches.[18] Photograph by author, 1997.

La Puerta Motor Lodge, 1949
Albuquerque

Next door to the Enchanted Mesa, and a year after its construction, Ralph and Sadie Smith built an equally striking building. The Smiths, who owned several motels in Albuquerque, modeled La Puerta Lodge on the Palace of the Governors in Santa Fe. They built a long, low building housing thirteen units and garages. It was fronted by a colonnade of rough-hewn posts with elaborately carved capitals and entablature, more elaborate than those on the palace even, as was the ornately carved door to the end unit of the motel.[19] Photograph by author, 1997.

El Jardin Lodge and Cafe, 1946
Albuquerque

David Bettin divided the fifty-four units of El Jardin Lodge and Cafe into two courtyards separated by the large office and café. He built long, irregular blocks to hold the units and a few garages. El Jardin was a modern post–World War II motel made to look like a pueblo. Bettin smoothed stucco over concrete block, a method that came into general use after the war. He installed steel-casement windows and mounted vigas to support the canopies over each door. At the rear of each wing he built a large outdoor oven with a chimney. Bettin sold El Jardin not long after he opened for business. He later took it back and sold it again, and again. The fourth time he sold it, it stayed sold, a fact that was to bother him the rest of his life.[20] Photograph by author, 1982, from *Route 66: The Highway and Its People,* photographs by Quinta Scott, text by Susan Croce Kelly (University of Oklahoma Press, 1988).

Gas Station and Garage, 1946
Albuquerque

Even when New Mexicans departed from the Pueblo Revival style and opted for the Streamline Moderne, they used stucco to mold the rounded forms. F. V. McCormick's Standard Service Station in the Nob Hill section of Albuquerque was the spiritual cousin of the Tower Station in Shamrock, Texas. Photograph by author, 1982.

Acoma Hotel, 1913
New Laguna

Folks who failed to stop in Albuquerque or Los Lunas found it was a long way to New Laguna—just west of the Laguna Pueblo—where the only place to stay was the ten-room Acoma Hotel next to the railroad station. Like the hotels and motels in Albuquerque, the Acoma was a variation on the Pueblo Revival. It was an adobe building plastered over with stucco. When U.S. 66 came to New Laguna, the old hotel found new life as a highway stop.[21] Photograph by author, 1982.

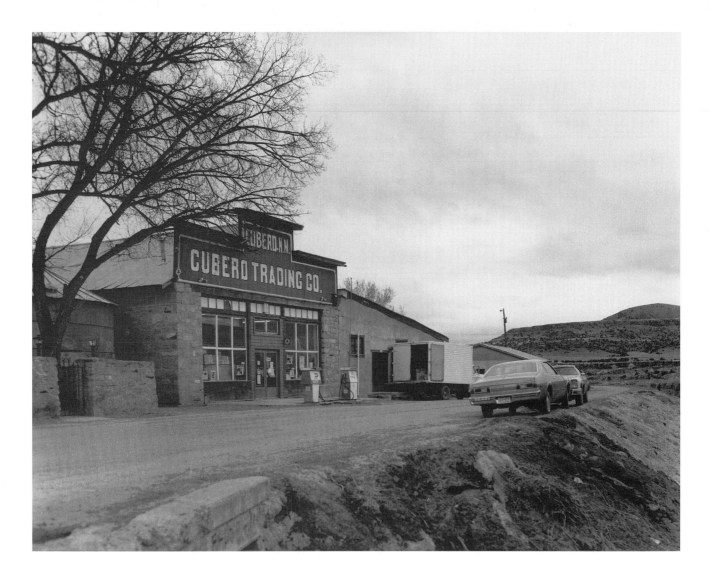

Cubero Trading Company, 1910
Cubero

U.S. 66 brought freewheeling auto tourists to western New Mexico and changed the trading business. Traders like Sidney Gottlieb at Cubero, C. K. Gunderson at Grants, the Richardson family at Gallup, and Leroy Atkinson at Gallup changed their businesses to take advantage of the tourists who came to their doors. Some had started in nineteenth-century stores on the Laguna, Navajo, or Zuni Reservations and then moved to town, locating first near the rail-road station and then near the hotels and motels on U.S. 66.

Sidney Gottlieb traded livestock with the Lagunas and Acomas at his trading post at Cubero. It was a credit business. He gave his customers credit for their livestock, which they in turn used to buy groceries and supplies. With the advent of automobile traffic, Gottlieb added gasoline pumps to the front of his trading post. When U.S. 66 was routed past his place, he went into a cash business, selling gas to passing tourists to whom he also offered fresh spring-water and free camping space.[22] Photograph by author, 1982.

La Villa de Cubero, 1936
Cubero

In 1928 Wallace Gunn went to work for Sidney Gottlieb at the Cubero Trading Post to learn the business. When U.S. 66 moved south of the trading post in 1936, Gunn and Gottlieb decided to keep the trading post for their credit business in livestock with the Lagunas and Acomas and to build La Villa de Cubero—a motel, grocery, and gas station—for their cash business with tourists on the highway. Gunn managed the new business and, in time, purchased it. Gottlieb built a café across the road from La Villa for his sister from Chicago, but Gunn and his wife, Mary, took it over after several years.

Wallace Gunn designed La Villa following Spanish Colonial models. He housed the office, gas station, and grocery in an imposing building with towers over the office and the owner's residence, which he set on either corner. He laid out the stucco, pueblolike cabins around the U-shaped driveway that circled the main building. He installed modern tile baths in each of the cabins. The café, where Ernest Hemingway wrote portions of *The Old Man and the Sea*, reflected the architecture of the motel.[23] Photograph by author, 1997.

Bond-Gunderson Trading Post, 1915
Grants

C. K. Gunderson started as a trader at Laguna and ended as the Standard Oil distributor for western New Mexico, with outlets on the I-40 interchanges. In 1928 he had moved to Grants, a shipping point and trading center west of Laguna, where he bought into the Bond-Sargent Trading Company. One of two such businesses in Grants, the store occupied a wood-frame building across U.S. 66 from the railroad depot. Setting it apart from other general stores of that era was a curved stepped false front that gave it a Spanish Colonial look, although thirty years later it would evolve into a Streamline Moderne look.

Gunderson's new company, now called Bond-Gunderson, traded with the livestock ranchers and, later, with the carrot farmers around Grants. Almost immediately after buying into the trading post, Gunderson took the company into the gasoline business, opening a service station that supplied ranchers and farmers with fuel for their trucks. Traffic picked up, bringing tourists who needed gas and tires to replace those blown out bouncing across the railroad spur that served Gunderson's store. In 1931, when Standard Oil of California made him a distributor, Gunderson added a station a mile west of the trading post, using a standardized building supplied in a kit by the oil company. In 1958 he built the first shopping center at Grants, converting the original trading post to a furniture store, and in 1966 he opened his first service station at an I-40 interchange.[24] Photograph by author, 1982.

Uranium Cafe, 1956
Grants

When Paddy Martinez discovered uranium in Haystack Mountain in 1950, Grants boomed. Hearing of the boom, Eugene Woo pulled up stakes in Winslow, Arizona, where he worked at the National Restaurant, and joined the rush to Grants. There he bought a simple block-and-stucco café from Wilbur Thigpen, erected a sign in honor of Paddy's discovery, and served chop suey, burritos, and burgers.[25] Photograph by author, 1982, from *Route 66: The Highway and Its People,* photographs by Quinta Scott, text by Susan Croce Kelly (University of Oklahoma Press, 1988).

Franciscan Lodge, 1950
Grants

Grants did not become a tourist center in the 1930s and 1940s even though the drive from Albuquerque took a day and there was a demand for motels. As late as the mid-'40s, a traveler stranded for the night in Grants had only four options for overnight accommodations: Mother Whiteside and Mother Wilson operated boarding-houses at the east and west ends of town, where they served family-style meals and provided a few rooms; the Allen family operated the local campground; and George Aide operated the Yucca, a two-story hotel he had built in 1929.

Land was cheap in Grants in 1950 just before Paddy Martinez discovered uranium. That's when Auro and Nellie Cattaneo bought a plot at the east end of town. It was said that Auro "really didn't like the public," but he loved making buildings, and in 1950 he made the most modern motel in Grants. A contractor from Gallup, Auro and

his brother Felix designed and constructed the Franciscan Lodge with the help of local Navajo and Mexican workers. They adapted a plan and materials that came into common use after World War II, replacing individual cabins with attached units under one low roof and eliminating garages. They used concrete block finished in stucco rather than adobe or structural clay tile and installed broad steel-casement windows instead of small wood-frame windows.

When it was done, Nellie Cattaneo agreed to move her family to Grants and run the motel for a year. When the year was up, the family sold the motel and returned to Gallup. Grants was poor, they realized, and their children were falling behind in school. And, it turns out, Auro really did hate dealing with the public.[26] Photograph by author, 1982.

Monte Carlo Restaurant, 1947
Grants

Eskie Mazon built the two-story Monte Carlo on Santa Fe Avenue in 1947. He managed a restaurant on the ground floor and rented apartments on the second floor when housing was tight during Grants' boom time. In 1955 the city widened Santa Fe Avenue, cutting ten feet from the Monte Carlo facade. When Mazon rebuilt the facade, he hung the tall Streamline Moderne sign out over the street.[27] Photograph by author, 1982.

Milan Motel, 1947
Milan

Salvador and Mary Milan, brother and sister, were born in Mexico of parents who had emigrated from Valencia, Spain, in 1898. Expelled from Mexico during the 1913 revolution, the family moved to New Mexico to do contract work in the coal mines. Mary eventually married Wallace Gunn and moved to Cubero, while Salvador married Veneranda Mirabal, daughter of a sheep rancher near Grants. In 1939, Salvador established Milan three miles west of Grants on land Veneranda inherited from her father. He became mayor of the new town, a title he held until he died in the late 1970s.

When Salvador gave up sheep ranching in 1946, he decided to build the Milan Motel. With the help of his brother-in-law, Wallace Gunn, he studied several different layouts and settled on one very similar to Gunn's La Villa de Cubero—a central building housed the motel office, gas station office, and snack bar, with a series of duplex cabins laid out along a U-shaped driveway that circled the main building. But instead of following the style of La Villa, Milan built log cabin duplexes.[28] Photograph by author, 1982.

Bay Oil, ca. 1940
Milan

New York investment banker Charles Ulrick Bay entered the gasoline business when he purchased a refinery in McPherson, Kansas,
in 1934. He set up Bay Petroleum three years later, with headquarters in Denver, and sold a complete line of petroleum products—
gasoline, motor oil, diesel and tractor fuels, and kerosene—to
independent dealers throughout the Midwest, the Southwest, and
along the Gulf Coast. He advertised extensively, urging drivers to
"Buy Bay Gas at Independent Service Stations and Garages."

But the independents found it hard going after folks started pay-
ing for gas with credit cards and the major brands came to dominate
the gasoline market on U.S. 66. Small independent dealers, who
could not offer credit cards, went after the cash business and "low-
balled" their prices. But they couldn't overcome brand loyalty built
on credit cards nor did they have a highly recognizable architecture
to attract customers. In Milan they had only the Bay Oil sign that
alternately flashed, SAVE and BAY OIL CO. As a result, one operator after
another went bust at the west end of Milan.[29] Photograph by author,
1982.

Tomahawk Bar, 1947
Prewitt

With the end of World War II, the Great Lakes Steel Company of Detroit began looking for new markets for its Quonset hut, which was based on a manufactured building of British design used in World War I. The U.S. Navy had built the first American corrugated-arch steel building at Quonset, Rhode Island, in 1941, but when demand grew beyond the navy's capacity to produce the metal building, its manufacture had been turned over to Great Lakes Steel. After the war, Great Lakes continued to manufacture the hut in two sizes: a twenty-by-forty building that sold for nine hundred dollars and a forty-by-forty building that sold for two thousand. The total cost for a finished building in 1946 was about two dollars a square foot, as opposed to seven dollars a square foot for a standard building of the same size. Ex-GIs, who had grown accustomed to sleeping,

eating, and even praying in Quonset huts during the war, bought them and set them up as houses, movie theaters, churches, beauty shops, and roadside businesses.

Navy swabbie "Pistol Pete" South, for one, had lived in a Quonset hut when he was stationed in the South Pacific. When he returned to Prewitt after the war, he purchased a small adobe bar on U.S. 66. It burned. He wanted a new building, something fireproof. He had fond memories of the Quonset hut. He ordered a twenty-by-forty hut from Great Lakes Steel, assembled it with the help of friends, added a concrete-block facade, painted the whole structure hot pink, wrote BAR in big black and red letters on the front and the side of the hut, and opened for business.[30] Photograph by author, 1997.

Herman's Garage, 1931
Thoreau

In 1914 Standard Oil of California introduced its prototype for a standardized, prefabricated steel-and-glass gas station. It had a small office with an attached canopy covering the pumps; the building was enameled in Standard's white with red and blue trim and was topped by a uniform sign that was anchored to the ridge of the canopy. C. K. Gunderson, who operated Chevron stations in Grants for Standard Oil of California, purchased the 1931 version of the prefabricated station and erected it at the west end of town, a mile from his Bond-Gunderson Trading Post. The building contained a ten-by-ten-foot office, a small showroom for batteries and tires, and a "lube bay" in back.

In 1937, when the company needed a new station in Grants and an outlet in Thoreau, Gunderson sold the building to Joe Anderson, who carted it to the corner of U.S. 66 and New Mexico 371 on the outskirts of Thoreau, pronounced "threw." A dozen years later, Roy Herman bought the building from Anderson and moved it several hundred yards west of 66 and 371. "That building was built like a bridge. To move it all I had to do was brace the front poles, pick it up, and go," Herman said. In 1964, after I-40 had swallowed his location, Herman moved the station again. At the new place, he stopped pumping gas but added a large stucco garage behind the little building and continued repairing cars.[31] Photograph by author, 1997.

Top o' the World Hotel, Cafe, and Trading Post, ca. 1935
Continental Divide

Route 66 crossed the Continental Divide five miles west of Thoreau; at 7,275 feet it was the highest point on the highway. The Top o' the World complex at the divide never became the full-service tourist trap that Clines Corners was, even though it was on the eastern edge of Navajo country and the western edge of Pueblo country, with access to a large variety of American Indian arts. Maybe that was because its reputation was a little bit shady. A long, loaf-shaped stucco building, which originally housed a bar, was all that remained of a complex that once included a gas station, a hotel, a café, a trading post, and a dance hall that featured taxi dancers. There was also a dormitory for railroad workers and a boardinghouse that some thought might be a bawdy house, though no one could prove it.[32] Photograph by author, 1982.

Gallup

In 1879 the Santa Fe railroad sent mining engineers to western New Mexico to find coal and open mines. The following year the Blue Goose Saloon and Trading Post opened for business to serve the sheep and cattle ranchers scattered throughout the red hills in the region. And a year after that, the Santa Fe laid its tracks through the hills and built a station near the Blue Goose. Folks settled around the trading post, and the settlement grew into Gallup, which from the first thrived on ranching, coal mining, and railroad traffic.

The Santa Fe tracks and Railroad Avenue ran parallel on the north side of town. Then, in 1926, U.S. 66 came down Railroad Avenue, bringing additional business to the Main Street establishments that had catered to the railroad. When Indian traders opened their first outlets directed to the auto tourist, they set up shop near the motels that were springing up on 66 at the west end of town.[33]

Ideal Court, 1927–37
Gallup

Folks who stayed at places like the Ideal Court, the first motel in Gallup, spent their evenings walking to the cafés and trading posts that lined the street. The Ideal followed the standard motor-court plan—a service station/office fronted on the highway and attached units wrapped around a U-shaped driveway on a tight urban lot.

The rooms were plain, not much to look at. When the owner, Bert Eddies, switched brands from Sinclair to Texaco, Texaco came in and added Walter Dorwin Teague's distinctive portico to the service station.[34] Photograph by author, 1982.

Blue Spruce Lodge and East 66 Avenue, 1949
Gallup

The coal mines drew families like the Novaks and the Milosovichs to Gallup. John Novak brought his family from the copper mines in Bisbee, Arizona; John Milosovich was eighteen months old when his father brought the family from the iron mines in Hibbing, Minnesota. John Novak gave up mining and became a contractor. John Milosovich grew up to become the mayor of Gallup in 1935—at age twenty-one, the youngest mayor in the United States. With the end of World War II, Novak gave up the contracting business and opened a lumberyard. Milosovich returned from the military and became Gallup's city clerk.

The two men, born a generation apart, became great friends. From his desk at city hall, Milosovich watched the changes U.S. 66 brought to Gallup. From his counter in the lumberyard, Novak sold construction materials to the folks building motels along East 66. In 1949, when Novak persuaded his young friend to build a motel, he financed the project, designed the building, and supervised its construction.

Novak laid out the Blue Spruce in a U and covered the building with a low ranch roof that extended over the walkways and was supported with corbel-capped columns. When he finished, he and Milosovich planted a sign, a blue spruce tree outlined in neon, in the row of motel signs that stretched the length of East 66, each advertising the amenities the establishment offered the traveling public. Milosovich managed the Blue Spruce and paid off Novak quickly.[35] Photograph by author, 1982.

El Rancho, 1937
Gallup

Anything that happened in Gallup in the 1940s and 1950s happened at El Rancho. Local theater owner R. E. Griffith built the hotel, which served as the headquarters for the numerous movie companies that came to Gallup for location shooting in the red hills surrounding the city.

Before Nellie Cattaneo became an innkeeper in Grants, she had sold tickets at Griffith's movie theater in Gallup. Before Auro Cattaneo became a general contractor, he had been a stonemason. They married in 1937 just as Griffith was building El Rancho. When it came time to hire a stonemason for the job, Griffith turned to Auro, who did both the brickwork and stonework.

El Rancho was an imposing presence, with a tall white portico that welcomed travelers to the lobby. The lobby, a stone block attached to the crescent-shaped brick hotel, featured Auro's great stone fireplace and a two-story space that rose over a brick floor pol-

ished so bright "a lady could see her white slip in the shine." Navajo rugs hung from the mezzanine that surrounded the lobby. Outside, Auro laid the warm grey brick of the main body of El Rancho in irregular courses that waved up and down, with brick jutting in and out. Monterey-style balconies hung from second-story rooms on the rear.

The rest of the complex was huge, including a porch outside the dining room, a gas station, and smaller buildings housing a motel on Aztec, the next street over. Griffith furnished the public areas with western tables and chairs having carved tops and legs; he hung leather draperies over the windows. And when it was all done, he lit a neon sign on the portico, assuring travelers that they would enjoy the CONVENIENCE OF TOMORROW while basking in the CHARM OF YES-TERDAY.[36] Photograph by author, 1982.

Richardson Trading Post, 1913
Gallup

Gallup, surrounded by the Navajo and Zuni Reservations, has traditionally served as an outlet for American Indian arts. The traders in Gallup kept their main stores on the north side of the railroad tracks, where they traded with the Navajo and Zuni—jewelry and other crafts for groceries, hardware, and dry goods. Then, with the coming of U.S. 66 down Railroad Avenue, they opened new stores on the south side of the tracks. In the early 1990s only Richardson's was left on Railroad Avenue in downtown Gallup, where it continued to do business with the Navajo, the Zuni, and the tourists in a single-story shop built in the early part of the century.[37] Photograph by author, 1997.

Arizona

During the 1850s the War Department began work on a transportation corridor across the Southwest. In 1853 the secretary of war, Jefferson Davis, ordered surveys along the thirty-fifth parallel for a transcontinental rail line from Fort Smith, Arkansas, to the Colorado River on the California border. In 1857 and 1858 Edward F. Beale, leading a string of camels, surveyed along the thirty-fifth parallel for a wagon road. Between 1881 and 1883 the Atlantic and Pacific Railroad followed the trace surveyed by Beale when it laid its track from Albuquerque west to Needles, California. Along its route, a series of trading centers, spaced approximately sixty miles apart, grew into railroad towns named after the men who built the railroad.

When auto tourists started rambling across the Colorado Plateau in Arizona, the folks who tacked the signs on telephone poles for the National Old Trails Road followed the corridor from Gallup, New Mexico, along a good dirt track. At Kingman the National Old Trails Road turned south and west along the railroad around the Black Mountains, through flatlands laced with washes that swept away the road every time it rained.

When Cyrus Avery and the American Association of State Highway Officials laid out U.S. 66 in 1926, they followed Beale's corridor as far as Kingman. To avoid the washes south of Kingman, they directed 66 west across the Black Mountains and then south to Topock, the Colorado River crossing. When I-40 abandoned the section between Seligman, Arizona, and Barstow, California, that stretch of highway became a roadside museum.[1]

By 1926, Grants and Gallup, New Mexico, and Holbrook, Winslow, Flagstaff, Ash Fork, and Seligman, Arizona, were well established around elegant railroad depots and the hotels, restaurants, and stores that grew up along Main Street to serve railroad passengers and tourists. With the advent of 66, the Arizona Main Street business people turned their attention to the road in much the same way the traders did in Gallup, adding hotels, motels, and cafés first to the center of Main Street and then to its east and, occasionally, west fringes.

John Steinbeck and Bobby Troup have led us to see U.S. 66 as the road to California, to view everything between Chicago and Los Angeles as some place to get through on our way to the Golden State. We forget that long before the dust bowl or the postwar boom everything between Albuquerque and Williams, Arizona, was a destination: the Laguna, Acoma, Navajo, Hopi, and Zuni Reservations; the natural wonders—the Grand Canyon, the Petrified Forest, and the Painted Desert; and the annual Indian festivals in Gallup and Flagstaff. Fred Harvey, who began building restaurants in rail depots as early as 1876, recognized the appeal of the Southwest. He built hotels or restaurants in every city along the Santa Fe railroad and provided tours of the reservations and the natural wonders.

After World War II, when American travelers took to the road and headed down 66 to

New Mexico and Arizona, roadside businesses responded to the phenomenon with a flurry of motel building. Entrepreneurs lined their motels up on narrow lots along Main Street in one town after another from Grants to Kingman. After World War II, concrete block came into general use, easing the construction of a simple motel—a plain, rectangular building filled with attached units connected by an outside walkway and covered with a sloping roof to make the whole look like a ranch house. Postwar motel builders in Arizona had no time to explore the decorative possibilities of concrete block the way their counterparts had in prewar Shamrock, Texas.

Atkinson's Trading Post, 1942
Box Canyon

The competition for the dollar spent on American Indian arts was stiff in Gallup, but it was not so stiff west of town on the New Mexico–Arizona border. Leroy Atkinson, who started in the business in Gallup, moved out to Box Canyon just after the beginning of World War II. Prior to that, in 1935, Leroy, a nineteen-year-old Texas boy with eight dollars in his pocket, had piled his seventeen-year-old bride in his old car and moved to New Mexico. Three years later he had gone to work for Jack Hill at a trading post in Gallup where they took Navajo crafts—rugs and jewelry—in trade for groceries, hardware, and dry goods. To dispose of these craft items, Jack and Leroy opened a shop on 66, where they sold the artifacts to tourists coming down the road. It was their only source of cash.

Then, in 1942, Atkinson opened his own trading post in Box Canyon on the Arizona border. To attract the tourists, he housed the shop in a pair of log hogans, hexagonal Navajo huts tied together with another building. (The Navajo traditionally built their hogans around four posts, each one representing one of the sacred mountains of the Navajo homeland. The entrance faced east so occupants could greet the rising sun.)

Atkinson struggled in Box Canyon during World War II. Gas rationing kept tourists off the highway. But when the war ended, so did gas rationing, and business boomed. Tourists with money in their pockets and a desire to spend it hit the road. To get them to stop at Box Canyon, Atkinson set enormous statues of prehistoric characters out front and kept a herd of buffalo out back.[2] Photograph by author, 1982.

Brunswick Hotel/Arizona Rancho Motor Lodge/Tom's Rock Shop, ca. 1881
Holbrook

For more than a hundred years the pueblo/adobe image was successful in promoting tourism in Holbrook. The Brunswick Hotel served a series of businesses and reflected Holbrook's history as a rail center, a cowtown, a highway center, and a tourist stop. Located a block from the railroad station, it served the train travelers who stopped to visit the Painted Desert and Petrified Forest and the cattle barons of the Aztec Land and Cattle Company who drove their herds through town and maintained an office in the hotel.

In the 1930s Lloyd Taylor purchased the Brunswick and remodeled it into a motor lodge, adding a twelve-unit motel wing on the west side of the hotel. In keeping with the pueblo/adobe tradition, Lloyd built the wing in stucco painted white and used vigas to support the roof of the motel and its veranda. In the 1980s, Lloyd's eldest son, Tom, sold petrified wood to folks returning to Holbrook from the Petrified Forest.[3] Photograph by author, 1982.

Wigwam Motel, 1950
Holbrook

The Plains Indians dragged their shelters—tipis—from site to site as they roamed across the grasslands of the Great Plains. The Sioux, from whom the word "tipi" comes, fixed three long poles together in a tripod with the feet set on the circumference of a circle. They set additional poles at equal intervals around the circle and laid them up against the tripod, forming the basic structure for the tipi. Then they wrapped the cone-shaped skeleton in a semicircle of animal hides, folding back the ends for a door and chimney.

Frank Redford designed his tipis to make American sightseers wandering the land from tourist site to tourist site stop and stay the night. He erected his first tipi in 1933. Sixty feet tall, it lured tourists leaving Mammoth Cave to his gas station and café at Horse Cave, Kentucky. He installed rest rooms in a matching pair of little tipis. In 1935, at the request of his customers, he added six thirty-foot tipis, "sleeping rooms" he called them, to the complex he named Wigwam Village.

After several false starts in constructing his tipis, Redford settled on a steel skeleton to form a cone over which he laid a layer of wood, then a layer of felt, and finally a layer of canvas. He rubbed generous quantities of linseed oil into the cloth to shrink it tight to the frame and sealed it with stucco. He rolled back the canvas on either side of the door and cut diamond-shaped windows. He painted the whole structure white and added red rickrack around the top, the middle, and the windows. Realizing that while children might clamor to sleep in a tipi, their parents would want all the modern conveniences, Redford outfitted each tipi with a tile bath and a comfortable bedroom. He patented the structure in 1936 and in the following years built a chain of Wigwam Villages. Village No. 6 is in Holbrook, Arizona, and Village No. 7 in Rialto, California, both on U.S. 66. Redford owned No. 7; his friend Chester Lewis owned No. 6.

Lewis had never considered going into the motel business, even while motels mushroomed around his Holbrook Texaco station. He was doing well enough pumping gas and towing wrecks. But in 1946, on a trip to Horse Cave, he was struck by Frank Redford's tipis. He purchased the blueprints, returned to Holbrook, and built fifteen stucco tipis along a semicircular drive around his gas station.[4] Photograph by author, 1982.

Sitting Bull Trading Post, 1950
Joseph City

That the architecture of the trading posts, curio shops, and other tourist traps that dotted the roadside between Gallup and Flagstaff was so striking may have been due to the talents of Jack Fuss and other Arizona sign painters. The cheapest sign was always black paint on a simple whitewashed building. Leon Little used such a sign on his motel and café at Hinton Junction, Oklahoma. But Jack Fuss and sign painters like him turned whitewashed sheds into something special.

In 1919 Fuss pocketed his degree from the Philadelphia Academy of Fine Arts and set out for Flagstaff, where he worked as a cowhand and taxi driver. In 1925 he began putting his talents to work painting signs along U.S. 66. He built, painted, and maintained billboards and rented them to local businesses that advertised Arizona's scenic wonders, grand hotels, and gaudy trading posts. But Fuss also painted colorful signs on whitewashed sheds for anyone who could pay.

Many of Arizona's trading posts—parents called them tourist traps—were housed in shedlike structures decorated with paintings of Hopi kachina figures, Navajo rugs, Acoma pots, and dancing chieftains. If Jack Fuss did not establish the tradition, he certainly contributed to it. Fuss quit painting signs in 1972, but the tradition of using colorful figures to advertise roadside businesses, particularly those selling American Indian arts, continued across Arizona.

The Sitting Bull Trading Post was such an operation. "Howdy Hank" owned it, and, like so many proprietors along 66, he offered the traveler a little bit of everything—a motel with a few units and a swimming pool, a café, and a gift shop. He eventually sold it all to V. P. Richards, who sold it to Max Ortega, an Indian trader, who built the fence, added dancing Indian cherubs to the top of the fence, and painted the rest with colorful figures.[5] Photograph by author, 1982.

Ella's Frontier, n.d.
Joseph City

Mormons established five villages on the Little Colorado River after 1873. Joseph City, settled in 1876, is the sole survivor. If Ella Blackwell had her facts straight, her trading post was built by Mormons, but then, Ella claimed that God talked to her through her television set. She also claimed that she ran the oldest trading post on Route 66. She staked that claim on a painted-over Coke sign that said, EST. 1873, but Ella only came into possession of the old log building in 1956. She added this and that—wagon wheels and large chunks of petrified wood—to the exterior of the building to lure tourists inside. In the late 1990s, Ella's Frontier lay rotting on a dead-end strip of 66 just west of Joseph City.[6] Photograph by author, 1982.

Pacific Motel, Gas Station, and Cafe, 1947
Joseph City

"That's what radios looked like," Phil Blansett said, explaining his father's choice of the Streamline Moderne style for the Pacific Motel. Everything had rounded corners on it in 1947—radios, refrigerators, stoves, gas stations, and the newly completed Pacific Motel.

Glenn Blansett finished his stint with the army air corps in 1944 and moved from Arkansas to California, where he and his wife worked in an airplane factory. With the end of the war, Glenn went to work for the San Fernando Sheriff's Department, but he had his heart set on building a motel. In 1947 he moved his family to Joseph City, purchased a piece of property, set up housekeeping in a tent, and went to work building a motel with the help of his sons Phil, eleven, and Rand, thirteen. They made their own cinder blocks, compressing a dry mix of cinders, portland cement, and a little water into an eight-by-eight-by-sixteen-inch mold with collapsible sides for easy removal. The only place they used brick was to turn the rounded corners at the ends of the east and west wings.

The Blansetts built as money became available and eventually developed a full-service motel that operated twenty-four hours a day. They started with a line of attached units on the east side of the property, then added another row across the back, and a third on the west side until they had twenty-one units in a U around a parking court. In 1949 they added a gas station and four years after that a café across the road. Phil noted that the café, built with premanufactured concrete block, was much easier to build than the cinder-block motel had been. Tired of the grind, the Blansetts sold the motel in 1958. Then Glenn turned around and leased, and later bought, the Jack Rabbit Trading Post five miles down the road. Its proprietor, James Taylor, had also grown tired of the grind.[7] Photograph by author, 1998.

Let's Eat Cafe, 1946
Joseph City

Stormy Niles had the Let's Eat Cafe with a few gas pumps out front and a little motel, no more than six units, out back. He housed the café/gas station in a Western Bungalow covered in stucco. To attract attention to his café he painted LET'S EAT on the roof of the canopy over the service area. Stormy provided the competition for the Blansetts. A half-dozen times every summer he got in his truck and motored down the road to check out business at the Pacific. He would be pleased and proud if he filled his six units before the Blansetts filled their twenty-one.[8] Photograph by author, 1982.

Jack Rabbit Trading Post, 1949
Joseph City

James H. Taylor, who sold the kind of junk kids love at the Jack Rabbit Trading Post five miles west of Joseph City, and Wayne L. Troutner, purveyor of men's clothing at the For Men Only Store in Winslow, traveled U.S. 66 as far east as Springfield, Missouri, erecting billboards advertising their respective businesses. Taylor's black silhouette of a jack rabbit on a yellow background and Troutner's skimpily clad cowgirl were as much icons for their businesses as the Fat Man was for the Club Cafe in Santa Rosa, New Mexico. And the billboards worked. When folks traveling down 66 finally reached the Jack Rabbit, there was no question where they were: The big yellow sign announced, HERE IT IS.

James Taylor was a Texas boy who got into the trading business first in New Mexico and then in Arizona. Before opening the Jack Rabbit in 1949, Taylor had trading posts west and east of Albuquerque. When he moved to Joseph City, he bought the local snake farm, turned out the snakes—much to the alarm of the residents of Winslow fifteen miles to the west—and set about turning the asphalt-shingled shack into the Jack Rabbit.

First he whitewashed the building. Then he hired sign painter Charlie Miller to freehand a pair of dancing chiefs on either side of the door and a big arrow that said, REST ROOMS. Taylor jigsawed thirty rabbits from a one-by-twelve plank and set them hopping along the roofline. A big rabbit sat on the roof above the door. But Taylor also wanted one huge rabbit for the kids. He found a man who said he could build a wooden structure for such a rabbit, pad it with straw, and cover it with horsehide, but first he would have to kill the horse. Hired to do the job, he did in fact kill the horse. The rabbit, hunkered down in a corral near the entrance, welcomed tourists and provided a photo opportunity for three generations of children who rode the saddle on its back.

Inside the store, Taylor crowded the large open space with counters—like those in old-time dime stores—that were covered with geodes; bits of turquoise, quartz, petrified wood, and other kinds of rock; and cheap imitations of the real thing—Indian jewelry and beadwork, cowboy hats and Indian headdresses, tomahawks and rubber bowie knives. The good stuff, the real stuff? He kept that in a back room.[9] Photograph by author, 1997.

Modern Sign, ca. 1926
Winslow

This sign, boasting MODERN in a handsome script surrounded by the legend, "A Temporary Home for Those Who Roam," was possibly painted by Jack Fuss. Its black letters on green-painted stucco advertised a motel long since razed. Photograph by author, 1982.

Lorenzo Hubbell Trading Post, ca. 1885
Winslow

Lorenzo Hubbell saw the commercial value of Indian arts as early as 1876, when he purchased a trading post at Pueblo Colorado in Navajo country. He renamed the place Ganado to prevent confusion with Pueblo, Colorado. In the late 1880s he purchased a warehouse and store in Winslow, which he turned over to his son, Lorenzo, Jr.

This was the trading post that served travelers on U.S. 66 in Winslow after 1926. It was a brick building on a stone foundation with a deep porch and a raised false front over the porch that acted as a signboard.[10] Photograph by author, 1982.

Beacon Motel, 1946
Winslow

Concrete block came into general use after World War II. It was, as Phil Blansett noted, easy to handle, certainly easier than frame and siding, and it didn't crack like adobe and stucco. As highway travel increased after the war and into the 1950s, and the demand for motels exploded, it became possible to build and make money on a motel that offered no-frills accommodations. Proprietors like those who built the Beacon set down basic motels of concrete block one after another along the edges of southwestern towns from Amarillo, Texas, west to Kingman, Arizona. They were even frugal with neon, mounting fragile glass tubes directly onto concrete block facades with no background painting. Only the shadow of the writing on the wall or the glint of the tubes in the sunlight made the signs readable in daylight. So at Winslow the Beacon Motel scrawled WELCOME across its lime-green facade. Photograph by author, 1982.

Service Station and Garage, n.d.
Winslow

By early summer, the folks who operated gas stations and garages in eastern Arizona needed a means of shading their workers and customers from the heat of the sun. Where their counterparts in Oklahoma and Texas used deep canopies attached to the main building, Arizonans and Californians extended the building out over the service area and removed the walls and windows between the columns that supported the roof, providing deep shade for both the service area and the office. In Winslow the Spanish Colonial canopy was a building unto itself. Photograph by author, 1982.

La Posada, 1930
Winslow

"The mention of 'Fred Harvey' makes no other comment necessary," stated Duncan Hines in his first *Lodging for a Night*. In 1902 the Fred Harvey Company made Mary Elizabeth Jane Colter its architect and interior designer. It was she who created the Harvey style of architecture using Spanish Colonial, Pueblo, Navajo, and other southwestern Indian motifs. Her favorite work, La Posada at Winslow, was the last of the great Fred Harvey hotels built along the Santa Fe line through New Mexico and Arizona. Colter gave La Posada two facades, one for train travelers and one for automobile tourists. She designed a seventy-room Spanish Casa, a ranch house finished in stucco, and turned its best face toward the railroad. Low colonnades flanked an arched entry and overlooked a garden. One colonnade stretched east to provide cover for passengers coming from the adjacent railway station. A Tudor-arched portal faced Winslow's Main Street and U.S. 66. Colter capped La Posada with a series of red-tiled, cross-gabled roofs.

The Harvey system designated La Posada as the Arizona headquarters for the Harveycar Indian Detours, auto tours of the Petrified Forest and Painted Desert, the Meteor Crater, the Grand Canyon, and the Hopi Pueblo. The auto tours, started in 1926 in New Mexico, had been hugely successful in opening the Grand Canyon and the pueblos of New Mexico to tourism. Wealthy tourists arrived by train in Santa Fe and Albuquerque and toured the sights, staying in Harvey hotels along the way.

The Harvey system had the same hopes for the Indian Detours in Arizona. But La Posada did not open until 1930, a year after the 1929 stock market crash. The rich tourists stopped coming, and Harvey discontinued the Indian Detours in 1931. After the hotel closed in 1957, only the decision by the Santa Fe railway to make Winslow a division headquarters kept La Posada from being razed along with the rest of the great Fred Harvey hotels on the Santa Fe line.[11] Photograph by author, 1997.

Let's Eat, aka Miz Zip's, 1942
Flagstaff

There was nothing on the east side of Flagstaff in 1942, only a wrecking business with a motel and a café. When it came available at a sheriff's sale, Joe and Lila Lockhard sold their house, bought it, and went into business with Lila's sons, Howard and Bob Leonard, and Bob's wife, Norma, and their two boys. They all moved into the big house that came with motel and the café. And they all worked at the business, the men at the garage, which they converted to a gas station, and the women at the motel. Lila, Bob, and Norma ran the café.

Bob's boys, Craig and Kent, washed dishes, standing on milk crates to reach the sink.

Bob and Norma wanted to name the café "Let's Eat," but Bob's uncle, who was in the restaurant business in Nogales, Arizona, suggested they needed something zippier—like "Miz Zip's." So they used both names and scrawled "Let's Eat" in neon on the stepped false front above the door.[12] Photograph by author, 1982.

Jesus Garcia's Tourist Home, 1926
Flagstaff

After 1870, when drought forced them out of California, many Basque sheepherders settled in the mountains around Flagstaff. At the same time, a Basque community grew up around the railroad station in southeast Flagstaff. Married shepherds bought houses in the neighborhood. Unmarried shepherds lived in boardinghouses like Jesus Garcia's Tourist Home. Garcia located his boardinghouse at the corner of San Francisco and East Phoenix, one block south of Santa Fe, U.S. 66. He built a single-story, shotgun structure with rooms double-loaded on either side of a long corridor. From the street the structure's appearance was that of a Craftsman-style house, with a string of wraparound windows. This front area contained the office and possibly a dining room. When the boardinghouse was opened to tourists, probably in the 1940s, a simple sign with small Streamline Moderne details was hung out over San Francisco Avenue.[13] Photograph by author, 1998.

Du Beau's Motor Inn, 1929
Flagstaff

The intersection of Santa Fe Avenue and San Francisco marked the center of Flagstaff. That is where the Santa Fe railroad built its station in 1889, and the town expanded north and south from there. Then, in 1926, Route 66 came through downtown Flagstaff on Santa Fe to Beaver. Soon thereafter, Albert N. Du Beau located his motor inn on the corner of Beaver and East Phoenix, one block south of Santa Fe.

When folks tired of hauling the comforts of home—linens—with them, they looked for places like the Du Beau, the first fully equipped motel in Arizona. At the Du Beau, housekeepers smoothed cool, freshly laundered sheets on the beds and hung clean white towels in the tiled bathrooms. Du Beau crammed twenty-eight units, a separate garage, and a Western Bungalow–style office and owner's residence onto his lot. He set the rather large bungalow right on the street and wrapped the units around it. Heat came from the city's steam plant. Du Beau supplied kitchens in four units, but he also served dinners. His daughter, Clara, owned and operated the Black Cat Cafe, one block over on Santa Fe.[14] Photograph by author, 1982.

Nackard's Downtowner Motel, 1929, expanded 1950
Flagstaff

In 1912 K. J. Nackard opened a dry goods store on Front Street in Flagstaff. When Marie Sutter, a madam known as Dutch May, was murdered in 1916, Nackard bought the one-story Craftsman-style brothel at the corner of San Francisco Street and East Phoenix from her estate, moved in, and set up housekeeping with his young family. In 1919 he bought Rosie Harkahus's one-story brothel next door, added a second story to it, and opened the Nackard Hotel. The fam-ily lived in Dutch May's house until 1929, when Nackard saw the need for a motel. He moved his family out, converted the house to a motel office, and built Nackard's Downtowner Auto Court around it. Nackard's first Downtowner was a series of small cabins that he updated into a ranch-style motel, adding a rising canopy over the office in the fifties.[15] Photograph by author, 1982.

Sierra Vista Motel, 1937–42
Flagstaff

Taken together, the three motels on East Phoenix—the Downtowner, the Du Beau, and Salvador Esparza's Sierra Vista—make a tight urban setting. Salvador Esparza came to Flagstaff from Mexico in 1924 and learned to be a carpenter. When it came to building the Sierra Vista in 1937, he used stone—red Coconino sandstone, the traditional building material in Flagstaff, and malpais fieldstone. Mexican workers cut the sandstone and gathered fieldstone for the two-story hotel. Salvador saved the sandstone for the front third of the building and used the fieldstone for the rear. Stonemasons laid the Coconino stone in a coursed pattern on the first floor and in a random pattern over the arched portico. They piled up the malpais fieldstone like rubble on the rear two-thirds of the building. The arched porch set into the first story of the hotel provided shade for those guests who wished to sit outside in the evening. When Esparza added a string of attached motel units on the west side and at the rear of the property, he continued his use of stone but added a walkway supported with concrete-block columns.[16] Photograph by author, 1982.

Grand Canyon Cafe, 1950
Flagstaff

Eddie Wong opened the Grand Canyon Cafe—twelve stools and six tables—on Santa Fe in 1938. His brother, Albert, joined him two years later. They managed to stay open through wartime food rationing. After the war, business boomed. In 1950 they expanded into the shop next door, adding a Streamline Moderne tile facade. They installed windows that were flat next to the entrance but rounded on the end. Over the entrance they installed a shallow stain-less steel canopy that was outlined in neon, more for decoration than function. On the white false front the Wongs wrote GRAND CANYON CAFE in neon with a background painting to set off the letters. Over the street, they hung a neon sign with the name of the café. The Wongs stayed open eighteen hours a day and drew customers from the highway, the railroad, and downtown Flagstaff.[17] Photograph by author, 1982.

Old Smokys Pancake House and Restaurant, 1945
Williams

Rod Graves owned two restaurants in Williams. He served breakfast and lunch at Old Smokys on the western edge of town and lunch and dinner at Rod's Steak House in the center of town. Travelers in a hurry could get the "Quick Lunch" advertised on the painted sign in the gable at Old Smokys. Those at leisure could enjoy an elegant dinner served on white linen and eaten with "clean silver" at the Steak House. Rod constructed Old Smokys in colorful flat flagstones, reminiscent of Ozark giraffe stone, quarried down the road at Ash Fork.[18] Photograph by author, 1982.

Copper State Motor Court, 1928
Ash Fork

In winter, good business in Ash Fork depended on bad weather. Otherwise, folks passed through to a bigger place—Kingman or Flagstaff. Travelers coming from the east or west along Lewis Avenue could sum up the services available in town with one glance. The Copper State, the Green Door Bar, the Arizona Cafe, the White House Hotel: All had huge signs that hung out over the street. Those tourists who decided to stay found E. A. Nelson's Copper State Motor Court at the east end of town.

For years, the Santa Fe ran a single track between Kingman and Flagstaff. But in 1924 the railroad started laying a second one, and the gandy dancers who did the work needed housing. Ezell Nelson responded with the Copper State Motor Court. It took him four years to build it—four years of collecting cobblestones from the hills around Ash Fork and from the nearby creek beds, four years of painstakingly laying up the walls and cementing the rocks together with black mortar, four years of slathering layer upon layer of port-land cement plaster on the inside walls to smooth the finish in the rooms. When he was done, he had twelve rooms arranged in an L under a flat roof and with walls eighteen inches thick. Each room had a garage wide enough to park a Model T Ford. In 1935 when the gandy dancers finished their work and left town, Ezell went after the auto tourist, erecting a big sign at the corner of his lot at Lewis and Park.[19] Photograph by author, 1998.

Arizona Cafe, 1920/Green Door Bar, 1926
Ash Fork

The cafés that opened up in the one- and two-story commercial blocks that lined Lewis Avenue were designed to serve the railroad. The buildings changed hands frequently as one owner after another failed in spite of the huge signs they used to draw in tourists. The Winchester Dickerson store was the first business to occupy the two-story Arizona Cafe block at the west end of Lewis; a drugstore followed and then came the café and bar. The Arizona Cafe wrote its name in neon across the front of its building; mounted a large sign proclaiming, CAFE, on the roof; and added a sign on the front of the building announcing, COCKTAILS.

East on Lewis the Crow Bar replaced the Green Door in the 1990s in a building erected in 1926 or 1956, depending on whom you ask. The builder of the Green Door added a stepped parapet to give the building more height. The sign, an upside-down, off-center T, almost as tall as the building and parapet, made the building a half-story taller.[20] Photograph by author, 1982.

Seligman Garage, 1933
Seligman

When I-40 bypassed the old section of 66 between Seligman and Kingman, it put Seligman in a unique position: It was the last town for seventy-four miles along I-40. The location of the highway proved a bonanza for local motel and gas station owners. This time the plans of the highway department worked in favor of Seligman businesses. But local proprietors had learned much earlier that you cannot fight the highway department. When it wants to move the highway, it will move the highway.

Guy Sykes and Tom Cook had built a large stone garage along Railroad Avenue in Seligman in 1923. Three years later Railroad carried U.S. 66 through Seligman, and Sykes and Cook did a good business. They never closed; they towed cars for fifty cents a mile; they built a reputation for good, honest repair work; they maintained a campsite supplying water, fuel, and rest rooms. They came to depend on 66 for their business. But in 1933 the Arizona Highway

Department decided to pave Chino Avenue, one block north of Railroad, and move 66 to Chino. One proprietor on Railroad was so upset that he offered to pay for the paving of Railroad if the highway department would only leave 66 where it was. Other owners, like Guy Sykes and Tom Cook, just moved their businesses.

Sykes and Cook built a new Seligman Garage, duplicating the old, and added a huge, deep canopy that allowed their customers to get out of the sun, get out of the wind, and get out of the rain while Sykes and Cook pumped their gas, checked their oil, and washed their windows. There were two islands under this canopy—and when business exploded, one was added on the outside. Proud of their new building, the partners splashed SELIGMAN GARAGE across the front of the canopy and outlined it in neon. Then they hung the first neon sign in Seligman out over the street.[21] Photograph by author, 1982.

Snow Cap, 1958
Seligman

Route 66 brought economic stability to the Delgadillo family. Angel Delgadillo came to Seligman from Mexico in 1917 and worked on the railroad until a strike erupted in 1922. Two years later, he opened a barbershop and pool hall, drawing a good business from the highway after 1926. When the highway moved to Chino Avenue in 1933, he moved with it.

Delgadillo's nine children, including sons Angel and Juan, all grew up in Seligman. Angel eventually took over the barbershop and pool hall. Juan went his own way. But after a stint playing in a band during the depression, and another stint working on the railroad, Juan settled down and built the Snow Cap. Like Red Chaney in Springfield, Missouri, everything Juan did to his basic roadside food stand was designed to call attention to it: He wrote his menu on the cornice—MALTS, TACOS, BURRITOS, DEAD CHICKEN, AND CONES. He painted pictures of his menu below the front windows and around the doors. And, like Red, who parked an old Buick in front of his food stand, Juan parked a 1936 Chevy convertible in front of his stand, painted it white, and set a Christmas tree crowned with a pumpkin in the back seat. He provided shaded picnic areas outside the Snow Cap where his customers could wash down their tacos, burritos, and dead chicken with a malt and a smile.[22] Photograph by author, 1998.

Osterman's Shell Station, 1932
Peach Springs

Swedish sailor John Osterman wanted to captain his own ship. Toward that goal, he set sail in 1914 around the world, as was required by the Swedish Merchant Marine—but on a German ship. When the ship was interned at Santa Rosalia, Mexico, on the Baja Peninsula at the beginning of World War I, Osterman jumped ship, ferried across the Gulf of California, made his way to Nogales, crossed the border into Arizona, and followed the railroad north to Phoenix, where he went to work in a dairy. He hated the work. When the dairy shipped its cows, and John, north to summer pastures near Flagstaff, he took off and hopped a freight train to San Francisco with the intention of going back to sea. But the railroad cops caught him and threw him off at Peach Springs, where the largest body of water was a dry wash.

Osterman stayed, worked on a ranch, became a citizen, and was drafted when the United States went to war in 1917. After the war, he returned to Peach Springs, opened a small gas station and quickly developed a reputation for honest work. He would tow a car day or night. He stocked Ford parts, particularly springs—six were deliv-

ered daily from Los Angeles for folks who busted theirs on the rough road.

Things were so good John persuaded his brother Oscar to join him, sold him the gas station in 1925, and moved to Kingman. A year later the highway department designated the road in front of Oscar's station U.S. Highway 66. Six years later, they moved the highway a block north. In the face of all of this, Oscar needed a new location and a new building. He built a jagged Alamo. He poured a two-story concrete frame, four bays wide, and filled it with concrete block, formed to look like quarried stone. He was taking advantage of new technology: By 1920 the reinforced-concrete frame had come into general use in large industrial buildings—flour mills and factories, for instance—but it was unusual to see one on such a small scale as Osterman's. Oscar housed his office and workroom in the west half of the building and the garage in the east half. Behind the stepped facade over the garage, he provided a second-story sleeping room for the help. He finished the building with a wide, spreading canopy that covered the pumps.[23] Photograph by author, 1998.

Peach Springs Auto Court, 1932
Peach Springs

Beatrice Boyd came to Peach Springs as a bride in 1938 to run the motel her groom had just purchased from Oscar Osterman. Her husband, Frank, who hated farming, had left their native Kansas to go to college in California in 1934. In the summers he would join his brother in Peach Springs, where they worked at Osterman's service station and lived in the sleeping room over the garage. After Oscar had finished building his new gas station, he decided to add a motor court to his holdings. He built little wooden shacks next to the dry wash east of the station. Charging a dollar a night for the rooms, he had paid for the shacks by the end of the first summer. Then he built sixteen attached units, covered the long building in clapboard, and added a false front.

In 1938 Frank Boyd decided to settle in Peach Springs and went back to Kansas to claim his bride. Bride and groom returned to Arizona and purchased Osterman's motor court. Peach Springs was a good location, and the young couple saw a good living in the motor court. They understood that in the winter they were far enough from Kingman and Williams for people to stop and that in the summer they were close enough to the Grand Canyon for rafters to rest before

heading down the Colorado River. But they couldn't predict a fire, and they didn't understand that Arizona has two kinds of rivers: perennial rivers that run all year long and ephemeral rivers that are dry washes, that run only when it rains, and it doesn't rain much.

Business was good for the Boyds during World War II, but just as the postwar boom began in 1946, fire destroyed half their units. Frank and Beatrice rebuilt fast and made other changes. They set up housekeeping in a clapboard bungalow with a clipped-gable roof that they moved from across the wash. They took Osterman's old office shack, which sat next to the wash, moved it to the edge of the highway, and opened a gas station. They started pumping Sunoco gas but switched to Mobil to take advantage of the credit card business the flying red horse would bring to their pumps.

Finally, in 1966, when life seemed settled and business was good, the dry wash ran. The Boyds came home from a day in Kingman to find thirty-seven inches of water in the units and ten inches in their house. Undaunted, they replaced everything.[24] Photograph by author, 1982.

Carrow's Cabins, 1935
Valentine

Ed Carrow and his six brothers ran the Seven Bar V Ranch in Valentine, halfway between Hackberry and Truxton. Ed did a little bit of everything: He ran cattle, which he butchered in his slaughterhouse in Slaughter House Canyon; he had a dairy; he kept a vegetable garden and an orchard; he dug a few gold nuggets from his mining claim. And finally, he ran a restaurant and swimming pool, a garage and service station, and an auto court.

In 1924 when the Santa Fe had moved its tracks out of the floodplain of Crozier Creek—a perennial stream—to higher ground, it abandoned its stone bridges across the creek and allowed Carrow to salvage the stone for a restaurant, which he built on Old Beale Road. The place looked like a fort. He sank a spring-fed swimming pool and built dressing rooms next to it. Buses took their meal stops at the restaurant, where the passengers had a bite and a dip—very refreshing in the hot desert—dried off, and resumed their trip. For a snack before their next meal stop, Ed sold them fruits and vegetables from his garden.

When Old Beale Road became U.S. 66 and traffic picked up, Ed added a garage and gas station to his restaurant. Then, along Crozier Creek, he built eight little Western Bungalow–style cabins with hipped roofs. Each cabin housed two units. Crozier Creek flooded in 1939, washing out the garage, the service station, and a piece of the restaurant and filling the little cabins with four feet of water. Eventually, 66, like the Santa Fe, moved out of the floodplain of Crozier Creek, leaving the little row of cabins stranded down by the stream.[25] Photograph by author, 1982.

Hotel Beale, 1900
Kingman

In 1900 Johanna and Frances Wilkerson opened a restaurant to serve workers on the Santa Fe railroad. The sisters soon added a two-story boardinghouse with rooms to let. When Johanna married Harvey Hubbs, they named the boardinghouse the Hubbs House. It burned. The Hubbses then built a two-story brick hotel with corbeling at the cornice, later adding a third story at the rear.

The couple eventually sold the hotel to Thomas and Amy Devine, parents of Andy Devine, who would be known to children of the 1950s as Jingles B. Jones, the gravelly voiced sidekick to Guy Madison's Wild Bill Hickok in the television series of the same name. The Devines renamed the hotel the Beale. In 1923, when the Beale was the leading hotel in Kingman, the Devines charged their guests, mostly rail passengers, between $1.50 and $4 for any one of the seventy rooms. They sold the Beale in 1926, just as auto tourists started checking in.[26] Photograph by author, 1982.

Bungalow Court, 1939
Kingman

In 1938 Duncan Hines recommended to tourists arriving in Kingman, "While it may be hot up here, it is nothing to what it is down in Needles. So better hang around until 'long about sunset." It was good advice, and the people of Kingman supplied plenty of motels to hang around in. The December 22, 1939, issue of the *Mohave County Miner* announced, "Auto Courts Becoming One of Most Important Businesses Here, Huge Sums Invested." By the end of 1939 Kingman had accommodations for eight hundred visitors.

Jack Sapp was one of those who had invested in Kingman's tourist business that year, adding twenty-four cabins to the town's stock of overnight housing. Sapp built simply, possibly using the design for a ten-foot-by-twelve-foot cabin that had been published in *Popular Mechanics* four years earlier, although Sapp added a larger building to house his office and residence. He finished the whole in stucco.[27] Photograph by author, 1982.

White Rock Court, 1935
Kingman

There was nothing simple about Conrad Minka's White Rock Court. Before Minka constructed his stone motel, he dug tunnels under the site so he could heat it from a central furnace. Most stone motels along U.S. 66 were rock-veneered buildings, like those slabstone auto courts in the Missouri Ozarks, but Minka used masonry construction and tufa stone quarried from the region. He laid stone lintels over the doors and windows of the units, and he spanned the spaces between the units with stone arches, roofed the spaces, and used them as the garages. He arranged two blocks of rooms and garages in an L on a narrow lot and added a two-story office and owner's residence.[28] Photograph by author, 1998.

El Trovatore, 1939
Kingman

By December 1939, John F. Miller had completed thirty units at El Trovatore and was working on another twenty-four. The man had a passion for reinforced concrete; he built to last. In 1905, on his way home to Iowa from California, he had passed through Las Vegas, Nevada, a dusty place of no importance, where the town proprietor was auctioning off lots. Even then Miller saw possibilities in the desert and bid successfully on a site at the corner of Main and Fremont. There he built his first hotel, the two-story Nevada, constructed with reinforced-concrete walls. Over the years Miller changed the name and the facade of the hotel, but the concrete struc- ture endured, evolving into the Golden Gate Casino by the 1990s.

After Hoover Dam was completed across the Colorado River, Miller saw new opportunity in the desert in northwestern Arizona. He bought a ranch north of Kingman in 1935, moved into town sev- eral years later, purchased the site of El Trovatore, and started con- struction. He began with ranch-style motel buildings with concrete walls and shingle-roofed porches. Later he experimented with the urbane Streamline Moderne, adding a handsome reinforced- concrete, curved-front unit to El Trovatore.[29] Photograph by author, 1998.

Gas Station, ca. 1926
Gold Hill Summit

When Cyrus Avery and his colleagues routed 66 through the Black Mountains rather than around them, they laid out a difficult drive. From the foot of the mountains to Gold Hill Summit, 66 climbed fourteen hundred feet over nine miles, beginning with a gentle grade and ending in several sharp switchback turns. The reward at Gold Hill Summit was a gas station, an ice cream parlor, and a grand view. The descent from the summit was downright scary, seven hundred feet in two miles, hugging the side of the mountain in outside turns and inside turns, into Goldroad, an abandoned mining town. For eastbound cars that couldn't make the grade, the gas station at the summit provided a tow. From Goldroad, it was a quick trip down the mountain to Oatman. From there, old 66 descended into the Colorado River Valley and ran parallel to the river to Topock, where it crossed into Needles and the Mojave Desert.

In 1953 the Arizona Highway Department rerouted 66 south from Kingman through the flatlands along the route of the National Old Trails Road to Topock and abandoned the road through Sitgreaves Pass in the Black Mountains. Businesses and buildings along the old section of road disappeared. What remained were remnants of buildings, piles of stones that hinted at gas stations. The Ford Motor Company, which opened a testing ground at Yucca in 1955, began using old 66 to test its cars.[30] Photograph by author, 1982.

California

At Needles he drove into a service station, checked the worn tires for air, checked the spares tied to the back. He had the gas tank filled, and he bought two five-gallon cans of gasoline and a two-gallon can of oil. He filled the radiator.

—John Steinbeck[1]

Needles, the hottest place in the country, was the first stop in California. Theoretically, 66 was a local road between Needles and Los Angeles. Theoretically, it was a day's drive between the two cities. Theoretically, there was no need for many motels. Theory was great; reality was the Mojave Desert. Needles rested in the Colorado Valley. As hot as it was, it was a green place after the Black Mountains and before the Mojave Desert. The Joad family of Steinbeck's novel did what all travelers did in Needles, prepared for their nighttime run across the desert. They needed gas and water, plenty of water—for the car, for the people, and for the canvas water bag they purchased to hang on the radiator.

In California, Route 66 fell into four distinct sections: the Mojave Desert between Needles and Barstow; the Mojave River Valley between Barstow and San Bernardino; Foothill Boulevard between San Bernardino and Pasadena; and Los Angeles, where the road spread out like a river delta. Between Needles and San Bernardino, only Barstow and Victorville offered a wide selection of roadside businesses. Each of the desert stops between Needles and Barstow was dominated by a single business geared to helping folks cross the desert. There was nothing fancy about the architecture of the desert. The most important criterion for a building was to keep it cool. Therefore roadside builders added broad canopies to their gas stations and cut small windows into their motel walls.

The architectural turnover between San Bernardino and Los Angeles was so great that few buildings from the 1926–56 period remained in the 1990s. Those motels and gas stations that survived drew on the architecture of the Los Angeles suburbs—the Craftsman style and variations on the Spanish Colonial. In Los Angeles, where there are two seasons—day and night—open-air food stands, the precursors of the McDonald brothers' golden-arched pavilion, proliferated.

Havasu Court at Carty's Camp, 1925
Needles

Needles was isolated. Going west, the only way out was across the Mojave Desert—164 miles to Barstow, a four-hour drive. Going east, the only way out was over the Black Mountains—69 miles to Kingman, a four-hour drive.

In 1925 Bill Carty drove east to the Grand Canyon, stayed in a tent-and-cabin camp, came home to Needles, and raved to his friend Ernest Mansker about the camp. Mansker responded with enthusiasm for the idea and with a site for a gas station and camp at the east end of Needles. Carty's Camp would be the first place the auto travelers stopped after the difficult trip over the Black Mountains. It would prepare them for the hard drive across the Mojave Desert.

Carty and Mansker built a large gas station and added a motel next door. Like so many of the gas stations in the desert, this one was a simple frame-and-clapboard building with a deep canopy to provide shade in the pumping area. The Joads drove past Carty and Mansker's gas station in the film version of *The Grapes of Wrath*. The motel, which the partners named the Havasu Court, consisted of fourteen units set back to back in seven wood-frame-and-fiberboard gabled cabins with tin roofs. The dimensions of each cabin were determined by the size of the sheets of fiberboard and the width of the door. Only in the Mojave could anyone build cabins of fiberboard and expect them not to dissolve in the rain or even go soggy and smelly in the humidity. This was, after all, a desert. Photograph by author, 1998.

Robinson Motor Inn, 1928
Needles

In 1940 Duncan Hines recommended that travelers check in to Robinson's Motor Inn because "other good accommodations are far, far away." Sarah Robinson and her husband had come from Scotland to Needles, where he worked in the local quarry. It was from the quarry that he pillaged huge fourteen-by-fourteen-inch wooden beams to build their motor inn. The Robinsons drew on two California styles—the Monterey house and the Craftsman Bungalow—when they wedged eight bungalows and a two-story house onto a tight city block in Needles. Built of adobe brick and finished in stucco, the Monterey house was an Anglo variation on the Spanish Colonial house. It had evolved in Monterey, California, at the end of the nineteenth century. A second-story balcony the width of the house served as a hallway between rooms.

The Robinsons built their Monterey house of masonry finished in stucco and set it in the center of the complex. They surrounded it with eight Craftsman-style bungalows in a city where similar houses lined the streets. The small wooden duplexes were characterized by roof rafters that were exposed under the eaves. The style was an outgrowth of Henry and Charles Greene's explorations of Japanese architecture in Pasadena in the early 1900s.[2] Photograph by author, 1998.

Names in rocks, 1942–72
Mojave Desert between Essex and Ludlow

World War II brought great excitement to the Mojave Desert. The U.S. Army established the Mojave Anti-Aircraft Range at Fort Irwin in 1938. General George S. Patton trained his tank troops for action in North Africa in this desert. Douglas Aircraft tested A-20 attack bombers at Daggett. When Douglas moved out, the U.S. Army Air Corps moved in and trained pilots to fly P-38s. The U.S. Navy opened a supply depot at Nebo, which it turned over to the marines in 1943. The place was hopping. "There were so many soldiers out there you could stir them with a stick," one observer noted.

Patton's tank troops learned the desert was a dangerous place; they learned not to sleep in dry washes, to shake scorpions out of their shoes in the morning, and to watch out for rattlesnakes. One hundred ninety-one thousand troops stayed for four months, only to be followed by another group. But, before they departed, they left their marks on the desert—their names in rocks along the road. Patton's soldiers didn't start the practice; they only did what others before them had done when they found themselves stuck along 66

in the Mojave: They wrote their names with small rocks on the low berm that followed the road between Essex and Ludlow.

With World War II over, civilian travelers learned that Route 66 in the Mojave Desert was a dangerous place. The eighteen-foot bridges that crossed the washes were too narrow for two speeding cars to pass safely in opposite directions. One car would hit another or, worse, impale itself, and sometimes its driver, on the wooden guardrail. Every wrecker had a litany of horror stories. But vapor-locked gas lines and overheated radiators stopped more cars than did guardrails. Folks sat on the roadside, their radiators boiling, waiting for a wrecker to tow them to the nearest garage. Bored, they collected small stones and laid them on the roadside berms in the shape of big letters spelling out their names.

What was the purpose of the low berms? They were levees. When it rains in the desert, it floods. The berms that lined the north side of the highway funneled floodwater away from the road and into the washes.[3] Photograph by author, 1982.

Chambless Camp, 1932
Cadiz

With few gas stations in the desert, places like Chambless Camp and Roy's, on west at Amboy, grew into full-service enterprises geared to helping naïve travelers cross the Mojave. Wreckers were the center of their businesses, with repair shops to fix cars, cafés to feed stranded motorists, and cabins to bed them down while they waited—sometimes for days, the press of business was so great.

James Albert Chambless, a widower, and his children, Melvane and Pearl, came west from Arkansas in the 1920s and settled near Amboy. When they saw opportunity in the Cadiz Valley, each family member took a desert homestead—160 acres—and improved it. They mined their land and built a roadside business along the newly designated U.S. 66. When the highway moved to Cadiz in 1932, the family moved with it and built Chambless Camp, a business similar to Carty's Camp. In the late 1930s James married Fannie Gould. She ran the place, turning the camp into an oasis, complete with rose garden and fishpond.

Like the Seligman Garage, Chambless Camp also provided a massive canopy—a trussed roof four bays wide and two deep, supported by seven columns set on stone bases. Inside the large, dim building, Fannie presided over a café, a grocery, and a service station. She refused to sell beer, but during World War II, she made gallons and gallons of lemonade for soldiers who chugged it down in a picnic area located in a grove of acacia trees. Out back James Chambless lined up a series of small concrete-block cabins with tin roofs.[4] Photograph by author, 1982.

Roy's, 1926–72
Amboy

Buster Burris hauled away the wrecks that happened in the desert, picked up the vapor-locked automobiles and their owners, and took them to his garage/café/motel complex in Amboy. Buster came to Amboy from Texas in 1938, went to work for Roy Crowe, drove Roy's wrecker, and married Roy's daughter. At first the business was only a service station and garage with the wrecker, but in 1945 Buster added the café to feed Roy's customers while they waited for their cars to be repaired. In 1948 when he tired of seeing those same customers sleep in their cars while they waited, Buster built the cabins.

He had a 100 percent occupancy day and night. He built both the cabins and the café of concrete block and stucco; he added the familiar deep canopy to the front of the café and a low gable over the entrance of each cabin. The six stucco cabins, lined up like little houses stretching out into the desert, were dominated by Buster's enormous sign, which pointed to the complex. As business increased, Buster added eighteen motel units in a two-story block in back.[5] Photograph by author, 1982.

Railroad Workers' Cabins, 1920
Ludlow

Ludlow was the only town of any substance between Needles and Barstow. Its major business was the Tonopah and Tidewater Railroad, a narrow-gauge line that ran between Ludlow and Beatty, Nevada. Francis Marion "Borax" Smith of the Pacific Coast Borax Company began building the line from the Santa Fe siding at Ludlow in 1905. It took him two years to run his tracks 167 miles in a straight line across the Mojave Desert through Broadwell Lake, Soda Lake, and Silver Lake—all dry lakes except when it rained and they flooded, halting rail traffic. The Tonopah and Tidewater, which hauled three hundred thousand tons of borax from the mines near Death Valley, maintained its shops at Ludlow, where Smith built stucco-and-brick cabins with clipped gables to house his workers. Never profitable, the Tonopah and Tidewater made its last run on June 14, 1940. Its tracks were then abandoned and dismantled; the cabins were sold and converted to motel units.[6] Photograph by author, 1982.

Ludlow Mercantile, aka Murphy Brothers' Store, 1908
Ludlow

Ludlow was founded in 1882 as a water stop for steam engines on the Southern Pacific Railroad, and later the Santa Fe. Real prosperity came to the town in 1905 when the Tonopah and Tidewater made Ludlow its southern terminus. Mother Preston moved to Ludlow from Calico and opened a saloon, where workers on the T & T imbibed in their afterhours, and a rooming house, where they slept it off. She got rich, rich enough to lend John Denair the money to build the Ludlow Mercantile in 1908. He built a two-story building of reinforced concrete and raised a low false front over the canopy. When Denair went broke competing with the Murphy Brothers' store next door, Ma Preston took possession of the building, forgave

the loan, and ran the store until 1918, when she sold it to the Murphy brothers and left town.

Tom and Mike Murphy owned general stores at the southern and northern terminals of the T & T—Tom in Ludlow and Mike in Tonopah. When Ma handed over the Ludlow Mercantile, Tom moved into Denair's handsome two-story concrete building. When auto tourists began crossing the desert, Tom added a garage and an auto camp next to the store. He stayed open twenty-four hours a day at the garage, changing tires, replacing batteries, and welding broken axles. At the camp he provided "Free-W-C-L-Shade"—free water, comfort stations, lights, and shade.[7] Photograph by author, 1982.

Kelley's Restaurant Sign, 1948
Daggett

Daggett has had two cafés—Ma Millet's Cafe and Kelley's. With the arrival of auto tourism, the California Department of Agriculture set up its inspection station at Daggett. There inspectors stopped all cars coming from the east to check for and confiscate all fruit and plant materials that might be carrying diseases and parasites. Marie Millett opened a café in her kitchen to serve lunch to the inspectors. The tourists followed, filling themselves on all-you-can-eat meals for fifty cents. Room by room Marie turned her house over to the café until she and her husband, Newton, had to build a new house for themselves next door. Marie Millett closed her doors on May 1, 1947, the day James and Elsie Kelley opened their café.

The Kelleys came from Sigourney, Iowa, in 1942 and went to work in the Douglas Aircraft plant at the Barstow-Daggett airfield. After the end of World War II, the Kelleys stayed, and James, called Mike, fulfilled a dream and built a restaurant, a gas station, and a motel. The restaurant was a concrete-block box with picture windows overlooking 66. Mike cooked, and the rest of the family, Elsie and the five children, served food, pumped gas, and made beds. To get the attention of the passing traveler, the Kelleys erected a huge sign across 66—a curved arrow with a shamrock on which they wrote RESTAURANT. Lit with running lights and neon, the sign pointed to the café across the road and demanded that travelers stop.[8] Photograph by author, 1985.

Greystone Auto and Trailer Camp, 1935
Barstow

Between Daggett and Barstow, Route 66 followed the Mojave River. At one time, the site of the Greystone was a watering hole for the twenty-mule teams that hauled borax from the mines in Death Valley. In time the Greystone itself became a watering hole for marines stationed at the Daggett depot and airmen from the army airfield.

A man named Grey, whose first name is long forgotten, homesteaded the site of the Greystone at the turn of the century. Like so many people in isolated regions along 66, Grey found more than one way to make a dollar once the highway was routed past his homestead. In 1935 he built the Greystone: a service station and garage; a café with an outdoor patio that served as a dance hall; an auto and trailer camp. It was all housed in a rambling collection of cottages built of grey and purple and pink stones that reflected the colors of the surrounding mountains and that had been rolled smooth by the Mojave River.

The service station and garage catered to locals and tourists. The café and dance hall catered to local teenagers, the marines, and the airmen. The auto and trailer camp catered to passing travelers. And finally, the tin-roofed stone cottages catered to prostitutes who, in turn, catered to the soldiers and pilots.[9] Photograph by author, 1982.

El Rancho, 1947
Barstow

Barstow was a crossroads a hundred or more miles from everywhere. From here 66 turned south to Victorville and San Bernardino, while 466 continued west to Bakersfield and northeast to Las Vegas. For folks arriving from Needles, Barstow was a relief. On the other hand, everybody traveling east stopped in Barstow to prepare for the trek across the desert. Motels and gas stations, squeezed onto urban lots, stretched from one end of town to the other.

Before the highways turned Barstow into a roadside oasis, it was a rail center, the division point of all Santa Fe lines from southern California, San Francisco, and the San Joaquin Valley. Casa Desierto, the Santa Fe station and hotel, was elegant, but the employees of the Santa Fe stayed at Cliff Chase's El Rancho.

Cliff Chase salvaged the ties from the Tonopah and Tidewater Railroad and modeled El Rancho on the Spanish Colonial ranch house or California Casa. Between 1769 and 1823 Spanish Franciscan missionaries had established twenty-one missions along the Camino Real between San Diego and San Francisco. Ranchers in the backcountry of Los Angeles had then modeled the Casa on the missions, surrounding a courtyard with adobe or rubble-stone buildings. Like the Mission style, the Casa was the perfect model for motel builders on U.S. 66 who needed to tuck their units onto tight urban lots. Breaking from the flat roofs, so familiar on Pueblo/Adobe buildings in New Mexico, Californians built low-pitched roofs, which they covered in heavy, red clay tiles. Often they extended the roof over a veranda, much like the porches at El Rancho, and supported the heavy tile roofs with large wooden columns or adobe piers.[10] Photograph by author, 1998.

Texaco Station, ca. 1940
Lenwood

From Barstow the road turned south along the eastern edge of the Mojave River Valley. In early spring the east side of the road was a desert landscape; tan and grey hills were sprinkled with yellow flowers on pale green stems. The west side of the highway was a bottomland floodplain, lush and emerald green with young spring wheat. This stretch was a local road between Barstow, Victorville, and San Bernardino. There were plenty of gas stations, a few motels, an occasional café or food stand, and lots of beer joints.

Jack Belsher, a Texaco consignee in Barstow, delivered gas to the four Texaco stations in the thirty-five miles between Barstow and Victorville. Texaco supplied the standard Walter Dorwin Teague canopy to a small brick office at the gas station at Lenwood. The owner added a sandwich shop using the same colors and forms as the Texaco station.[11] Photograph by author, 1982.

Oro Grande Motel
Oro Grande

Oro Grande may have been a thriving gold-mining town in the 1880s, but it never thrived as a highway town. Only four miles north of Victorville, it was a good place for Moonshiner Wadsworth to set up his operation in two or three cabins and a gas station. In one of the cabins he installed a secret wall and a trapdoor from which he dispensed his brew. He built the Oro Grande using the same round chunks of Mojave River stone as Grey used at his auto camp. Wadsworth set the stone in a coursed rubble pattern. Tapered columns of riveted steel set on stone piers supported the canopy. Out back, he kept a garage and an outhouse, both built of fiberboard.[12] Photograph by author, 1998.

New Corral Motel, 1947
Victorville

Victorville was the largest stop between Barstow and San Bernardino. The movie industry discovered the old mining town in 1914 and made it the backdrop for silent pictures. William S. Hart started making movies here in 1914; then came Tom Mix, Harry Carey, and Will Rogers.

Roy Rogers came to Victorville to make movies and stayed. He came as Len Slye. In 1930 he and his father quit their jobs in a shoe factory in Cincinnati, packed their belongings in a '23 Dodge, and set out for California to join Len's sister Mary. They crossed the Indiana and Illinois flatlands and picked up U.S. 66 at St. Louis. The trip took two weeks, several changes of tires, and one set of bearings salvaged from a junker. They spent the summer of 1931 picking peaches near Bakersfield. When Mary encouraged Len to sing on a radio amateur show, he was noticed by the Rocky Mountaineers, who invited him to be their singer. Then he began taking bit parts in Westerns for Republic Pictures. The bit parts grew into bigger parts. Len changed his name to Roy Rogers, married Dale Evans, mounted a golden palomino named Trigger, and rode to fame and fortune. When Trigger died, Rogers had him stuffed and mounted—rearing up on his hind legs—and installed him at the Roy Rogers and Dale Evans Museum in Victorville. Trigger struck the same pose on the sign at the New Corral, a standard ranch-style motel.[13] Photograph by author, 1982.

Between Victorville and San Bernardino, 66 crosses the San Bernardino National Forest and descends south through Cajon Pass in the Sierra Madre. Since 1831, when William Wolfskill carved out the Spanish Trail, all roads between Los Angeles and Santa Fe have passed through Cajon Canyon. From San Bernardino 66 followed Foothill Boulevard west to Pasadena against a backdrop of Spanish Colonial architecture.[14]

Mission Auto Court and Cafe, 1935
San Bernardino

According to Duncan Hines, the Mission Auto Court and Cafe was the best of its kind in 1940. Thomas I. Proctor modeled his auto court on the Spanish Mission and the tiny flat-roofed Spanish Colonial houses in his San Bernardino neighborhood. He built churchlike towers to flank the entrance of the complex. Inside, fifty-eight attached stucco bungalows with raised parapets and red-tile canopies over their entrances lined the parking court. Some units had kitchenettes; others, attached garages.[15] Photograph by author, 1982.

Mitla Restaurant, 1937
San Bernardino

Vicente and Lucia Montano came to California in 1928 and settled in San Bernardino, where he went to work for the Santa Fe railroad. In 1937 Lucia opened a taco stand on Mount Vernon. Vicente opened a pool hall next door. Business boomed. Vicente quit the railroad, and Lucia bought the old drugstore at the corner of Mount Vernon and Sixth Street, installed a counter and some booths, and opened a full-scale restaurant where she served tacos, enchiladas, and burritos—Mexican fare so fine Duncan Hines took notice. She expanded again in 1949, opening a dining room.

One block north of the turn west onto Foothill Boulevard, the Mitla was a handy place to stop on a trip north to the mountains or west to the beach. In the evening long-distance travelers staying at the motels along Mount Vernon strolled down to the Mitla for dinner. Set on a busy corner right next to a bus stop, the Mitla was more big-city coffee shop than roadside café. It was a stucco building with a white tile base and corner entrance. A red Spanish tile awning shaded large picture windows.[16] Photograph by author, 1998.

Drive-in Food Stand, ca. 1935
Etiwanda

Farmers in the Los Angeles backcountry devoted their land to vineyards, citrus orchards, and olive groves. Folks in the towns along Foothill Boulevard picked and packed oranges and olives and shipped them east. They harvested grapes and turned them into wine. And they squeezed and sold fresh orange juice at stands along the roadside.

In the early 1930s Harry and Charles Carpenter built a large octagonal drive-in at Sunset and Vine in Hollywood. The octagonal shape served as the prototype for drive-in food stands in the Los Angeles region. Cars parked two or three to a side, depending on the size of the octagon. The kitchen was in the center. Carhops picked up the finished orders at the windows around the octagon. The owner of this food stand in Etiwanda used only half of an elongated octagon when he built his drive-in on a shallow lot off Foothill Boulevard.[17] Photograph by author, 1998.

Ancil Morris's Service Station, 1934
Cucamonga

Like motel builders along this stretch of 66, both oil companies and independent dealers like Ancil Morris and Duane Meyer drew on the Spanish Colonial style for their gas stations. Standard Oil of California, Union Oil, Ventura Oil, and finally, Richfield Oil of California: All used Spanish Colonial architecture. In Cucamonga, Ancil Morris built a stucco gas station and garage. He set his gas sta-

tion and office at the front of his property at Foothill and Archibald and built the garage at the rear. The high false front and broad arch that spanned the columns supporting the canopy and their red-tile caps gave the station its Spanish flavor.[18] Photograph by author, 1982.

Meyer's Service Station, 1950
Cucamonga

Duane Meyer, a Nebraska farm boy, migrated down 66 to California in 1937 to join his uncle in Cucamonga. He held a variety of jobs until he married and settled down to pump gas and fix cars in his father-in-law's service station at the intersection of 66 and Summit Avenue. Also called the Cajon Cutoff, Summit took the eastbound travelers north to Devore, allowing them to bypass San Bernardino and cut many miles from their trip. Traffic thickened. By 1950 Meyer and his father-in-law needed a new and larger station. At a time when the big oil companies in California were abandoning Spanish Colonial architecture for Streamline Moderne buildings or, occasionally, International Style boxes, Meyer and his father-in-law built a Spanish Colonial station. Their station was simple, basically a stucco box with tile roof that housed the office and garage. They extended a long, three-bay canopy out over the pumping area and lined up three pumping stations between the columns that supported the canopy.

By the late 1990s Cucamonga, Upland, Claremont, Glendora, and Duarte had become bedroom communities. Strip malls had replaced the orchards, olive groves, and vineyards as well as the motels, restaurants, and gas stations that served travelers on U.S. 66. Wal-Mart erected a supercenter across Foothill from Duane's, and the California Highway Department lopped off the canopy to accommodate a smooth right turn from Foothill onto Summit.[19] Photograph by author, 1982.

Upland Motel, 1935
Upland

It was possible to look at the Upland Motel two ways: It was a scaled-down version of the Craftsman Bungalow with exposed rafters and clapboard siding, or it was the little ten-by-twelve-foot cabin published in a 1935 issue of *Popular Mechanics*. In Upland, where the streets were lined with larger, fancier variations of the same style, it was a Craftsman Bungalow. William and Theresa Scholten built the tiny cabins in 1935 and sold them to Jack Burton ten years later.[20] Photograph by author, 1982.

Shamrock Motel, 1946
Glendora

On January 14, 1946, D. B. Salisbury of Paso Robles, California, took out a construction permit to build a motel in Glendora. He chose an unusual plan, dividing twenty units into six stucco buildings facing a courtyard. He wrapped the parking around the rear of the buildings and provided five entrances to the courtyard between the buildings. He set the two rear buildings at angles so that the courtyard came to a point. He united the whole with a continuous colonnade supported by wide stuccoed columns and covered with a red-tile roof. Salisbury molded phony stucco bricks, long and narrow, into the bottom half of each building and painted them deep red. He paved the walk under the colonnade with quarry tile and set a large shamrock in the tile in front of the office.[21] Photograph by author, 1998.

Kort Meier Chevrolet, ca. 1901
Azusa

Kort Meier and Charles and Ira Moon built the Spanish Colonial garage around 1901. The fancy tin front was a caricature of the facade of a Spanish Mission church with a high-arched false front. Meier and the Moons saved the fancy tin, stamped to look like stone, for the front and sheathed the sides and rear of the building in plain corrugated tin. In the 1930s Meier housed his auto agency on one side and an office of the Automobile Club of Southern California on the other. In the late 1990s, the Azusa Pawn Shop painted the building hot pink with electric blue trim.[22] Photograph by author, 1998.

McDonald's, 1954
Azusa

With its mild weather, southern California abounded in open-air food stands consisting of a small shelter, a service counter, and possibly a few stools. Maurice and Richard McDonald opened a classical octagonal orange juice stand in 1937 in Arcadia. In 1940 they cut the building in half, carted the pieces to San Bernardino, reassembled them, and opened a drive-in barbeque and hamburger stand with carhops. Eight years later they fired the carhops, threw out the crockery, pared down the menu, and opened walk-up windows through which they served burgers, fries, and shakes. Their customers hated the new arrangements, but slowly, slowly, they caught on to the speed and convenience of "fast food."

By 1953 the McDonald brothers were ready to expand. They hired Stanley Merston to design a food stand they could reproduce every time they expanded into a new place. Merston gave them a candy-striped building, which Richard McDonald modified, tipping the roof up and adding the golden arches that seemed to support the roof. The building became the model for food stands along 66 from Chicago to Los Angeles and everywhere else. By 1989 McDonald's had evolved into an eat-in restaurant with seating inside, and the red-and-white-striped building was obsolete. It was razed. By the late 1990s McDonald's had built a new, glitzier variation on the golden-arched building along Foothill Boulevard near Glendora.[23] Photograph by author, 1982.

BLVD Cafe, 1946
Duarte

Susie Tomasian and her family operated a food stand and café down the road at Duarte, several miles west of the Azusa McDonald's. The Tomasians had settled in Duarte in 1946 and opened the BLVD, where they served hamburgers at a counter with a few stools in an open-air lean-to. The lean-to was attached to a small stucco house in which customers could find table service. It was the family's inten- tion to name the restaurant the Boulevard, but they had the same problem Red Chaney had at Red's Hamburg in Springfield, Missouri: There was not enough room on the sign for "Boulevard," so they abbreviated it. Over the roof of the lean-to, a pole raised the sign, which on three lines carried the words BEER, BLVD, and CAFE.[24] Photograph by author, 1982.

Evergreen Motor Hotel, 1937
Duarte

Unique to this stretch of 66 was the occasional use of the Craftsman style in motels, mostly simple cabins like those at the Upland Motel. While related to the Spanish Colonial ranch house or Casa, the Craftsman Bungalow also reflected an interest in the Japanese house and in the use of low-pitched rooflines, broad overhangs, and wooden construction, which was expressed on the exterior by the extended support beams and wood fascia.

The Evergreen was a far more elaborate variation on the Crafts-man style than the Upland was. It was probably built as a private house by Yola Radabaugh in 1937 and then converted to a rest home in 1940. Frank Kempka bought it in 1948 and made it into a motel, adding sixteen units in two board-and-batten ranch-style blocks to the side and rear of the lot. He incorporated three more units into the house. In 1956 Kempka converted rooms in the house into a coffee shop, dining room, and bar.[25] Photograph by author, 1982.

Aztec Hotel, 1925
Monrovia

In the 1920s, 66 turned north and then west on Colorado Boulevard at Monrovia. In 1925, the year before U.S. 66 was designated, Robert B. Stacy-Judd, a British architect who worked in Hollywood, completed the Aztec Hotel on Colorado. Exotic architecture had long intrigued Stacy-Judd, who employed Egyptian and Islamic forms in the movie theaters and hotels he designed as he moved from London to Minot, North Dakota, to Los Angeles.

In 1923 a rare-book salesman had introduced Stacy-Judd to Mayan architecture, and he had developed a taste for it. At about this same time National Community Hotels, a chain based in Harris-burg, Pennsylvania, hired him to design the hotel in Monrovia. He presented his clients with two plans, one Spanish and one Mayan. They accepted the Mayan. Once called the pièce de resistance of the short-lived Aztec revival movement, the Aztec was for a few years the most exclusive hotel in the region serving the nearby Santa Anita racetrack. Stacy-Judd appliquéed elaborate Mayan forms to the otherwise simple stucco facade of the two-story hotel. Inside, stained-glass windows, patterned tile floors, murals, and Mayan sculptures decorated the public rooms.[26] Photograph by author, 1998.

Grand Motel, 1938
Pasadena

In Pasadena, where land values were high and the lots tight, Abraham Koslow, the owner of the Grand, squeezed twenty-eight units with garages onto a beautifully landscaped site with a turnaround oval in the center. The cabins were a series of stucco ranch houses with deep overhangs, each set a little higher than the last, stepping up a slight incline. From the street, the Grand was all greenery and shingled rooftops, very appealing after a trip through the desert and the long haul from San Bernardino. An urban motel, the Grand did not have a café or a gas station; rather, Koslow recommended folks eat at places like Brotherton's.[27] Photograph by author, 1982.

Brotherton's Farm House Dinners, 1937
Pasadena

Brotherton's fit right in on Colorado Boulevard in Pasadena, where the feel of the street was suburban residential in spite of the motels that catered to tourists. The Brotherton family migrated to California from Iowa in 1937. They set up residence on the second floor of a classic California-style bungalow. The house was fronted by a heavy porch supported by short wooden columns mounted on massive brick piers. On the first floor the family opened the Farm House Dinners. On the sign in the front yard, they advertised that they served up farm dinners and tourist information. While they depended on locals for the core of their business, they also hosted tourists who were staying in nearby motels, places like the Grand.[28] Photograph by author, 1982.

From Pasadena, various alignments of U.S. 66 spread out like a river delta. From Colorado Boulevard the road turned south to downtown Los Angeles on Fair Oaks and Huntington to North Broadway, then west on Sunset Boulevard—or it continued west on Colorado to Eagle Rock and south on Figueroa to Sunset, where it ended. In 1935 the California Highway Department extended U.S. 66 to Santa Monica along Santa Monica Boulevard.[29]

Gas Station, ca. 1910
Los Angeles

Located on Figueroa near Sunset, this old gas station somehow survived, at least until 1982, while a larger garage grew up around it. In 1910 it provided the basic necessities for pumping gas—a tiny office and a canopy over the service area made of small, decorative pieces of metal. It is possible the original owner purchased the station from a catalog of standardized gas stations, had the materials shipped to the site, and assembled them in a day or two by bolting the four steel posts to prepoured concrete islands, erecting the trusses that sup-

ported the tile roof, attaching the decorative tin fascia to the roof, building the tiny steel-and-glass office, and finally, painting it all silver. The building probably survived in downtown Los Angeles because later owners wrapped a garage and convenience store around the rear of the site and painted the new buildings white, thus providing a setting for the little silver station.[30] Photograph by author, 1982.

Jay's Jay Burgers, 1934
Santa Monica and Virgil

Walk-up, open-air food stands proliferated in Los Angeles, where the weather was always mild. The most famous of the food stands was the Tail o' the Pup, a walk-up hot dog stand in the shape of a hot dog on a bun built by Milton Black in 1938. Sometimes the stands provided an outdoor seating area with tables, and sometimes, like Jay's Jay Burgers, they provided several stools at a shaded counter. Bill Morgan built the stand in 1934 on the corner of Santa Monica and Virgil and sold it to Jay Coffin in 1968 for eleven thousand dollars. It was not much more than a counter wrapped around a little kitchen with scalloped tin awnings attached to a hipped roof.[31] Photograph by author, 1998.

Grave of Douglas Fairbanks, Sr.
Hollywood Memorial Cemetery

Tinsel Town, where the sun always shines and the weather is mild, was not the final stop on U.S. 66, but it was an important destination after World War II when Americans hopped in their cars and became tourists. They toured the Hollywood studios and watched movies being made. Armed with maps, they cruised the streets on the lookout for movie stars' houses. Finally, they visited the Hollywood Memorial Cemetery, just off Santa Monica Boulevard, which housed the shrines of the stars and the producers who invented Hollywood.

The Horsley brothers made the first Hollywood movie in 1910 in a tavern and barn they converted to a studio, but the great Cecil B. De Mille and Douglas Fairbanks, Sr., and the other stars of the teens and twenties made Hollywood. De Mille began his movie career as an actor in New York, then moved on to directing and pro-

ducing. In 1913 he decided to move west—legend has it to Flagstaff, Arizona, which he decided did not look western enough. So he continued west to Hollywood, where he, like the Horsley brothers, purchased an old barn and made *The Squaw Man,* released in 1914.

Douglas Fairbanks, Sr., began his career on the Broadway stage in 1902 and in 1915 moved on to Hollywood, where he learned the business from D. W. Griffith. During the 1920s movie making boomed into a billion-dollar business led by producers De Mille and Griffith. When De Mille died in 1959, he was buried in Hollywood Memorial Cemetery among the stars of his generation: Rudolph Valentino, John Gilbert, and Douglas Fairbanks, Sr., whose famous profile was sculpted in bronze and mounted on the marble peristyle that surrounded his sarcophagus set at the end of a great reflecting pool.[32] Photograph by author, 1982.

Motel, 1940
Lincoln Boulevard, Santa Monica

In the 1860s Angelenos discovered the beach at Santa Monica. They made their weekend excursions first by buggy and later by trolley. A beach community developed, and a residential community followed. Not until 1935 did the California Highway Department extend U.S. 66 along Santa Monica Boulevard to Santa Monica, where it turned left on Lincoln and ended a few blocks south at Olympia, U.S. 101A.

Roadside builders responded with small motels along Santa Monica, Lincoln, and Olympia. The Spanish Colonial style prevailed. While there were hints of Streamline Moderne architecture, an outgrowth of the Spanish Colonial, in the hexagonal office of the motel on Lincoln the overall effect was Spanish.[33] Photograph by author, 1982.

Belle Vue Restaurant Building, 1919
Santa Monica at Ocean Avenue, Santa Monica

In 1952 the U.S. Highway 66 Association made the intersection of Santa Monica and Ocean Avenue the unofficial end of Route 66. Led by Lyle Overman, owner of the Carlyle Motel in Oklahoma City and president of the association, members traveled in a caravan the length of 66, picking up fellow pilgrims as they progressed from town to town. Warner Brothers Studio actually staged the caravan to publicize their film, *The Will Rogers Story,* but members of the 66 Association went along for the ride and to publicize their highway. At the end of the road they erected a plaque in Palisades Park dedicating their highway to Will Rogers, whose hometown was Claremore, Oklahoma.

Across Ocean Avenue in the Belle Vue Restaurant, which was itself in one of the large hotels and apartment houses that line Ocean and face Palisades Park, Ann and Jimmy Wallace had been serving abalone steaks—not your standard roadside fare—since 1937. Some time in the late 1930s or 1940s, the 1919 building was given a Hollywood Deco facade with details—the scroll over the door and the Streamline Moderne canopy and sign—that came straight from the romantic movies of the period.[34] Photograph by author, 1982.

Merry-go-round, Santa Monica Pier, 1909–26, reconstructed 1983
Santa Monica

Where did the road end? It depended on your vantage point. Just as 66 did not start at Lake Michigan in Chicago, it did not end at the Pacific Ocean. In 1926 it ended in downtown Los Angeles; in 1935 highway engineers extended it to Santa Monica; then, in 1952 Lyle Overman and company put its terminus at Santa Monica Boulevard and Ocean Avenue.

At the end of the twentieth century the highway's spiritual end was three blocks south of Santa Monica and Ocean, at the Santa Monica Pier, a playground where the merry-go-round still entertained people much as it had in 1916 when Charles Looff, a carousel maker from Long Beach, constructed the pier.[35] Photograph by author, 1982.

The Ultimate Road Trip

66—the long concrete path across the country, waving gently up and down on the map, from the Mississippi to Bakersfield—over the red lands and the gray lands, twisting up into the mountains, crossing the Divide and down into the bright and terrible desert, across the desert to the mountains again, and into the rich California valleys.

—John Steinbeck[1]

Route 66 was defined by the great road trips of its day. The Bunion Derby, followed by newspapers across the nation, fixed Route 66 in the American imagination. John Steinbeck gave it a name—"the mother road."[2] The dust bowl migration down 66 from the wind-whipped Midwest was the first great automobile migration west. Other migrations followed, and Bobby Troup provided the map. His song came at the beginning of the post–World War II boom, when Americans, having survived the depression and won the war, jumped in their cars and started traveling for fun, using Troup's song as a guide. Then, barely more than a decade later, Sterling Silliphant made Route 66 the road to adventure. His show glowed on the nation's television screens in an era when American opportunity seemed limitless.

Route 66, the highway, may have lost its economic viability with the passage of the Federal Aid Highway Act in 1956, but Route 66, the myth, did not. In the late 1980s the first histories of U.S. 66 were published.[3] Travel down what is left of the highway at the turn of the century, and you will find a whole industry devoted to the myth of Route 66. Cruise the Internet, and you will find the same thing. Lucille Hamons, who started pumping gas outside Hydro, Oklahoma, in 1941, fashioned her own web site with links to other Route 66 sites.[4] In 1995 the Oklahoma Historical Society opened a museum in Clinton dedicated to the myth, and Elk City, Oklahoma, followed with its own museum in 1998. Shops selling Route 66 memorabilia—calendars, cookbooks, coffee mugs, buttons, belt buckles, tee-shirts, and even a chessboard—have replaced the old-time souvenir stands, proving that the old road is still a good source of cash money. Old motels and cafés invoke the name of Route 66 in hopes of bringing in business. Restaurants like the Ariston in Litchfield, Illinois, and the Mitla in San Bernardino, California, and food stands like the Cozy Dog in Springfield, Illinois, and the Snow Cap in Seligman, Arizona, all still in the hands of the families that built them, have found new life in the myth of the old road.

Route 66 is still the ultimate road trip. While the road has ceased to be a highway to somewhere, it has become its own destination. Angel Delgadillo, the barber in Seligman, Arizona, understood that and started the Arizona Route 66 Association in 1987 to promote travel along the old highway. In 1989 Jack Rittenhouse reprinted his 1946 guide, and other guide-books followed.[5] In the spring of 1995, a pair of French cyclists set out to write a guidebook for French and other European travelers who come to this country to visit Route 66 and search out the "real America."[6] Finally, in 1995, sixty-one years after the great migration along 66 began, Oklahomans, who previously had been loath to even discuss John Steinbeck and *The Grapes of Wrath,* invited Americans to come to Oklahoma, "where the 'Mother Road'—Route 66—beckons travelers with endless adventure."[7]

Notes

The Architecture of America's Highway

1. Dorothea Lange and Paul Taylor, *American Exodus;* Woody Guthrie, *Dust Bowl Ballads;* John Steinbeck, *Grapes of Wrath.*
2. Bobby Troup, interview by author and Susan Croce Kelly, Encino, Calif., June 25, 1982; Bobby Troupe, "Get Your Kicks."
3. *Route 66,* CBS, 1960–64.
4. Robert Venturi, Denise Scott-Brown, and Steven Izenour, *Learning from Las Vegas,* 13.
5. Ibid., 13, 90; Peter Blake, *God's Own Junkyard,* 101.
6. Allen Noble, *Houses,* 123; Virginia McAlester and Lee McAlester, *Field Guide,* 100, 129–37.
7. Alan Gowans, *Comfortable House,* 199; McAlester and McAlester, *Field Guide,* 454.
8. Quinta Scott and Susan Croce Kelly, *Route 66,* 23–24.
9. Gowans, *Comfortable House,* 116.
10. Cliff May, *Western Ranch Houses,* 8–10.
11. Donald Bush, *Streamlined Decade,* 154–59; Chester Liebs, *Main Street,* 57.
12. Gowans, *Comfortable House,* 120; Alan Gowans, *Styles and Types,* 251.
13. Liebs, *Main Street,* 61.
14. Kurt Gottlieb, interview by author and Kelly, Cubero, N.Mex., March 1, 1982; Charles H. "Bud" Gunderson, interview by author and Kelly, Grants, N.Mex., March 2, 1982; Arthur Whiting, interview by author, Holbrook, Ariz., June 29, 1982.
15. John Jakle and Keith Sculle, *Gas Station,* 131–33; Liebs, *Main Street,* 100; Charles H. "Bud" Gunderson, telephone interview by author, January 19, 1998.
16. Jakle and Sculle, *Gas Station,* 132–33.
17. John Margolies, *Pump and Circumstance,* 43; Daniel Vieyra, "*Fill'er Up,*" 7–10, 69–71.
18. Jakle and Sculle, *Gas Station,* 147–48.
19. Leon and Ann Little, interview by author, Hinton, Okla., March 8, 1982.
20. Jessie Hudson, interview by author and Kelly, Lebanon, Mo., March 20, 1981; Littles, interview; Whiting, interview.
21. Warren Belasco, *Americans on the Road,* 3–5, 152.
22. John Jakle, Keith Sculle, and Jefferson Rogers, *Motel,* 38; "Tourist Cabins," *Popular Mechanics* 64, July 1935, 151–53.
23. Noble, *Houses,* 123–24; McAlester and McAlester, *Field Guide,* 100.
24. Gowans, *Comfortable House,* 22–25.
25. Noble, *Houses,* 82; McAlester and McAlester, *Field Guide,* 417; Gowans, *Comfortable House,* 118.
26. Joy Spears Fischel, interview by author and Kelly, Marshfield, Mo., March 15, 1981.
27. Works Progress Administration, *New Mexico,* 193–94.
28. Gowans, *Comfortable House,* 116.
29. Virginia Grattan, *Mary Colter,* 58–67; Matilda McQuaid with Karen Bartlett, "Building an Image of the Southwest," in Marta Weigle and Barbara Babcock, eds., *Great Southwest,* 25.
30. Sue Flanagan, Alamo, www.drtl.org/webchrol.html.
31. Jakle, Sculle, and Rogers, *Motel,* 102–5.
32. Jakle, Sculle, and Rogers, *Motel,* 93–95.
33. Mickey Stroud, telephone interview by author, May 8, 1998; Keith Sculle, letters to author, February 6 and 7, 1998.
34. G. Waide Sibley, telephone interview by author, February 19, 1998; Michael Witzel, *Route 66 Remembered,* 152; William Yost, telephone interview by author, July 25, 1998.
35. Scott and Kelly, *Route 66,* 57; Amy Thompson, interview by author and Kelly, Clementine, Mo., March 18, 1981; Jiggs Miller, interview by author and Kelly, Devils Elbow, Mo., March 18, 1981; Glenn Johnson, interview by author and Kelly, Kingman, Ariz., June 20, 1982; Buster Burris, interview by author and Kelly, Amboy, Calif., June 21, 1982.
36. McAlester and McAlester, *Field Guide,* 130; John Burchard and Albert Bush-Brown, *Architecture of America,* 58.
37. Liebs, *Main Street,* 181–84.
38. Hudson, interview.
39. Burris, interview.
40. Belasco, *Americans on the Road,* 52; Duncan Hines, *Adventures* (1938).
41. Tobe Turpin, interview by author and Kelly, Gallup, N.Mex., March 2, 1982.
42. Belasco, *Americans on the Road,* 167.
43. Scott and Kelly, *Route 66,* 62.
44. Wallace and Mary Gunn, interview by author and Kelly, New Laguna, N.Mex., March 1, 1982.
45. Elizabeth Threatt, interview by author, Luther, Okla., March 10, 1982.
46. Michael Witzel, *American Drive-in,* 161; Philip Langdon, *Orange Roofs,* 67.
47. Alan Hess, *Googie,* 97–107; Witzel, *American Drive-in,* 90.
48. "William C. Wyatt," *St. Louis Post-Dispatch,* May 3, 1995.
49. Liebs, *Main Street,* 212–14; Hess, *Googie,* 97–107.
50. Langdon, *Orange Roofs,* 86–87.
51. Marian Clark, *Route 66 Cookbook,* 17, 158; Ruby Denton, interview by author, Groom, Tex., August 19, 1997.

Illinois

1. David Keene, *Illinois Historic Route 66,* B-19.
2. Dorothy Seratt, telephone interview by author, May 12, 1998; Harry Schlechte, telephone interview by author, May 14, 1998; Scott and Kelly, *Route 66,* 25.
3. Works Progress Administration, *Illinois,* 223; Kathleen Howard and Diana Pardue, *Inventing the Southwest,* ix.
4. Bob Henry, telephone interview by author, May 11, 1998; Hess, *Googie,* 106.
5. Scott and Kelly, *Route 66,* 38–39; Peter Rossi, interview by author and Kelly, Braidwood, Ill., July 15, 1983.
6. Burt Parkinson, telephone interview by author, February 12, 1996.
7. Ibid.
8. Seratt, interview.
9. Marian Rodino, interview by author and Kelly, Pontiac, Ill., July 16, 1983; Michael Wallis, *Route 66,* 37.
10. Liebs, *Main Street,* 208.
11. Witzel, *American Drive-in,* 161; Langdon, *Orange Roofs,* 67; Scott and Kelly, *Route 66,* 64.
12. Scott and Kelly, *Route 66,* 40–42; Clark, *Route 66 Cookbook,* 17.
13. Clark, *Route 66 Cookbook,* 17; Venturi, Scott-Brown, and Izenour, *Learning from Las Vegas,* 13.
14. Clark, *Route 66 Cookbook,* 18.
15. Fenton Craner, interview by author, Elkhart, Ill., August 1979; Fenton Craner, interview by author and Kelly, Elkhart, Ill., July 16, 1983.
16. Silver Suarez, telephone interview by author, May 13, 1998; *Springfield (Ill.) City Directory, 1934, 1940–66, 1986; Illinois Times,* February 17, 1978; Keith Sculle, "Diners," *Historic Illinois,* April 1983, 3.
17. Raymond Joseph McAnarney, telephone interview by author, November 19, 1997; E. Paul McAnarney, telephone interview by author, November 19, 1997; Howard McAnarney, telephone interview by author, November 18, 1997; Clark, *Route 66 Cookbook,* 21.
18. Nick Adam, interview by author and Kelly, Litchfiled, Ill., July 1979; Susan Croce Kelly, "There Are No More Kicks," *Midwest Motorist 51,* no. 3 (January-February 1980), 19; Clark, *Route 66 Cookbook,* 23.
19. Kelly, "There Are No More Kicks," 19.
20. Scott and Kelly, *Route 66,* 179–81; John McGuire, "One for the Road," *POSTnet,* 4.
21. Bud Tarro, interview by author, Benld, Ill., May 15, 1998; *Spotlighting the Coliseum Ballroom.*
22. Scott and Kelly, *Route 66,* 77, 168; Bill Roseman, interview by author and Kelly, St. Louis, Mo., February 1, 1983; American Automobile Association, *What to See, . . .: 1943 Guide to Illinois, . . .,* 25.
23. Harry Schlechte, telephone interview by author, May 14, 1998; Russell Soulsby, telephone interview by author, May 14, 1998.
24. Rickey Miller, *Kitchen Memories,* 15; "Albert Cassens," www.edwpub.com/route66/cassens.html.
25. Chester Wyers, interview by author, Mitchell, Ill., June 1979; Bud Eberhardt, telephone interview by author, May 27, 1998.
26. *St. Louis Globe-Democrat,* February 8 and 15, 1927, March 2, 1927, July 20, 1929, March 20, 1932; John R. Scott, Jr., telephone interview by author, June 1980; Tom Teague, *Searching for 66,* 33.

St. Louis

1. Missouri State Highway Commission, *Map of Missouri,* January 1, 1936; *St. Louis City Directory, 1930,* 1931.
2. Liebs, *Main Street,* 206–7; Langdon, *Orange Roofs,* 33.
3. Teague, *Searching for 66,* 33–37.
4. Office of Historic Preservation, Historic Inventory, 1.
5. Susan Croce Kelly, "From Campgrounds to Cottages," *Midwest Motorist 54,* no. 4 (March-April 1983), 8.
6. Gowans, *Comfortable House,* 22–23; C. H. Curtis, *Missouri U.S. 66,* 35.
7. Liebs, *Main Street,* 153–59; Ronald Krueger, telephone interview by author, January 21, 1994.
8. George Guernsey, interview by author and Kelly, St. Louis, Mo., July 1982.
9. Ginger Smith Gallagher, telephone interview by author, March 19, 1998; Clark, *Route 66 Cookbook,* 26.
10. Curtis, *Missouri U.S. 66,* 62; Works Progress Administration, *Missouri,* 406; Architectural/Historic Inventory Survey Form, 2.
11. Steve Eckelkamp, telephone interview by author, July 14, 1995; Susan Croce Kelly, "Haven of the Road," *St. Louis Post-Dispatch,* September 30, 1979, 9.
12. Curtis, *Missouri U.S. 66,* 68.
13. Ibid., 66–67.

Missouri

1. Larry Baggett, interview by author, Arlington, Mo., August 15, 1997.
2. Lynn Morrow and David Quick, "Slab Rock Dwelling," *Pioneer America Society Transactions* 12 (1990), 35–43; Linda Becker and Cydney Millstein, *Ozark Native Rock Masonry Survey,* 29–33; Jerry Berti, telephone interview by author, October 7, 1997.
3. Works Progress Administration, *Missouri,* 15, 408–409.
4. Scott and Kelly, *Route 66,* 165–67; Al Foster, telephone interview by author, August 1980; sign at St. Clair, Mo.
5. Berti, interview.
6. William Yost, interview; Chris Yost, telephone interview by author, July 21, 1998; Fred Snell, Jr., telephone interview by author, July 21, 1998.
7. Curtis, *Missouri U.S. 66,* 87; George McCue, *Guide to Architecture,* 101; Pauline Roberts Armstrong, interview by author, Cuba, Mo., August 6, 1997; Marie Friesenhan Davis, telephone interview by author, August 7, 1997; Frank Jansen, telephone interview by author, August 8, 1997; Robert Helmich, telephone interview by author, September 15, 1997.
8. Gail Lierman, telephone interview by author, February 12, 1998; Lee Lutz, telephone interview by author, February 11, 1998; Curtis, *Missouri U.S. 66,* 110.

9. Lynna Aaron and Bill Aaron, interview by author and Kelly, Rolla, Mo., September 18, 1980.

10. Curtis, *Missouri U.S. 66,* 14; Bill Aaron, telephone interview by author, August 3, 1999; Skip Curtis, telephone interview by author, August 3, 1999.

11. Jessie Hudson, interview by author and Kelly, Lebanon, Mo., March 20, 1981; Curtis, *Missouri U.S. 66,* 117, 118; George Branson, "Munger-Moss Sandwich Shop," *Show Me Route 66* 5, no. 2 (November 1993) n.p.; Nancy Smith [psued.], interview by author, March 1981.

12. Genevieve Jones, telephone interview by author, August 28, 1997.

13. Curtis, *Missouri U.S. 66,* 143.

14. Ibid., 149.

15. Fischel, interview.

16. Scott and Kelly, *Route 66,* 150–53; Hudson, interview; Jessie Hudson, telephone interview by author, March 1994.

17. William Otto August Lenz, interview by author, Lebanon, Mo., August 10, 1979; Curtis, *Missouri U.S. 66,* 153.

18. Frank Campbell, interview by author and Kelly, Springfield, Mo., March 23, 1981.

19. Curtis, *Missouri U.S. 66,* 164.

20. John Margolies, *End of the Road,* 17; Jakle and Sculle, *Gas Station,* 39–40.

21. Lowell Wilson, telephone interview by author, September 2, 1997; Curtis, *Missouri U.S. 66,* 201.

22. Mary Brightwell, telephone interview by author, August 27, 1997; Hillary Brightwell, telephone interview by author, August 29, 1997; Curtis, *Missouri U.S. 66,* 175–76.

23. Sheldon "Red" Chaney, interview by author and Kelly, Springfield, Mo., March 21, 1981.

24. Kenneth and Cleo Goodman, interview by author and Kelly, Halltown, Mo., March 22, 1981; Ina Rainey, interview by author, Springfield, Mo., August 16, 1997.

25. Goodmans, interview.

26. Curtis, *Missouri U.S. 66,* 212.

27. Rachel Asplin, interview by author and Kelly, Carthage, Mo., March 22, 1981; Curtis, *Missouri U.S. 66,* 215.

28. John Dobrauc, interview by author and Kelly, Joplin, Mo., March 23, 1981; Witzel, *Route 66 Remembered,* 151; Curtis, *Missouri U.S. 66,* 223; AAA, *What to See, . . .: 1943 Guide to Illinois . . .,* 70; *Joplin (Mo.) City Directory, 1942.*

Kansas and Oklahoma

1. Scott and Kelly, *Route 66,* 59.

2. Noble, *Houses,* 123.

3. Works Progress Administration, *Oklahoma,* 219.

4. Clark, *Route 66 Cookbook,* 61, 64.

5. Duncan Hines, *Lodging* (1956), 182.

6. LaVerne Harris, interview by author, Miami, Okla., August 1979.

7. "Coleman Theatre Beautiful," www.coleman.miami.ok.us/.

8. Alleene Kay, interview by author, Afton, Okla., March 5, 1982; Scott and Kelly, *Route 66,* 154.

9. Maryjo Meacham, ed., *Route 66,* 9–12.

10. Publicity mailer, Will Rogers Hotel, Claremore, Okla.

11. Sibley, interview; G. Waide Sibley, letter to author, February 23, 1998; Jakle, Sculle, and Rogers, *Motel,* 92–97; Sculle, letter, January 30, 1998; Keith Sculle, telephone interview by author, March 5, 1998.

12. Glenal Davis Hunt and Hugh Davis, interview by author, Catoosa, Okla., October 6, 1981.

13. Hunt and Davis, interview; Zelda and Hugh Davis, interview by author and Kelly, Catoosa, Okla., August 14, 1981.

14. Scott and Kelly, *Route 66,* 37-38; Clark, *Route 66 Cookbook,* 73-74; Ruth Sigler Avery, telephone interview by author, August 16, 1999.

15. Hope Colpitts Timmons, telephone interview by author, May 11, 1998; Theresa Smith, telephone interview by author, May 11, 1998; Jakle, Sculle, and Rogers, *Motel,* 38; "Tourist Cabins," 151–53; Charles Lee Cook, telephone interview by author, June 18, 1998.

16. *Tulsa (Okla.) City Directory, 1935–60.*

17. Stroud, interview; Jakle, Sculle, and Rogers, *Motel,* 93–98; Dorothy Harrison, interview by author and Kelly, Tulsa, Okla., August 14, 1981.

18. Stroud, interview.

19. *Tulsa (Okla.) City Directory 1958;* Mary Ann Anders, ed., *Route 66,* 18.

20. WPA, *Oklahoma,* 9; Clark, *Route 66 Cookbook,* 84; Emmie Parrick, "History of Rock Cafe," 1.

21. McAlester and McAlester, *Field Guide,* 100; Jack Rittenhouse, *Guide Book,* 50; Hines, *Lodging* (1946), 206; Jim Crouch, interview by author, Chandler, Okla., August 17, 1997.

22. Clark, *Route 66 Cookbook,* 83; Hines, *Adventures* (1951), 258.

23. Elizabeth Threatt, interview by author, Luther, Okla., March 9, 1982; Edna Prokupt, interview by author and Kelly, Luther, Okla., August 15, 1981; Anders, *Route 66,* 56; Meacham, *Route 66,* 11–12.

24. Prokupt, interview; Anders, *Route 66,* 57.

25. Grady Jones, interview by author and Kelly, Arcadia, Okla., August 13, 1981; Kent Ruth, *Oklahoma Travel,* 38; Wallis, *Route 66,* 113.

26. Christopher Caporal, telephone interview by author, July 29, 1998; Reyner Banham, *Concrete Atlantis,* 139–42.

27. Gladys Cutberth, interview by author and Kelly, Clinton, Olka., August 10, 1981; Hines, *Lodging* (1938), 150, (1940), 255, (1946), 208, (1956), 182; American Automobile Association, *What to See, . . .: 1943 Guide to Arkansas, . . .,* 41; Tandy Smoot, interview by author, Amarillo, Tex., June 1, 1982.

28. Atmer Taylor, interview by author and Kelly, El Reno, Olka., August 13, 1981.

29. Steinbeck, *Grapes of Wrath,* 166–67.

30. Ross H. Davis, telephone interview by author, September 10, 1997.

31. Ann Little, telephone interview by author, August 18, 1999; U.S. Geological Survey (1939), Fort Reno and Geary.

32. Littles, interview; Bob Little, telephone interview by author, September 7, 1999.

33. Ibid.

34. Elnora Shanklin, telephone interview by author, May 20, 1998; Warren Cusick, telephone interview by author, May 20, 1998; Ann Little, telephone interview by author, May 21, 1998.

35. Lucille Hamons, interview by author and Kelly, Hydro, Okla.,

August 12, 1981; Scott and Kelly, *Route 66,* 183.

36. Juanita Snow, interview by author and Kelly, Weatherford, Okla., August 12, 1981.
37. Cutberth, interview; Charles Engleman, telephone interview by author, June 15, 1998.
38. Gladys Glancy Sweeny, telephone interview by author, June 17, 1998; Clark, *Route 66 Cookbook,* 103; Friends of Oklahoma Route 66 brochure.
39. Joe Morgan, telephone interview by author, October 15, 1997; John R. Hill, telephone interview by author, October 15, 1997; Friends of Oklahoma Route 66 brochure.
40. "Andy" Andrewkowski, telephone interview by author, September 12, 1997; AAA, *What to See, . . .: 1943 Guide to Arkansas, . . .,* 37.
41. Wanda Queenan, interview by the author, Elk City, Okla., August 20, 1997.
42. Hines, *Lodging* (1956), 183.

Texas

1. Robert Lee, interview by author, Oklahoma City, Okla., June 10, 1982.
2. James Ray Tindall, telephone interview by author, July 13, 1998; Works Progress Administration, *Texas,* 20, 490.
3. R. C. Lewis, interview by author, Shamrock, Tex., October 8, 1981.
4. Mamie Tindall, interview by author, Shamrock, Tex., October 8, 1981; James Ray Tindall, interview.
5. Bebe Nunn, interview by author and Kelly, Shamrock, Tex., August 11, 1981; Scott and Kelly, *Route 66,* 65; Clark, *Route 66 Cookbook,* 108–13.
6. James Ray Tindall, interview; Lewis, interview.
7. Whiting, interview.
8. Ray Barker, telephone interview by author, September 18, 1997.
9. Jesse Smith, interview by author and Kelly, McLean, Tex., October 9, 1981; R. J. Turner, telephone interview by author, August 12, 1999; Nathaniel Bybee, telephone interview by author, August 13, 1999.
10. Scott and Kelly, *Route 66,* 111; Adie Alred, interview by author, Alanreed, Tex., October 9, 1981.
11. Historical sign on the "66" Super Service Station, 1997.
12. Pete Ford, telephone interview by author, September 15, 1997.
13. Rittenhouse, *Guide Book,* 65.
14. Marita Bumpers and Maria Taylor, interview by author and Kelly, Shamrock, Tex., October 8, 1981; Scott and Kelly, *Route 66,* 29; Pauline Bauer, interview by author, Albuquerque, N.Mex., March 5, 1982; Ray Franks and Jay Ketelle, *Amarillo,* item 156; Lee, interview.
15. *Amarillo City Directory, 1940.*
16. Albert Urqhart, telephone interview by author, September 16, 1997; Noble, *Houses,* 86; McAlester and McAlester, *Field Guide,* 130.
17. Rittenhouse, *Guide Book,* 66; Ethel Carpenter, interview by author and Kelly, Amarillo, Tex., October 10, 1981.
18. Franks and Ketelle, *Amarillo,* item 152.
19. Auline Rice, telephone interview by author, October 16, 1995;

Clark, *Route 66 Cookbook,* 117; Hines, *Adventures* (1956), 261.
20. Tommy Loveless, telephone interview by author, October 18, 1995.
21. Loveless, interview; Clark, *Route 66 Cookbook,* 127.
22. Vieyra, "*Fill'er Up,*" 69–71; Scott and Kelly, *Route 66,* 67; Rittenhouse, *Guide Book,* 69.

New Mexico

1. Whiting, interview; Automobile Blue Book, *Blue Book,* 845, 854, 906; David Kammer, *Historical and Architectural Resources,* 8; M. F. Hobbs, *Grade and Surface Guide,* 14.
2. Jill Schneider, *Route 66,* 204–6.
3. WPA, *New Mexico,* 149–53.
4. Gowans, *Comfortable House,* 118–19.
5. Charles Ramsey and Harold Sleeper, *Architectural Graphic Standards,* 33; Robert Packard, *Ramsey and Sleeper,* 246–47; "Pressing Bricks into Shape," www2.pok.ibm.com/library/i78.htm; "Drying Adobe Bricks," www2.pok.ibm.com/library/i77htm; Joseph M. Smith, telephone interview by author, January 26, 1998.
6. Bob Burnham, interview by author, Tucumcari, N.Mex., June 12, 1982.
7. Hines, *Lodging* (1946), 182.
8. Marjorie Wegner, telephone interview by author, January 13, 1998; Burnham, interview; Hines, *Lodging* (1946), 182.
9. Lillian Redman, interview by author, Tucumcari, N.Mex., August 19, 1997.
10. Newt Sanchez, interview by author, Santa Rosa, N.Mex., December 19, 1997; Joseph M. Smith, telephone interview by author, January 9, 1998.
11. Floyd Shaw, interview by author, Santa Rosa, N.Mex., April 2, 1985; Wallis, *Route 66,* 155–57; Michael Sanson and Mary Pritchard, "Hard Times," *Restaurant Hospitality* 76, no. 10 (October 1992), 74–76.
12. Jakle and Sculle, *Gas Station,* 65–66; Joseph M. Smith, interview by author and Kelly, Albuquerque, N.Mex., March 5, 1982; Smith, interview, January 9, 1998.
13. Smith, interview, January 9, 1998; Roy Cline, Jr., interview by author and Kelly, Albuquerque, N.Mex., March 5, 1982; Scott and Kelly, *Route 66,* 67–69.
14. Schneider, *Route 66,* 159; Wallis, *Route 66,* 160.
15. Schneider, *Route 66,* 143.
16. Bauer, interview; Rittenhouse, *Guide Book,* 78.
17. Hines, *Lodging* (1938), 173; Rittenhouse, *Guide Book,* 79; Wallis, *Route 66,* 165.
18. Carla Breeze, *Pueblo Deco,* 8–12; Pauline Bauer, telephone interview by author, April 14, 1998.
19. WPA, *New Mexico,* 194; Gowans, *Styles and Types,* 23–24; Bauer, interview, April 14, 1998.
20. Pauline Bauer, telephone interview by author, February 2, 1998.
21. Gunns, interview; Hobbs, *Grade and Surface Guide,* 13.
22. Gunns, interview; Gottlieb, interview; Hobbs, *Grade and Surface Guide,* 13.
23. Gunns, interview.
24. Gunderson, interview, March 2, 1982.

25. Yee Woo, interview by author, Grants, N.Mex., December 22, 1997; Paul L. Milan, interview by author, Grants, N.Mex., December 22, 1997; Marvel Prestridge, interview by author and Kelly, Grants, N.Mex., March 2, 1982; Wallis, *Route 66,* 172.

26. Prestridge, interview; Nellie Cattaneo, telephone interview by author, January 26, 1998; John and Jacqueline Cattaneo, telephone interview by author, January 26, 1998.

27. Clark, *Route 66 Cookbook,* 158; Prestridge, interview.

28. Milan, interview; Prestridge, interview.

29. Fred Bay, telephone interview by author, June, 1994; "Banker Says City Is Destined to Be a Manufacturing Center," *Denver Post,* July 8, 1937; Gunderson, interview, January 19, 1998; Jakle and Sculle, *Gas Station,* 66.

30. David South, interview by author, Prewitt, N.Mex., December 21, 1997; "Try Waldvogel Brothers, Inc.," *New Yorker,* March 16, 1946, 21; "Quonset Huts," *Business Week,* October 6, 1945, 19; Lucy Greenbaum, "Be It Ever So Humble," *New York Times Magazine,* May 5, 1946, 31.

31. Jakle and Sculle, *Gas Station,* 132–33; Gunderson, interview, January 19, 1998; Roy Herman, interview by author, Thoreau, N.Mex., December 21, 1997.

32. Schneider, *Route 66,* 110–11.

33. Turpin, interview; WPA, *New Mexico,* 323.

34. Turpin, interview; Albertine and Rudy Menini, interview by author and Kelly, Gallup, N.Mex., June 13, 1982.

35. Olga Novak Baird, telephone interview by author, January 29, 1998; Stephena Milosovich Radosovich, telephone interview by author, January 30, 1998.

36. Nellie Cattaneo, interview; Meninis, interview; Schneider, *Route 66,* 121.

37. Turpin, interview; Marge Richardson, interview by author and Kelly, Gallup, N.Mex., March 3, 1982.

Arizona

1. Works Progress Administration, *Arizona,* 105; Automobile Blue Book, *Blue Book,* 856; Glenn Johnson, telephone interview by author, July 24, 1998.

2. National Park Service, "Traveling among Navajos," www.nps.gov/hutr/travel.htm; "Navajo Hogans," www.uwec.edu/Academic/Geography/Ivogeler/w188/il4.htm; Leroy Atkinson, interview by author and Kelly, Gallup, N.Mex., March 3, 1982; Velma Christiansen, interview by author and Kelly, Gallup, N.Mex., March 3, 1982.

3. Garnet Franklin, telephone interview by author, January 12, 1998; WPA, *Arizona,* 313.

4. Clifton Lewis, interview by author and Kelly, Holbrook, N.Mex., June 13, 1982; Keith Sculle, "Frank Redford's Wigwam Village," *Roadside America,* 125–35; *Constructing a Tepee,* 3, org/stl/others/test04.html; Witzel, *Route 66 Remembered,* 126–27; Dan Harlow, "Sleeping in a Wigwam," *Route 66 West,* www.kaiwan.com/`wem/r66/wtr96/051landmk.hmtl; Margolies, *End of the Road,* 19.

5. Scott and Kelly, *Route 66,* 52–54; Jack and Marie Fuss, interview by author and Kelly, Flagstaff, Ariz., June 17, 1982; Phil Blansett, interview by author and Kelly, Joseph City, Ariz., June 15, 1982.

6. Blansett, interview; WPA, *Arizona,* 314, 501.

7. Blansett, interview; Phil Blansett, interview by author, Joseph City, Ariz., December 24, 1997.

8. Blansett, interview, June 15, 1982.

9. James L. Taylor, telephone interview by author, December 26, 1997; Blansett, interview, June 15, 1982; Scott and Kelly, *Route 66,* 172.

10. Rittenhouse, *Guide Book,* 98; WPA, *Arizona,* 501; Frank McNitt, *Indian Traders,* 205, 275–76.

11. Grattan, *Mary Colter,* 58–67; Marta Weigle, "'Insisted on Authenticity,'" in Weigle and Babcock, eds., *Great Southwest,* 47–49; Gowans, *Styles and Types,* 238; Hines, *Lodging* (1938), 22; Allan Affeldt, interview by author, Winslow, Ariz., July 16, 1998.

12. Norma Leonard, telephone interview by author, April 15, 1998.

13. Arizona Historic Property Inventory, Flagstaff, Jesus Garcia's Tourist Home, June 1992.

14. Dorothy Robertson, telephone interview by author, April 22, 1998; Hines, *Lodging* (1938), 19; Arizona Historic Property Inventory, Flagstaff, Du Beau Motor Inn, June 1992.

15. Fred Nackard, interview by author and Kelly, Phoenix, Ariz., June 17, 1982; Arizona Historic Property Inventory, Flagstaff, Nackard's Hotel and Nackard's Downtowner, June 1992.

16. Hilario Esparza, Sr., telephone interview by author, February 10, 1998; Arizona Historic Property Inventory, Flagstaff, Sierra Vista Motel, June 1992.

17. Albert Wong, interview by author and Kelly, Flagstaff, Ariz., June 17, 1982.

18. Clark, *Route 66 Cookbook,* 185–86; Hines, *Adventures* (1951), 31.

19. George Bannister, telephone interview by author, February 17, 1998.

20. Arizona Historic Property Inventory, Ash Fork, Arizona Cafe and Green Door Bar, September 24, 1995.

21. Angel Delgadillo, telephone interview by author, February 18, 1998; Hobbs, *Grade and Surface Guide,* 9.

22. Juan Delgadillo, interview by author and Kelly, Seligman, Ariz., June 19, 1982.

23. Banham, *Concrete Atlantis,* 56–107; John Osterman, Jr., telephone interview by author, March 2, 1998; Beatrice Boyd, interview by author, Peach Springs, Ariz., April 26, 1982; Hobbs, *Grade and Surface Guide,* 8.

24. Boyd, interview; Beatrice Boyd, interview by author and Kelly, Peach Springs, Ariz., June 20, 1982.

25. Sharlynn Robinson, telephone interview by author, February 23, 1998.

26. Material from the Mohave Museum Library, Kingman, Ariz.; Hobbs, *Grade and Surface Guide,* 8.

27. Hines, *Adventures* (1938), 20; *Mohave County (Ariz.) Miner,* December 22, 1939; "Tourist Cabins," *Popular Mechanics* 64, July 1935, 151–53.

28. Glenn Johnson, telephone interview by the author, April 14, 1998; "Auto Courts," *Mohave County (Ariz.) Miner,* December 22, 1939.

29. Bill Nugent, telephone interview by author, June 3, 1998; Lin Miller Casey, telephone interview by author, June 2, 1998; Johnson, interview, April 14, 1998; Stanley Paher, *Las Vegas,* 105.

30. Rittenhouse, *Guide Book,* 110; Johnson, interview, June 20,

1982; Roger Ueda and Michael Goodwin, telephone interview by author, July 27, 1998.

California

1. Steinbeck, *Grapes of Wrath,* 242.
2. Shirley Johnson, telephone interview by author, April 27, 1998; Maggie McShan, telephone interview by author, April 24, 1998; Noble, *Houses,* 86; Gowans, *Comfortable House,* 199; McAlester and McAlester, *Field Guide,* 130, 454; Hines, *Lodging* (1940), 46.
3. Maggie McShan, interview by author, Needles, Calif., March 26, 1998; McShan, telephone interview, April 24, 1998; Carolyn Chambless, telephone interview by author, April 20, 1998; Burris, interview; David Darlington, *Mojave,* 152–54.
4. Chambless, interview; McShan, telephone interview, April 24, 1992.
5. Scott and Kelly, *Route 66,* 141, 179; Burris, interview.
6. Hobbs, *Grade and Surface Guide,* 5; Darlington, *Mojave,* 196–202; Phyliss Couch, "Ludlow," in Patricia Keeling, ed., *Once upon a Desert,* 147.
7. Couch, "Ludlow," 144–47, 174, 190; Hobbs, *Grade and Surface Guide,* 5; Delmer Ross, "Ma Preston," in Dennis Casebier, *Guide to East Mojave,* 113.
8. Beryl Bell, interview by author, Daggett, Calif., April 3, 1998; Margaret Kelley, telephone interview by author, April 16, 1998; Rittenhouse, *Guide Book,* 118; Clark, *Route 66 Cookbook,* 203; Hobbs, *Grade and Surface Guide,* 5.
9. Bill and Edith Butler, interview by author and Kelly, Barstow, Calif., June 20, 1982; Cliff Walker, telephone interview by author, January 12, 1996.
10. Scott and Kelly, *Route 66,* 143; Hines, *Lodging* (1956), 18; Butlers, interview; Hobbs, *Grade and Surface Guide,* 5.
11. J. F. Belsher, Jr., interview by author and Kelly, Barstow, Calif., June 21, 1982.
12. Walker, interview.
13. "Conversation with Roy Rogers," *Route 66 West,* www.kaiwan.com/`wem/r66west/fall96/royint.html; Works Progress Administration, *California,* 613.
14. WPA, *California,* 614; Reyner Banham, *Los Angeles,* 61.
15. May, *Western Ranch Houses,* 10; Gowans, *Comfortable House,* 111–12; Hines, *Lodging* (1938), 42, (1940), 52.
16. Irene Montano, telephone interview by author, April 21, 1998; Clark, *Route 66 Cookbook,* 206; Hines, *Adventures* (1951), 53.
17. Hess, *Googie,* 97–107; Witzel, *American Drive-in,* 161.
18. Jakle and Sculle, *Gas Station,* 158.
19. Duane Meyer, interview by author and Kelly, Rancho Cucamonga, June 24, 1982; Jakle and Sculle, *Gas Station,* 158.

20. *Upland (Calif.) City Directory, 1934, 1945;* Building permits, Building Department, Upland, Calif.; McAlester and McAlester, *Field Guide,* 454.
21. Building permits for Shamrock Motel, Building Department, Glendora, Calif.
22. Pete Thacher, interview by author, Azusa, Calif., March 28, 1998.
23. Witzel, *American Drive-in,* 161; Langdon, *Orange Roofs,* 67.
24. Susie Tomasian, interview by author and Kelly, Duarte, Calif., June 22, 1982; Wallis, *Route 66,* 227.
25. Building permits for Evergreen Rest Home and Motor Hotel, Community Development Office, Duarte, Calif.
26. David Gebhart, *Robert Stacy-Judd,* 37–60; Gowans, *Styles and Types,* 268n; Clark, *Route 66 Cookbook,* 214.
27. Hines, *Lodging* (1956), 30.
28. Jack and Louella Brotherton, interview by author and Kelly, Pasadena, Calif., June 24, 1982; McAlester and McAlester, *Field Guide,* 454.
29. Tom Snyder, *Route 66,* 113.
30. Jakle and Sculle, *Gas Station,* 138.
31. Jay Coffin, telephone interview by author, April 7, 1998; Richard Wurman, *LA/Access,* 37; Jim Heimann and Rip Georges, *California Crazy,* 23.
32. WPA, *California,* 195–97; Kari Leigh, "Tribute to Douglas Fairbanks, Sr.," *Hollywood Web of Fame,* www.web-star.com/hollywood/douglasfairbanks.html; Diane MacIntyre, "Cecil B. DeMille," *Silents Majority,* www.mdle.com/ClassicFilms/BTC/direct22.htm.
33. WPA, California, 417.
34. Scott and Kelly, *Route 66,* 168; Clark, *Route 66 Cookbook,* 224.
35. Snyder, *Route 66,* 115; Wurman, *LA/Access,* 49; "Santa Monica Pier," www.naid.sppsr.ucla.edu/venice/articles/santamonicapier.htm.

The Ultimate Road Trip

1. Steinbeck, *Grapes of Wrath,* 127–28.
2. Ibid., 128.
3. Scott and Kelly, *Route 66;* Wallis, *Route 66;* Teague, *Searching for 66;* Jill Schneider, *Route 66;* Witzel, *Route 66 Remembered.*
4. "Lucille's Route 66," www.geocities.com/`vegas-okie/index.html.
5. Rittenhouse, *Guide Book;* Snyder, *Route 66.*
6. "Two Frenchmen Bicycling," *St. Louis Post-Dispatch,* June 19, 1995; "New Oklahoma Museum," *Belleville (Ill.) News-Democrat,* September 24, 1995.
7. Advertisement, *Parade Magazine,* April 9, 1995.

Bibliography

Books

American Automobile Association. *What to See, Where to Stop: 1943 Guide to Arkansas, Louisiana, Oklahoma, Texas, Including Memphis, Tennessee.* Washington, D.C.: American Automobile Association, 1943.

———. *What to See, Where to Stay: 1943 Guide to Illinois, Iowa, Kansas, Missouri and Nebraska.* Washington, D.C.: American Automobile Association, 1943.

Anderson, Warren H. *Vanishing Roadside America.* Tucson: Unversity of Arizona Press, 1981.

Automobile Blue Book, Inc. *Automobile Blue Book, 1918.* Vol. 7. Chicago: Automobile Blue Book, Inc.

Banham, P. Reyner. *Concrete Atlantis.* Cambridge, Mass.: MIT Press, 1989.

———. *Los Angeles: The Architecture of Four Ecologies.* New York: Harper & Row, 1971.

———. *Scenes in America Deserta.* Cambridge, Mass.: MIT Press, 1982.

Belasco, Warren James. *Americans on the Road, 1910–1945.* Cambridge, Mass.: MIT Press, 1979.

Blake, Peter. *God's Own Junkyard: The Planned Deterioration of America's Landscape.* New York: Holt, Rinehart and Winston, 1964.

Breeze, Carla. *Pueblo Deco.* New York: Rizzoli International, 1990.

Burchard, John, and Albert Bush-Brown. *The Architecture of America, a Social and Cultural History.* Boston: Little, Brown, 1961.

Bush, Donald J. *The Streamlined Decade.* New York: George Braziller, 1975.

Casebier, Dennis G., and the Friends of the Mojave Road. *Guide to the East Mojave Heritage Trail: Rocky Ridge to Fenner.* Norco, Calif.: Tales of the Mojave Road Publishing Company, 1989.

Clark, Marian. *The Route 66 Cookbook.* Tulsa, Okla.: Council Oaks Books, 1993.

Condit, Carl. *American Building Art: The Nineteenth Century.* New York: Oxford Univeristy Press, 1960.

Curtis, C. H. *The Missouri U.S. 66 Tour Book.* Lake St. Louis: Curtis Enterprises, 1994.

Darlington, David. *The Mojave: A Portrait of the Definitive American Desert.* New York: Holt, 1996.

Franks, Ray, and Jay Ketelle. *Amarillo, Texas, II: A Picture Postcard History.* Amarillo: Ray Franks Publishing Ranch, 1987.

Gebhart, David. *Robert Stacy-Judd.* Santa Barbara, Calif.: Capra Press, 1993.

Gowans, Alan. *The Comfortable House: North American Suburban Architecture, 1890–1930.* Cambridge, Mass.: MIT Press, 1986.

———. *Styles and Types of North American Architecture: Social Function and Cultural Expression.* New York: Icon Editions, Harper-Collins, 1992.

Grattan, Virginia L. *Mary Colter: Builder upon Red Earth.* Flagstaff, Ariz.: Northland Press, 1980.

Gutman, Richard J. S. *American Diner, Then and Now.* New York: Harper Perennial, 1993.

Heimann, Jim, and Rip Georges. *California Crazy: Roadside Vernacular Architecture.* Introduction by David Gebhard. San Francisco: Chronicle Books, 1980.

Henderson, James David. *Meals by Fred Harvey: A Phenomenon of the American West.* Fort Worth, Tex.: Texas Christian University Press, 1969.

Hess, Alan. *Googie: Fifties Coffee Shop Architecture.* San Francisco: Chronicle Books, 1985.

Hines, Duncan. *Adventures in Good Eating: A Directory of Good Eating Places along the Highways and in Villages and Cities of America.* Chicago: Adventures in Good Eating, 1938, 1946, 1951, 1954, 1956.

———. *Lodging for a Night: A Directory of Hotels, Motels, Motor Courts, and Inns.* Chicago: Adventures in Good Eating, 1938, 1940, 1946, 1956.

Hobbs, M. F. *Grade and Surface Guide.* Akron, Ohio: Mohawk Rubber Company, 1923.

Howard, Kathleen L., and Diana F. Pardue. *Inventing the Southwest: The Fred Harvey Company and Native American Art.* Phoenix, Ariz.: Heard Museum, 1996.

Jackson, John Brinkerhoff. *Discovering the Vernacular Landscape.* New Haven, Conn.: Yale University Press, 1984.

Jakle, John A. *The Tourist.* Lincoln: University of Nebraska Press, 1985.

Jakle, John A., and Keith A. Sculle. *The Gas Station in America.* Baltimore, Md.: Johns Hopkins University Press, 1994.

Jakle, John A., Keith A. Sculle, and Jefferson S. Rogers. *The Motel in America.* Baltimore, Md.: Johns Hopkins University Press, 1996.

Jencks, Charles. *The Language of Post-Modern Architecture.* New York: Rizzoli International, 1977.

Jennings, Jan. *Roadside America: The Automobile in Design and Culture.* Ames: Iowa State University Press, 1990.

Keeling, Patricia Jernigan, ed. *Once upon a Desert.* Barstow, Calif.: Mojave River Valley Museum Association, 1994.

Kouwenhoven, John. *Made in America.* New York: Doubleday, 1946.

Langdon, Philip. *Orange Roofs, Golden Arches: The Architecture of*

American Chain Restaurants. New York: Knopf, 1986.

Lange, Dorothea, and Paul Taylor. *An American Exodus: A Record of Human Erosion.* New York: Reynal & Hitchcock, 1939.

Liebs, Chester. *Main Street to Miracle Mile.* Boston: Little, Brown, 1985.

Lowe, Joseph. *The National Old Trails Highway: The Great Historic Highway of America.* Kansas City, Mo.: Old Trails Road Association, 1925.

Margolies, John. *The End of the Road: Vanishing Highway Architecture in America.* New York: Penguin Books, 1981.

———. *Home away from Home: Motels in America.* Boston: Bullfinch Press Book, Little, Brown, 1995.

———. *Pump and Circumstance.* Boston: Bullfinch Press Book, Little, Brown, 1993.

Marling, Karal Ann. *The Colossus of Roads: Myth and Symbol along the American Highway.* Minneapolis: University of Minnesota Press, 1984.

May, Cliff. *Western Ranch Houses.* Menlo Park, Calif.: Sunset Books, 1958.

McAlester, Virginia, and Lee McAlester. *A Field Guide to American Houses.* New York: Knopf, 1986.

McCue, George. *A Guide to the Architecture of St. Louis.* Columbia: University of Missouri Press, 1989.

McNitt, Frank. *The Indian Traders.* Norman: University of Oklahoma Press, 1962.

Miller, Rickey. *Kitchen Memories from My Childhood.* Hamel, Ill.: Miller's Three and Company, 1994.

Noble, Allen G. *Wood, Brick, and Stone: The North American Settlement Landscape. Volume 1, Houses.* Amherst: University of Massachusetts Press, 1984.

Packard, Robert T. *Ramsey and Sleeper Architectural Graphic Standards.* 7th ed. New York: Wiley, 1981.

Paher, Stanley H. *Las Vegas As It Began and As It Grew.* Las Vegas: Nevada Publications, 1971.

Patton, Phil. *Open Road: A Celebration of the American Highway.* New York: Simon and Schuster, 1986.

Ramsey, Charles George, and Harold Reeve Sleeper. *Architectural Graphic Standards.* 3d ed. New York: Wiley, 1941.

Rittenhouse, Jack D. *A Guide Book to Highway 66.* A facsimile of the 1946 first edition. Albuquerque: University of New Mexico Press, 1989.

Ruth, Kent. *Oklahoma Travel Handbook.* Norman: University of Oklahoma Press, 1977.

Schneider, Jill. *Route 66 across New Mexico: A Wanderer's Guide.* Albuquerque: University of New Mexico Presss, 1991.

Scott, Quinta, and Susan Croce Kelly. *Route 66: The Highway and Its People.* Norman: University of Oklahoma Press, 1988.

Snyder, Tom. *Route 66 Traveler's Guide and Roadside Companion.* New York: St. Martin's Griffen, 1990.

Steinbeck, John. *The Grapes of Wrath.* New York: Viking Press, 1939.

Teague, Tom. *Searching for 66.* Illustrated by Bob Waldmire. Springfield, Ill.: Samizdat Press, 1991.

Thomas, James H. *The Bunion Derby: Andy Payne and the Transcontinental Footrace.* Oklahoma City: Southwestern Heritage Books, 1980.

Venturi, Robert, Denise Scott-Brown, and Steven Izenour. *Learning from Las Vegas.* Rev. ed. Cambridge, Mass.: MIT Press, 1972, 1977.

Vieyra, Daniel I. *"Fill'er Up": An Architectural History of America's Gas Stations.* New York: Collier Books, 1979. Wallis, Michael. *Route 66, the Mother Road.* New York: St. Martin's Press, 1990.

Weigle, Marta, and Barbara A. Babcock, eds. *The Great Southwest of the Fred Harvey Company and the Sante Fe Railway.* Phoenix, Ariz.: Heard Museum, 1996.

Witzel, Michael Karl. *American Drive-in.* Oseola, Wisc.: Motorbooks International, 1994.

———. *Route 66 Remembered.* Osceola, Wisc.: Motorbooks International, 1996.

Works Progress Administration. Federal Writers' Project. *Arizona: The Grand Canyon State.* Rev. ed. New York: Hastings House, 1956.

———. *California: A Guide to the Golden State.* New York: Hastings House, 1939.

———. *Illinois: The WPA Guide to Illinois.* 1939. Reprint, New York: Pantheon Books, 1983.

———. *Missouri: A Guide to the "Show Me" State.* New York: Duell, Sloan and Pearce, 1941.

———. *New Mexico: The WPA Guide to 1930s New Mexico.* 1940. Reprint, Tucson: University of Arizona Press, 1989.

———. *Texas: A Guide to the Lone Star State.* New York: Hastings House, 1969.

———. *The WPA Guide to 1930s Oklahoma.* 1941. Reprint, Lawrence: University of Kansas Press, 1986.

Wurman, Richard Saul. *LA/Access: The Official Los Angeles Guidebook.* Los Angeles: Access Press, 1980.

Surveys, Inventories, Maps, and City Directories

Anders, Mary Ann, ed. *Route 66 in Oklahoma: An Historic Preservation Survey.* Stillwater: History Department, Oklahoma State University, 1984.

Architectural/Historic Inventory Survey Form. Route 66 in Missouri. Jefferson City, Mo.

Arizona Historic Property Inventory Forms for the Southside/Old Town Historic Building Survey. Flagstaff.

Arizona Historic Property Inventory Forms for Williams and Ash Fork.

Becker, Linda F., and Cydney E. Millstein. *Ozark Native Rock Masonry Survey.* Prepared for the South Central Ozark Council of Governments. Project No. 29-91-60032-197-A. Jefferson City, Mo.: State Historic Preservation Office, 1992.

City Directories for Cucamonga, Glendora, Pasadena, and Upland, Calif.; Springfield, Ill.; Joplin and St. Louis, Mo.; Tulsa, Okla.; and Amarillo, Tex.

Kammer, David. *Historic and Architectural Resources of Route 66 through New Mexico.* National Register of Historic Places. Multiple Property Documentation Form. Albuquerque, 1993.

Keene, David. *Illinois Historic Route 66 Corridor Study.* Chicago: Illinois Office of Historic Preservation, 1994.

Meacham, Maryjo. *Route 66 and Associated Historic Resources in Oklahoma.* National Register of Historic Places. Multiple Property Documentation Form. Norman, 1992.

Missouri State Highway Commission. *Map of Missouri Showing State Road System.* Jefferson City: Missouri State Highway Commission, 1936.

Office of Historic Preservation, State of Missouri. Historic Inventory of the Coral Court Motel prepared by Esley Hamilton for the St. Louis County Parks Department. February 1987.

U.S. Geological Survey. 15-Minute Series. Fort Reno and Geary Quadrangles. Washington, D.C.: U.S. Geological Survey, 1939.

Articles and Pamphlets

"Auto Courts Becoming One of Most Important Businesses Here, Huge Sums Invested." *Mojave County (Ariz.) Miner,* December 22, 1939.

"Banker Says City Is Destined to Be a Manufacturing Center." *Denver Post,* July 8, 1937.

Branson, George E. "Munger-Moss Sandwich Shop." *Show Me Route 66* 5, no. 2 (November 1993), n.p.

Couch, Phyliss. "Ludlow." In Keeling, ed., Once Upon a Desert, 146–47.

Friends of Oklahoma Route 66 Museum Brochure.

Greenbaum, Lucy. "Be It Ever So Humble." *New York Times Magazine,* May 5, 1946, 31.

Kelly, Susan Croce. "From Campgrounds to Cottages, to 'Ma and Pa' Motels, to Today's Luxurious Motor Inn." *Midwest Motorist* 54, no. 4 (March-April 1983): 6–11.

———. "Haven of the Road." *Sunday Pictures, St. Louis Post-Dispatch,* September 30, 1979.

———. "There Are No More Kicks on Old Route 66." *Midwest Motorist* 51, no. 3 (January-February 1980): 16–19.

McQuaid, Matilda, with Karen Bartlett. "Building an Image of the Southwest: Mary Colter: Fred Harvey Architect." In Weigle and Babcock, eds., The Great Southwest, 24–35.

Morrow, Lynn, and David Quick. "The Slab Rock Dwelling of Thayer, Missouri." *Pioneer America Society Transactions* 12 (1990): 35–43.

"New Oklahoma Museum Recalls Route 66 Glory Years." *Belleville (Ill.) News-Democrat,* September 24, 1995.

Parade Magazine, St. Louis Post-Dispatch. April 9, 1995. Ad placed by the Oklahoma Tourist Department.

Parrick, Emmie. "History of the Rock Cafe." Handout from the Rock Cafe, Stroud, Okla.

"Quonset Huts: Retail Peace Offering." *Business Week,* October 6, 1945, 19.

Ross, Delmer G. "Ma Preston, Ludlow's Legendary "Queen of 'the Desert.'" In Casebier and Friends, *Guide to the East Mojave Heritage Trail,* 99–114.

St. Louis Globe-Democrat, February 8 and 15, 1927, March 2, 1927, July 20, 1929, March 20, 1932. Clippings file, Mercantile Library, St. Louis.

Sanson, Michael, and Mary Pritchard. "Hard Times on Route 66." *Restaurant Hospitality* 76, no. 10 (October 1992): 74–76.

Sculle, Keith A. "Diners." *Historic Illinois* 5, no. 6 (April 1983): 3.

———. "Frank Redford's Wigwam Village." In Jennings, *Roadside America,* 125–35.

Spotlighting the Coliseum Ballroom on Its Twenty-fifth Anniversary, Benld, Ill., October 29, 1949.

"Tourist Cabins That Get Business." *Popular Mechanics* 64 (July 1935): 151–53.

"Try Waldvogel Brothers, Inc." *New Yorker,* March 16, 1946, 21.

"Two Frenchmen Bicycling on Route 66." *St. Louis Post-Dispatch,* June 19, 1995.

Weigle, Marta. "'Insisted on Authenticity': Harveycar Indian Detours, 1925–1926." In Weigle and Babcock, eds., *The Great Southwest,* 47–49.

"William C. Wyatt, 80; Introduced Missouri to McDonald's in '58." *St. Louis Post-Dispatch,* May 3, 1995.

Will Rogers Hotel, Claremore, Okla., publicity mailer.

Music and Television

Guthrie, Woody. *Dust Bowl Ballads.* Words and music by Woody Guthrie. New York: Folkways Records, 1964.

Silliphant, Sterling, producer. *Route 66.* CBS Television, 1960–64.

Troup, Bobby. *Get Your Kicks on Route 66.* Words and music by Bobby Troup. Londontown Music. Copyright 1946, renewed, 1973.

Internet Sites

"Albert Cassens Inducted into Illinois Route 66 Hall of Fame." www.edwpub.com/route66/cassens.html.

"The Coleman Theatre Beautiful." www.coleman.miami.ok.us/.

"A Conversation with Roy Rogers, King of the Cowboys." *Route 66 West—On Line Edition.* www.kaiwan.com/`wem/r66_west/fall96/royint.html.

"Drying Adobe Bricks." *New Deal Network Library.* www2.pok.ibm.com/library/i77htm.

Flanagan, Sue. *The Alamo: An Illustrated Chronology.* www.drtl.org/webchro1.html.

Harlow, Dan. "Sleeping in a Wigwam." *Route 66 West—On Line Edition.* www.kaiwan.com/`wem/r66/wtr96/051landmk.html.

Leigh, Kari. "A Tribute to Douglas Fairbanks, Sr." *Hollywood Web of Fame.* www.web-star.com/hollywood/douglasfairbanks.html.

"Lucille's Route 66." www.geocities.com/`vegas-okie/index.html.

MacIntyre, Diane. "Cecil B. DeMille." *The Silents Majority, On-Line Journal of Silent Films.* www.mdle.com/ClassicFilms/BTC/direct22.htm.

McGuire, John. "One for the Road." *POSTnet: An Information Exchange. St. Louis' Daily Newspaper Online,* 1997.

National Park Service. "Traveling among the Navajos." www.nps.gov/hutr/travel.htm.

"Navajo Hogans." www.uwec.edu/Academic/Geography/Ivogeler/w188/il4.htm.

"Pressing Bricks into Shape." *New Deal Network Library.* www2.pok.ibm.com/library/i78.htm.

"Santa Monica Pier." www.naid.sppsr.ucla.edu/venice/articles/santamonicapier.htm.

Index

Bill and Bessie's (Doolittle, Mo.), 78

Billboards, 5, 221; and building permits for drive-in theater screen towers, 61; and Highway Beautification Act of 1965, 5–6

Bill's Station (Phelps, Mo.), 97

Black, Milton, 281

Black Mountains, 249–51

Blackwell, Ella, 222

Blake, Peter: *God's Own Junkyard*, 5–6

Blansett, Glenn, 223–24

Blansett, Phil, 223, 228

Blansett, Rand, 223

Blue Mill (Lincoln, Ill.), 22, 25, 39

Blue Spruce Lodge (Gallup, N.Mex.), 213

Blue Swallow Motel (Tucumcari, N.Mex.), 186

Blue Whale Swimming Hole (Catoosa, Okla.), 118

BLVD Café (Duarte, Calif.), 274

Boardinghouses, 204, 210, 245. *See also* Tourist homes

Bond-Gunderson Trading Post (Grants, N.Mex.), 7–8, 202

Boots, Arthur G., 100

Boots' Court (Carthage, Mo.), 100

Bowser, Sylanus F., 8; and the "Filling Station," 8

Boyd, Beatrice and Frank, 243

Bridgeport, Okla., 11, 137–40; Swinging Bridge at, 137–40

Bridges: Chain of Rocks Bridge (St. Louis, Mo.), 52–54; McKinley Bridge (Madison, Ill.), 52–53, Swinging Bridge (Bridgeport, Okla.), 137–40

Brightwell, Hillary and Mary, 92

Bromley, Eli, 34

Brotherton family, 278

Brotherton's Farm House Dinners (Pasadena, Calif.), 277–78

Brunswick Hotel/Arizona Rancho Lodge/Tom's Rock Shop (Holbrook, Ariz.), 219

Brushingham, Mr., 32

Buddy's Grocery and Cabins (Conway, Tex.), 166

Buffalo Ranch (Afton, Okla.), 110

Building codes, 25

Building types: cafés and food stands, 21–25; gas stations, 8–11; motels, 11–21. *See also individual building types*

Bungalow Court (Kingman, Ariz.), 246

Bunion Derby, 3

Burnaman, Isaac, 121

Burris, Buster, 20, 255

Burton, Jack, 270

Bus Stop (Gardner, Ill.), 32

Bus stops, 32, 131; operating a bus stop, 131

Bybee, Edith Smith, 161

Cabins. *See* Motels and motor courts; *names of individual cabins*

Café and Gas Station (Conway, Tex.), 167

Cafés, 21–25, 78, 123, 130, 188; architecture of, 22–23; conversion of old gas stations into, 22–23, 92, 176; effect of franchise restaurants on, 24, 188; fire and, 22, 38, 43, 147; in motor courts, 21; rural, 22

Café sign (Texola, Okla.), 153

California Department of Agriculture, 258

Campbell, Frank, 87

Campbell 66 Express (Lebanon, Mo.), 87

Campgrounds: 11–12, 21, 257; and evolution into motels, 84; kitchens in, 21

Camp Joy (Lebanon, Mo.), 21, 84

Capone, Al, 47

Caporal, Sam (neé Kapriolotis), and family, 133

Carlyle Court (Oklahoma City, Okla.), 19, 134

Carpenter, Harry and Charles, 267

Carr, John, 19, 58

Carrow, Ed, 244

Carrow's Cabins (Valentine, Ariz.), 244

Carty, Bill, 251

Carty's Camp (Needles, Calif.), 251

Casa of Mission of San Gabriel Archangel (San Gabriel, Calif.), 20

Cassens, George, and family, 50

Cattaneo, Auro and Nellie, 204, 214

Caves, 70; Cathedral Cave, 70; Missouri Caverns, 70; Onondaga

Cave (Mo.), 70–71. *See also* Meramec Caverns

Chain of Rocks Bridge (St. Louis, Mo.), 52–54

Chambless, James Albert, and family, 11, 254

Chambless Camp (Cadiz, Calif.), 11, 254

Chaney, Red, 23, 92, 241, 274

Chapel of San Antonio de Valero, the Alamo (San Antonio, Tex.), 17

Chase, Cliff, 260

Chase, Fred and Margaret, 195

Chavez, Ron, 188

Cherokee Motel (Miami, Okla.), 108

Chicago World's Fair, 7, 28, 45

Chief Wolf Robe's Trading Post (Catoosa, Okla.), 117

Circle Inn (Cuba, Mo.), 74

Cities Service Station (Afton, Okla.), 113

Clayton, S. M. and Cora, 174

Cliffhouse Diner (Weatherford, Okla.), 142, 181

Cline, Roy, Jr., 22, 190

Cline, Roy, Sr., 22, 190

Clines Corners (N.Mex.), 5, 22, 190; and Rand McNally Company, 190

Club Café (Santa Rosa, N.Mex.), 22, 188

Coal miners, 10, 30, 46, 49, 76, 211, 213

Food stands, 21–25, 29, 36, 42, 56–57, 74, 79, 110, 136, 142–43, 177, 241, 250, 274, 277, 281; carhops, 23, 36–37, 273; Carpenter brothers, 267; chains, 24, 29, 136, 142, 273; drive-in, 22; in Los Angeles, 22, 24; McDonald brothers and, 24, 29, 273; octagonal plan, 267, 273; as precursor of fast food franchise, 22–23, 250, 267; prefabricated, 56, 142

Ford, John: *Grapes of Wrath* (film), 3–4; in Needles, Calif., 251; in Oklahoma, 22

Ford, Pete, 165

Ford Motor Company, 249

Forest Hills Tourist Court (Amarillo, Tex.), 170

Forest Park Camp (Avilla, Mo.), 98–99

4 Acre Court (Lebanon, Mo.), 83

Franciscan Lodge (Grants, N.Mex.), 204

Fred Harvey hotels and restaurants, 193, 230; Alvarado (Albuquerque, N.Mex.), 193; architecture of, 15–16, 230; and auto tourists, 21, 230; and Harvey House (Bridgeport, Okla.), 140; La Posada (Winslow, Ariz.), 230

Fuss, Jack, 221, 226

Gallagher, Ginger Smith, 63

Gallup, 211–15

Gambling, 31, 43, 47, 185

Garcia, Jesus, 232

Gardenway Motel (Gray Summit, Mo.), 23, 64

Gas Station: (Albuquerque, N.Mex.), 198; (Davenport, Okla.), 126; (Galena, Kans.), 104; (Gold Hill Summit, Ariz.), 249; (Los Angeles, Calif.), 280. *See also individual names of gas stations*

Gas stations: apartments over, 141, 242; architectural elements of, 8, 132, 141; as building type, 8–11; canopies of, 11, 103–104, 112–13, 126, 141, 160, 162, 229, 240, 254; as company logos, 8, 9, 209; development of, 8–10; effect of the interstates on, 11; gasoline taxes, 189; independent dealers, 189, 207; prefabricated, 8, 9, 209, 280; profit margin of, 41, 94, 169, 189; regional character of, 10–11, 160, 242, 254; site plans, 104, 160; vernacular in Illinois, 27, 32–33, 46

Geske, John, 38

Gibson, Joe, 127

Gift Shop and Gas Station (McLean, Tex.), 161

Girot, Jim, 31

Glancy, Chester and Gladys, 147

Glancy Motor Hotel (Clinton, Okla.), 147

Go-Kart Track (Bloomington, Ill.), 35

Golden Drumstick (Tulsa, Okla.), 123

Golden Spread Motel (Groom, Tex.), 165

Good Roads movement, 11; Ozark Trails, 69, 103. *See also* National Old Trails Road, Pioneer trails

Gorman, Marty, 43

Gottlieb, Sidney, 8, 22, 200–201

Gould, Fannie (Mrs. James Albert Chambless), 254

Graham, George, 161

Grand Canyon Café (Flagstaff, Ariz.), 23, 236

Grand Motel (Pasadena, Calif.), 277

Granot, Frank, 146

Granot Lodge (Clinton, Okla.), 146

Grave: of Douglas Fairbanks, Sr. (Hollywood Memorial Cemetery, Hollywood, Calif.), 282

Graves, Rod, 237

Grayfish, Johnny, 151

Great Lakes Steel Company, 208

Green Door Bar (Ash Fork, Ariz.), 238–39

Grey, Mr. (Greystone Camp, Barstow, Calif.), 259

Greystone Auto and Trailer Camp (Barstow, Calif.), 259

Griffith, R. E., 214

Groff, Spencer, 65

Gunderson, C. K., 200, 202, 209; Bond-Gunderson Trading Post, 7–8

Gunn, Mary and Wallace, 22, 201, 206

Guthrie, Woody: *Dust Bowl Ballads*, 3, 103

Hamburger Inn (El Reno, Okla.), 136

Hamburger stands. *See* Food stands

Hammond, Mr. (Avila, Mo.), 98–99

Hamons, Lucille, 141, 286

Hamons' Gas Station and Court (Hydro, Okla.), 141

Hannett, A. T., 182, 190

Happy Jack, 140

Hardwick, Thomas, 121

Harkahus, Rosie, 234

Harris, Bobby, 179–80

Harrison, Dorothy, 122

Harrison, Morton, 114

Harty, Roger, 67

Harty's Dine-O-Tel (St. Clair, Mo.), 67

Harvey, Fred, 216, 230

Harveycar Indian Detours, 230

Harvey House (Bridgeport, Okla.), 140

Havasu Court at Carty's Camp (Needles, Calif.), 251

Hendy, Lawrence, 136

Henry, Bill, 29, 42

Henry, Bob (son), 29

Henry Shaw Gardenway (Gray Summit, Mo.), 64

Henry's Hot Dog (Cicero, Ill.), 29

Herman, Roy, 209

Herman's Garage (Thoreau, N.Mex.), 209

Hicks, Ethan "Pop," 147

Higgins, W. A., 186

Highway Beautification Act of 1965, 5

Oil companies: Bay Petroleum, 207; credit cards, 207, 243; Hedges Oil Company, 189; Mobil, 89, 243; Pierce-Pennant Oil Company, 15, 62; Phillips 66, 8, 33, 89; Pure Oil, 8; Richfield Oil of California, 268; Rose Gas, 132; Shell Oil, 8, 46, 89, 242; Sinclair Refining Company, 33, 62, 212; Site Oil Company, 7, 51; SOCONY, 89; Standard Oil of California, 8, 209, 268; Standard Oil of Indiana, 33; Sunoco, 243; Texaco, 8–10, 41, 89, 212, 261; Union Oil, 268; Ventura Oil, 268

Oklahoma land opening (1889), 130, 132

Old Smokeys Pancake House and Restaurant (Williams, Ariz.), 237

Old State Road (Mo.), 54, 65, 69

Old Wire Road (Mo.), 54, 65, 69, 103

Oro Grande Motel (Oro Grande, Calif.), 262

Osterman, John and Oscar (brothers), 242–43

Osterman's Shell Station (Peach Springs, Ariz.), 242

Overman, Lyle and Ruby, 19, 134, 284–85

O-W Root Beer (Bloomington, Ill.), 36

Ozark Trail, 69, 103, 182

Ozark Trails Association, 69

Pacific Coast Borax Company, 256

Pacific Motel, Gas station, and Café (Joseph City, Ariz.), 223

Palace of the Governors (Sante Fe, N.Mex.), 12, 15, 15; construction of, 12, 15; as model for motels, 12, 196

Panhandle Gas and Garage (McLean, Tex.), 160

Pantex ordnance plant (Amarillo, Tex.), 169

Park Motel (Joplin, Mo.), 101

Park Plaza Courts (St. Louis, Mo.), 18

Park Plaza Courts (West Tulsa, Okla.), 122, 124

Patton, Gen. George S., 253

Payne, Andy, 3

P. B. Wooldridge Gas Station (Shamrock, Tex.), 158

Peach Springs Auto Court (Peach Springs, Ariz.), 243

Pennant No. 2 (Amarillo, Tex.), 177

Peter Rossi's Service Station (Braidwood, Ill.), 30

Pie House (Zamora, N.Mex.), 192

Pierce, William Clay, 15, 62

Pierce-Pennant Oil Company, 15, 62

Pig Hip Restaurant (Broadwell, Ill.), 40

Pioneer Tourist Court (Wellston, Okla.), 129

Pioneer trails: Pontiac Trail (Illinois), 27; Santa Fe Trail (Kansas, New Mexico), 5; Spanish Trail (California), 264

Pop Hicks' Restaurant (Clinton, Okla.), 147

Porter, Marvin, 23, 142

Prefabricated Gas Station (Carthage, Mo.), 9

Preston, "Mother," 257

Proctor, Thomas, 265

Prohibition, 43, 47; bootleggers during, 63, 262

Prokupt, Edna, 131

Prokupt's Gas Station and Bus Stop (Luther, Okla.), 131

Pyle, C. C., 3

Queenan, Reese and Wanda, 151

Queenan Indian Trading Post (Elk City, Okla.), 151

Quonset Huts, 208

Radabaugh, Yola, 275

Rafalala, Irma, 52

Railroad towns, 183, 187; along Atlantic and Pacific Railroad, 216; along Tonopah and Tidewater, 256

Railroad Workers' Cabins (Ludlow, Calif.), 256

Railroaders, 34, 77, 131, 210, 266

Rainey, Bert and Ina, 94

Rainey's Wrecker Service (Springfield, Mo.), 94

R Boy Drive-in (Weatherford, Okla.), 143

Red Cedar Inn (Pacific, Mo.), 63

Redford, Frank, 220

Redman, Floyd and Lillian, 186

Red's Hamburg (Springfield, Mo.), 93

Regal Reptile Ranch (Alanreed, Tex.), 162

Reptile farms, 118, 162

Restaurants: in hotels, 21; in railroad stations, 21. *See also names of individual restaurants or cafés*

Rest Haven Court (Springfield, Mo.), 92

Rice, Auline and Homer, 176

Rice's Dining Salon (Amarillo, Tex.), 176

Richards, V. P., 221

Richardson family, 200, 215

Richardson Trading Post (Gallup, N.Mex.), 215

Rieves, Roy, 125

Riley, Lyman, 162

Rio Siesta Motel (Clinton, Okla.), 144

Rischbieter family, 59

Rittenhouse, Jack: *A Guide Book to Highway 66*, 166, 173, 181, 287

Rivers and streams: Big Piney (Mo.), 79; Colorado (Calif.), 249–50; Crozier Creek (Ariz.), 244; ephemeral, 243; dry washes, 243, 253; Gasconade (Mo.), 81–82; Kankakee (Ill.), 27; Meramec (Mo.), 54, 62–63, 134; Mississippi (Ill.-Mo.), 52–53; Mojave (Calif.), 250, 259, 261–62; perennial, 243–44; Rio Grande (N.Mex.), 193; Sangamon (Ill.), 47; South Canadian (Okla.), 11, 137

Riviera Roadhouse (Gardner, Ill.), 31

Roadside architecture: deterioration of, 6, 25; "Duck" in, 4, 35; as stage set design, 150; standardization of, 8, 24–25

Roadside businesses: competition between, 98–99; evolution of, 11, 14, 21–22, 82, 98–99, 190–91, 254–59; selecting a site for, 84, 110, 217

Star Courts (Elk City, Okla.), 150

Star Motel (Claremore, Okla.), 116

Steak 'n' Shake (Bloomington, Normal, Ill.), 22, 23–24, 36–37

Steak 'n' Shake (St. Louis, Mo.), 54, 57

Steinbeck, John: *Grapes of Wrath*, 3–4, 103, 136, 250–51, 286–87

Stonemasons: Berti, "Grandpa," 72; Friesenhan, Leo, 75. *See also* Rock men

Streamline Moderne style: and cafés, 23, 36–37, 42, 65, 236; characteristics of, 18–19, 100, 175–76, 223; and food stands, 23, 57; materials used in, 19, 23, 30; 41, 48, 58; as an outgrowth of Spanish Colonial, 7, 25, 30, 44–45, 51, 81, 123, 135, 195, 198, 202, 283; St. Louis style, 54, 58–59, 68–69; signs, 64, 68; slabstone, 76, 81

Stroud, Lemuel and Milton, Sr., 18, 122–23

Stroud, Mickey and Milton, Jr., 122

Suarez, Manuel, 42

Sunset Motel (Sayre, Okla.), 152

Sunset Motel (Villa Ridge, Mo.), 66, 72

Surf Lounge (St. Clair, Mo.), 67

Sutter, Marie ("Dutch May"), 234

Sykes, Guy, 11, 240

Tarro, Ben and Dominic, 47

Tavern (West of El Reno, Okla.), 137

Taverns: Ill., 22, 27, 31, 32, 39, 50, 52; Mo., 67, 78; Okla., 137, 148; Tex., 161; N.Mex., 208

Taylor, James H., 223, 225

Taylor, Lloyd, 219

Taylor, Marie, 22

Taylor, Tom, 219

Teague, Walter Dorwin, 7, 8, 41, 169, 212, 261

Ted Drewes' Frozen Custard (St. Louis, Mo.), 54, 57

Texaco Gas Station (Glenrio, Tex.), 10

Texaco Station (Lenwood, Calif.), 261

Theaters: drive-in, 61, 133, 175; movie, 109; vaudeville, 109

Thigpen, Wilbur, 203

Thirty-fifth parallel, 216; and transcontinental railroad, 216

Threatt, Alan, and family, 130; quarry, 130–31

Threatt, Elizabeth, 22, 130

Threatt's Grocery and Gas Station (Luther, Okla.), 130

Tiller, Bill, 97

Tindall, J. M. and Mamie, 156

Tomahawk Bar (Prewitt, N.Mex.), 208

Tomasian, Susie, and family, 274

Tom's Rock Shop. *See* Brunswick Hotel

Tonopah and Tidewater Railroad, 256–57, 260

Top o' the World Hotel, Café, and Trading Post (Continental Divide, N.Mex.), 210

Torrence, Lee, 16–18, 122

Tourist Haven (Hamel, Ill.), 50

Tourist homes, 12, 86, 204, 232

Tourist sites: Grand Canyon, 216; Harveycar Indian Detours, 230; Hopi and Navajo reservations, 216, 230; Meteor Crater, 230; Painted Desert, 216, 219; Petrified Forest, 216, 219

Tower Station (Shamrock, Tex.), 23, 156–58, 198

Trading Posts, 110, 117, 151, 195, 200–202, 210, 215; evolution into tourist businesses, 200–202, 211, 218, 221, 227

Trail Drive-in Theatre (Amarillo, Tex.), 175

Trailer parks, 145, 259

Trail's End Motel (Springfield, Mo.), 90

Triangle Motel (Amarillo, Tex.), 174

Tri-county Truck Stop (Villa Ridge, Mo.), 65

Trigger (Roy Rogers's horse), 263

Troup, Bobby: "Get Your Kicks on Route 66," 3–4, 286

Troup, Cynthia, 3

Truck stops, 7, 23, 38, 38, 65; evolution of, 38, 48

Tucumcari, 183–86

Tulsa: U.S. 66 alignment in, 119

U-Drop Inn (Shamrock, Tex.), 22, 157

Upland Motel (Upland, Calif.), 270, 275

Uranium Café (Grants, N.Mex.), 203

Urick, Flick, 49

U.S. Highways: U.S. 30, 3, 5; U.S. 40, 3, 5; U.S. 50, 3, 5; U.S. 59, 110; U.S. 60, 3, 110, 174; U.S. 69, 110; U.S. 83, 155–56; U.S. 466, 260

U.S. Highway 66: alignment of, 3, 5, 27–28, 54, 69, 103, 182–83, 216, 233, 249–50, 260, 264, 266, 269, 276, 279, 283–85; changes in alignment to, 27, 28, 44, 46, 52–54, 62–63, 80, 85, 117, 119, 134, 137–40, 182, 240, 242, 244, 249; effect of Interstates on, 49, 64; Hannett's bypass (N.Mex.), 182, 188, 190; Hooker Cutoff (Mo.), 80, 85; at Kellyville, Okla., 125; Kingman to Barstow, 251; in New Mexico, 182–83; Old Beale Road, 244; regions along, 6; in St. Louis, 53–54; Shamrock to Amarillo, 168; weather along, 5, 155, 238

U.S. Highway 66 Association, 3, 5, 284

Valentine Systems of Wichita, 142, 181

Venturi, Robert: *Learning from Las Vegas*, 4

Vernacular architectural styles, 6; adobe house, 12, 182–83; California bungalow, 6, 234, 278; California Casa, 6, 19, 20, 171, 230, 260, 277; clapboard house, 12, 31, 45, 46, 67, 84; false front building, 52, 162; Great Plains, 137, 140, 154, 164–65, 167; Hollywood Deco, 284; log buildings, 63, 78, 206, 218, 222; Monterey house, 171, 252; motor courts and, 12; Ozark slabstone house, 6, 12, 69, 76–77, 81, 237; Navajo hogan, 218; Pueblo, 182–83, 185, 193–97, 219, 230; Russian-German house, 12; St. Louis Tudor house, 54, 60, 66, 69, 72, 75, 144; Spanish Colonial, 150, 166, 183; Spanish/Pueblo house, 6, 170,